Zinaida Vengerova: In Search of Beauty

Heidelberger Publikationen zur Slavistik

A. Linguistische Reihe
Hrsg.: Baldur Panzer (Heidelberg)

B. Literaturwissenschaftliche Reihe
Hrsg.: Horst-Jürgen Gerigk (Heidelberg)
Urs Heftrich (Heidelberg)
Wilfried Potthoff (Bonn)

PETER LANG
Frankfurt am Main · Berlin · Bern · Bruxelles · New York · Oxford · Wien

Heidelberger Publikationen zur Slavistik
B. Literaturwissenschaftliche Reihe · Band 27
Hrsg.: Horst-Jürgen Gerigk (Heidelberg)
Urs Heftrich (Heidelberg)
Wilfried Potthoff (Bonn)

Rosina Neginsky

Zinaida Vengerova: In Search of Beauty

A Literary Ambassador between East and West

PETER LANG
Europäischer Verlag der Wissenschaften

Bibliographic Information published by Die Deutsche
Bibliothek
Die Deutsche Bibliothek lists this publication in the Deutsche
Nationalbibliografie; detailed bibliographic data is available in
the internet at <http://dnb.ddb.de>.

ISSN 0930-729X
ISBN 3-631-53295-4
US-ISBN 0-8204-7396-2

© Peter Lang GmbH
Europäischer Verlag der Wissenschaften
Frankfurt am Main 2004
All rights reserved.

Printed in Germany 1 2 3 4 6 7

www.peterlang.de

To my father

TABLE OF CONTENTS

List of Illustrations   9
Preface   13
Introduction   19
Vengerova – Forgotten Trailblazer   20
Vengerova and Symbolism   21
Vengerova and Feminism   33
Vengerova and the 21st Century   35
Organization of the Book   37

Biographical Data   39

Chapter I: In the Beginning There Was. . .   41
Education   55

Chapter II: Saint Petersburg   63
The Northern Herald   65
Zinaida Nikolaevna Hippius   70
Religious and Philosophical Gatherings   73
The New Path   78
On Hippius in France and England   83
Literary Circles   86
The World of Art   86
Fridays at Sluchevsky   89
Pierre Weinberg   90
Baronessa Varvara Ivanovna Ixkul   91
Viacheslav Ivanov's Tower   91
Fedor Sologub   94
Anton Chekhov   96
Theater   97
New Life   102

Chapter III: Homeless and at Home: Across Europe 107

France 107
French Symbolism and Decadence 109
Belgian Symbolism 115
Symbolism and Feminism 117
Russian Novel and French Culture 119
Life in Paris and Minsky's Emigration 119
England 122
Oscar Wilde 123
The English Pre-Raphaelites 125
Dante Gabriel Rossetti 127
William Morris 128
Robert Browning 132
William Blake 133
Social Life in London 135
Fortnightly Review 137
"The Life and Death of Tolstoy" 137
Italy 140
"Sandro Botticelli" 142
"The Meaning of Dante for The Contemporary World" 146
"Francis of Assisi" 147
Contemporary Italian Literature 148
German Speaking Countries 149
Individualism and Symbolism 151

Chapter IV: Exodus 159

Berlin 161
The Parisian Archive of Prince Urusov 170
Vengerova's Memoirs of her Meetings with Eleonora Aveling 172
Last Years 172

Conclusion 175

Notes 181
Selected Bibliography 207
Index 217

ILLUSTRATIONS

Figure 1. Nikolai Ivanovich Gogolev, Foyer Saint Georges,
Meudon, France, 1996.   14
Figure 2. Zinaida Afanasievna Vengerova, around 1896.   18
Figure 3. Zinaida Afanasievna Vengerova, around 1890.   38
Figure 4. Isabelle Afansievna Vengerova.   46
Figure 5. Zinaida Afansievna Vengerova with Nikolai
Maksimovich Minsky, 1890.   56
Figure 6. Sofia Grigorievna Balakhovskaia-Petit, 1900.   59
Figure 7. Eugène Petit.   61
Figure 8. Zinaida Nikolaevna Hippius, around 1900.   74
Figure 9. Cover for *Angliiskie pisateli XIX veka* (*English
Writers of the Nineteen Century*), 1913.   131
Figure 10. Z.A. Vengerova's letter to S.G. Balakhovskaia:
18.11.923 (18.11.1923).   168

One who studies an artist especially loves him, because he understands him. The chosen one we usually put above the other creators, finding in him everybody and the whole world. The chosen one is understood, because the interpreter studied him and his biography well, looked into his facial features, studied the notes in his notebooks. To understand means to love.

Valery Briusov, "About Art" [1]

The interpreter of art is a guide in new worlds. He is not interested in what is only typical of one's time, in what the artist has in common with his contemporaries, but he is captivated by the desire to understand the soul itself of the creator. The interpretation of works of art is a new creativity: by discovering the soul of the creator, the interpreter will recreate it, not merely in fleeting moods, but he will penetrate the essence that establishes the moods. The interpreter of the artist can only be a sage.

Valery Briusov, "About Art" [2]

PREFACE

The seed for this book was planted in France, in Meudon, by Nikolai Ivanovich Gogolev, a scholar and a teacher. He was born at the turn of the 20th century in Russia, in a family of Russian intellectuals, and came to France at the end of the World War II. I met him in Meudon, at the Center for Russian Studies, Foyer Saint Georges in the 1980s, which belonged to and was operated by Jesuits. We both lived there at that time; he, as a senior well-respected teacher, already in his 80s, while I was a seventeen-year-old student, a freshman at the University of Paris.

Nikolai Ivanovich had many ideas and an outstanding knowledge and feel for literature. He was a giving and generous person, and fully shared his cornucopia of ideas, questions and tentative conclusions with his students, fellow colleagues, and friends. He had a rare gift of eloquence and an encyclopedic knowledge of literature, painting, and cinema. He could spend hours talking about those topics, but he did not like to write. Speaking and sharing his ideas was a way of disseminating them among people who had a potential to develop them in writing, and thus give them permanence. He had a special love, taste and understanding of turn-of-the-century culture, his culture, a culture that was a part of his life as a child. It was he who introduced me to the works of Zinaida Afanasievna Vengerova. When he was a child, she was well known to most Russian intellectuals: her articles and books as well as her translations were on the book shelves of most educated Russian families.

His enthusiasm inspired me, and I decided to learn more about Vengerova, especially because I was eager to explore *fin de siècle* culture to which I was inexplicably drawn as if I were, like him, a child of that culture. He wanted to return to his childhood by reconstructing that period; I wanted to rediscover that period as part of my emerging adulthood.

When I began my research, there was practically nothing written about Vengerova, except a few short encyclopedia articles. My only alternative was to search for archives. But where? Vengerova had lived all over Europe. Since I lived then in Paris, I started there. I

Figure 1. Nikolai Ivanovich Gogolev, Foyer Saint Georges, Meudon, France, 1996.

searched, but found very little. One day I called *Biliothèque de Documentation Internationale Contemporaine* (BDIC) in Nanterre and talked to the librarian, Madame Hélène Kaplan, who was known for being one of the best informed and most helpful librarians. Nevertheless, she was not aware of any material in their collection about Vengerova, nor was she familiar with that name. She told me, however, that recently they had received a donation, a large package of letters that they had not yet reviewed; and I was welcome to come and read them. The archive was a collection of material belonging to a woman with the surname of Balakhovskaia-Petit, and it was brought in by her niece Madame Alice Laurent. These two names were unfamiliar to me, but opening the package, I became speechless. It contained many letters, all addressed to "Sonichka," and they all were signed "Zina" – the diminutive of Zinaida. On the inside of the package was written, as I learned later, by the hand of Sonia Balakhovskaia-Petit, that "these were the letters of Zinaida Vengerova, the writer." This was a treasure trove!

Madame Kaplan introduced me to Madame Laurent, who shared with me the history of her aunt, and their family, and provided details about the relationship her aunt had with Vengerova and Vengerova's family. She also gave me a number of photographs and kindly authorized me to use them in my future publications. My gratitude goes to Madame Kaplan for her support of new enterprises, and to Madame Laurent for her help and cooperation.

A few years later, I participated in the National Endowment for Humanities Summer Seminar on Russian Orthodoxy led by the historian, Gregory Freeze. The seminar took place in Moscow, but we as a group went on a field trip to Saint Petersburg to work in the archives. Through acquaintances, I was given the name of the director of the department of archives, Larisa Nikolaevna Ivanova, at the Institute of Russian Literature, better known as The House of Pushkin, *Pushkinski dom*. She agreed to meet me, and subsequently provided entree to the Institute of Russian Literature, helped me to obtain the material I needed, and secured for me excellent working conditions.

Russia, for years, was a closed country and was very protective of its archives, especially with Western scholars. Russians wanted to be the first to explore and to publish their material. Larisa Nikolaevna had a different approach. She had spent a great deal of time in Rome, working on the archive of Viacheslav Ivanov, had traveled extensively in Western Europe, and was particularly familiar with Germany and France. She was aware of the wealth of the Russian culture abroad. She believed in cooperation between Russia and the West, and that an affirmation of Russian culture and access to archival material does not belong only to Russians in the Soviet Union, but also belongs to Russians abroad and to any scholar who has an interest in it and was ready to dedicate his or her time to its discovery and dissemination. I am deeply grateful to her. Without her cooperation and support this book would not be possible.

The Vengerova archives in *Pushkinski dom* were complementary to the Parisian material. There I read Zinaida's letters to her sister, Isabelle; letters to her life-long friend, Nikolai Minsky, letters to her parents, and a few of Sonia's letters to Vengerova, some of which were paired with Vengerova's letters in Balakhovskaia's collection. These Parisian and Saint Petersburg archives helped me to reconstruct "the puzzle" of Vengerova's life and to understand the role she played in turn-of-the-century culture.

After my return to the U. S., during a semester spent at the University of Chicago as a Visiting Scholar and, using the letters from both archives, I wrote an article on Vengerova and prepared for publication sixty four letters with my commentaries from the "Balakhovskaia-Petit" archive. That material was published in1995 by *Revue des Études Slaves* in Paris, whose head at that time was Monsieur Jacques Catteau, professor at the University of Sorbonne. After the publication of the article and the letters, I realized that I had enough material to write a book, in which Vengerova would be the centerpiece, and which would also be a turn-of-the-century cultural history.

Writing a book is a long process, but we are never alone in this process, and the final product is rarely possible without the support and the participation of friends. My first reader and constant support was Brian Wallen. He endlessly read and reread over several years different versions of my book always making helpful suggestions. I am also grateful to Frank O'Leary who read the Introduction and suggested a number of changes. I met many people at the University of Illinois at Springfield who provided substantial and varied support, necessary especially during the last steps of the completion of the book. My special thanks go to Professor Larry Shiner, my friend and mentor, for his help and advice. I owe a particular debt to Professor Jackie Jackson who proofread and edited the manuscript, and to my friend and colleague Professor Barbara Burkhardt for her valuable comments and suggestions. My gratitude also goes to Daniel Collet for his assistance at the final stages of this project. The help I have received, from the first to the last step, made this book possible.

Rosina Neginsky
Springfield, Illinois 2004

Figure 2. Zinaida Afanasievna Vengerova, around 1896.

INTRODUCTION

Stylistic schools in the fine arts tend to evolve as meandering tribu-
taries rather than monolithic channels of thought. The Symbolist
movement in the latter part of the 19th century was more diverse
than most others, because it was relatively long-lived and occurred
across Europe, sometimes under different names. Trying to track
the similarities and differences among the various currents of this
trend has confounded many. Zinaida Vengerova became one of the
most successful in this endeavor and was all the more remarkable
because she accomplished most of her interpretive work even as
Symbolist art and literature were still being created. That she is
little known today has more to do with the exodus of artists from
Russia at the end of the Symbolist period[1] than with the quality of
her thought or its expression.

Some writers are monumental; their creativity touches all chords
of the human soul. Others are less central, but still represent cases
of great interest. According to Zinaida's brother, Semen
Afanasievich Vengerov, himself a famous Russian literary figure,
the latter group reflects the life of the entire society and offers "an
excellent aid for creating a picture of a famous circle of people."[2]
Semen Afanasievich might have been describing his sister.

Indeed, Vengerova's life, soul, insights, perception of the *fin de
siècle* culture, and aspiration to better acquaint two disparate worlds
can help to enrich our grasp of the period of the *fin de siècle* in

Russia and in Western Europe. That understanding is especially timely now, in the twenty first century, as we attempt to summarize the nineteenth and twentieth centuries and to understand the influence of the nineteenth century's end to the overall culture of the twentieth and, in turn, to the future culture of the twenty first.

VENGEROVA – FORGOTTEN TRAILBLAZER

At the end of the 19th century, Vengerova's name was well known to the Russian reader. Her works appeared in many leading Russian journals and newspapers. Her translations of Western European literary works, her articles and her four books[3] were widely read, not only by the Russian intelligentsia, but also by the general reading public. Written in foreign languages, her essays about Russian literature and culture, were published and read in England, France, Germany, and Austria.

Since Vengerova spoke all major European languages and travelled extensively – spending long periods in England, France and Germany – she was able to immerse herself in the new spirit of Western European culture. As correspondence reveals,[4] she was fascinated by the European culture of the *fin de siècle*, and, perceiving it as kindred to her spirit, decided, very early in her career, to dedicate her energies to its promulgation to the Russian public.

After the revolution, however, Vengerova's name disappeared from the pages of Russian literary journals and newspapers and was quickly forgotten. Her association with the Russian Symbolist movement, considered by Soviets as "conservative and bourgeois," and her emigration, made her unfashionable in Soviet Russia. At the present time, Vengerova's name is often associated with critical analysis of Western, especially Modernist literature, and with the dissemination of that literature in Russia.[5]

Yet Vengerova was more than a propagator of Western European literature. In her way of thinking and writing, in her lifestyle and in her artistic and literary tastes, she represented *fin de siècle* culture. Yet, serving as a kind of literary emissary, she also became a *de facto* educator, partly responsible for shaping the literary tastes of the Russian public of the end of the nineteenth century and some features of the Russian Symbolist movement. She knew how to introduce, in an interesting and accessible manner, Modernist writers and artists whose style and message had not yet piqued the public interest. As a measure of Vengerova's "ambassadorial" skills, Boris Glinsky, the Civic critic so furiously opposed to Symbolism that he called the representatives of the Symbolist movement "psychopaths," wrote of Vengerova's way of introducing Symbolism in Russia:

> Her [Vengerova's] essays are written with a real knowledge of the subject, in a quite literary manner, and to my great surprise, in simple and clear language, without any vagaries and screaming symbolisms. . . . Maybe the respectable publishing house of *The Herald of Europe (Vestnik Evropy)*, which for some reason willingly publishes these articles about literary psychopathy, corrects the style of their contributor, but the most probable to assume is that Mme. Vengerova finds herself still only in the earliest stages of the illness.[6]

By publishing articles on Western European writers and artists before their works reached Russia, Vengerova helped prepare the Russian public to receive Western Modernist ideas. More importantly, Vengerova's works, taken as a whole, can be interpreted as a first history of Western European Modernism written in Russian when this movement was being established, and was not yet very popular, and at a time when the public's sensibilities still needed considerable enlightenment to build even a minimal appreciation of the styles and ideas involved in Modernism, and especially Symbolism.

VENGEROVA AND SYMBOLISM

While still a student in Bestuzhev's Institute of Higher Learning for Women in St. Petersburg, in the early 1880s, Vengerova was captivated by Western European culture and chose the history of Western literature as her specialization. Her specific interest in art and literature of the *fin de siècle* did not develop, however, until her stay in Europe in the late 1880s and early 1890s, crucial years in her formation as a writer and literary critic. In her "Autobiographical Essay," written in 1914, she emphasizes the significance of the time spent in England, France, and Italy, as well as the importance of the role that English and French Symbolist art and literature played in her perception of the world and formation as a Symbolist:

My first article on contemporary Western European literature appeared during a few years abroad; . . . these years were important to me not because of the university lectures, but because I had an opportunity to learn more about French and English Modernism. It took place only at the beginning of the 1890s, at the time in France when Decadence and Symbolism blossomed, and in England when the Pre-Raphaelite Movement and the so-called Aesthetical Renaissance united artistic ideals with people's daily lives. In French Decadence I sharply felt its liberating element, its striking individualism, that breaks down the moral code of dead social interdictions in the name of the creation of new spiritual values. This revolt in the name of aesthetic ideals captivated me in the poetry of Baudelaire and in the creativity of his immediate followers, Verlaine, Rimbeau, Moréas and others. In my articles about these best representatives of French Decadence, published in *The Herald of Europe*, I tried, as much as I could, to emphasize that particular meaning of the French poets, the renovating influence of their tempestuous individualism. They seemed to me to be fighters in the area of spirituality, fighters for beauty, which was the essence of the freedom of individuality. In that element, their creativity had an importance for a certain part of Russian literature and influenced the young generation in Russia. . . .
    Being captivated by the courage of French Decadence, its campaign against outdated naturalism, its search for new paths in poetry, I personally, however, was more drawn toward the English Pre-Raphaelite Movement, a trend in literature and art that developed simultaneously with French Decadence. In this movement,

its idealistic content and the presence of spiritual values seduced me. Decadents disclaimed traditions – in that was their superiority. They created a cult of beauty and were putting it into practice. Reflecting on these trends at the present moment from an autobiographical point of view and how they reflected on my spiritual world, I record my deep emotional experiences related to the study of Rossetti and other poets and painters of English idealistic *fin de siècle*, as being the opposite of the amorality of French Decadence. [7]

Vengerova belonged to the first generation of Russian Symbolists. She came from a highly cultured family, in which two other children, her older brother, Semen, and her younger sister, Isabelle, made substantial contributions to Russian and world culture. Semen was a professor of literature at the St. Petersburg University and a respected literary critic, whereas Isabelle was a famous pianist and later became a piano teacher, who, from 1923 until her death in 1957, had an appointment at the prestigious Curtis Institute of Music in Philadelphia. Among her beloved pupils were the conductor Thomas Scherman, and the composers Leonard Bernstein, Samuel Barber, and Lukas Foss who, after graduating from Curtis Institute of Music, became stars of the American musical scene.

Zinaida Vengerova was a close friend of the poets and writers Zinaida Hippius, Dmitry Merezhkovsky and Poliksena Solovieva, a sister of the Russian philosopher Vladimir Soloviev, and a life-long friend of the poet and writer Nikolai Vilenkin-Minsky. She knew well Sergei Diaghilev, the publisher of the art journal, *The World of Art (Mir Iskusstva),* and the future ballet impresario, who was the first to take Russian ballet to Europe and make it known internationally.[8]

An active participant in the Symbolist-Decadent movements, Vengerova attended different *fin de siècle* gatherings and forums: the Philosophical and Religious Gatherings, founded by poets and writers, Hippius and Merezhkovsky; Wednesdays at the art journal, *The World of Art*; the Neo-Philological Society, known for its discussion of the latest events of Modernist literature and art; the

gatherings organized by and held at the Russian Hellinist poet
Viacheslav Ivanov's *Tower*. She wrote for the Symbolist journal, *The
Northern Herald (Severny Vestnik)*, published by writers Akim
Flekser-Volynsky and Liubov Gurevich; *The New Path (Novy Put')*,
started by Hippius and Merezhkovsky; and, as archival materials
show, collaborated with *The World of Art*[9] on a number of projects
that unfortunately did not come to fruition.

At the earliest stages of the appearance of Symbolism in Russia,
Vengerova was the one who emphasized the complex character of
the movement. Moréas defined Symbolism narrowly as a school of
French poets led by Mallarmé and Verlaine.[10] That definition
brought a certain confusion to the later understanding of different
sides of this movement. For Vengerova, the movement represented
a broader, more complex set of ideas.

As she tried to bring a universal flavor to the notion of
Symbolism, Vengerova received criticism from the representatives
of more traditional schools, especially from the Civic writers and
critics. She was one of the first to understand and to try to convey
to her audience that the notion of Symbolism could be traced to
much earlier times – to Dante Alighieri, Sandro Botticelli and
William Blake – and could encompass a variety of schools that, at
that time, were not necessarily aware of their kinship. As she mentions in her "Autobiographical Essay," Symbolism included the
school of the Pre-Raphaelites and its followers (Burne-Jones and
Morris); the schools of Aesthetes with Oscar Wilde at the head; and
the school of "Olympians" represented by Frederic Leighton and
Viacheslav Ivanov, who explored the Antique world and recons-
tructed it in its purity. Symbolism, as understood by Vengerova,
also included the beginning of German expressionism, the new
Scandinavian drama of Henrik Ibsen and August Strinberg, and
especially the mystical and idealistic works of Belgian writers, poets
and painters.

In the article "Symbolism in its Modern Understanding" ("Symvolizm v ego sovremennom ponimanii"),[11] Vengerova claims that
Symbolism is not a new notion in art and literature, but that it has

always existed – all great art is symbolistic. For her, however, it is important to distinguish between two types of Symbolism: the first, which always existed, represents an eternal and inseparable part of any kind of creativity; it is a method. It uses physical reality to emphasize the invisible, mystical reality that lives in each of us in a variety of forms – the life of the soul, emotion, thought, imagination, and faith. This type of Symbolism considers physical reality for its own sake and uses it as a background for the invisible reality, for creating an atmosphere.

The second type of Symbolism is preoccupied with the invisible reality *only* and uses physical reality *only* as an instrument to emphasize the importance and magnitude of the invisible. This type of Symbolism does not consider physical reality for its own sake. It explores dark sides of physical reality to stress the contrast between visible and invisible, and to emphasize the Beauty of the invisible. It is not only a method of creativity, but is also a trend in art and literature, and it includes the elements of the first type of Symbolism, that can be called the "primary Symbolism." In her "Autobiographical Essay," she summarized this distinction in the following way:

> Symbolism is dear to me because it represents the eternal beginning in all our modern perceptions and feelings. I do not perceive Symbolism only as a literary school, which had its beginning, its period of blossom and then was replaced by other trends.
>
> Symbolism is everything that reflects the essential as a sign of the unincarnated. The Symbolist is one who does not merge with the existing moment, is not immersed in it, but perceives it as a search for the purpose of existence, as a path. Under the sign of Symbolism, I perceive all the best that art created in the past and continues to create in the present. That is what I perceive as a main thread that unites everything that I have written about Western European Literature.[12]

In 1889, given this approach to Symbolism, Zinaida Vengerova began her literary career with the publication of "John Keats and his Poetry" ("John Keats i ego poeziia"), an article in *The Herald of Europe*. When she wrote this article, she was already aware of an interest in Keats manifested by the English Pre-Raphaelites, especially by Dante Gabriel Rossetti, whose poetic imagery was greatly influenced by Keats.[13] In this article, Vengerova demonstrates that Keats was a precursor of the Symbolist movement. She argues that the novelty of Keats' art of writing is in his glorification of the eternal aspects of life: its unresolved mystery, the life of the inner world, dreams, and beauty. His poetry builds on the world of thoughts and emotions. He glorifies those aspects of life that allow individuals to detach from the surrounding physical reality and to immerse themselves in the world of dreams and beauty – the world of a fuller, more perfect life. Vengerova emphasizes that, like the Symbolists, Keats also had an interest in the distant past, in the exotic, and in the fatal beauty of woman.

She continued to introduce Symbolism to the Russian public, and to shape Russian literary and artistic tastes, by publishing the first Russian article about the French Symbolist poets in 1892. "Poets-Symbolists in France" ("Poety-symvolisty vo Frantsii")[14] appeared long before translations of the works of French Symbolist poets – Laforgue, Mallarmé, Moréas, Rimbaud and others – were published in Russian. After he read her article, the future Russian Symbolist poet, Briusov, wrote in his diary: "Finally Nordau's *Degeneration* (*Entartgung*) has appeared, and we have Z. Vengerova's article in *The Herald of Europe*. I went to the bookstore and bought myself Verlaine, Mallarmé, A. Rimbaud, and several of Maeterlinck's dramas. This was an entire revelation for me."[15]

In 1893, Vengerova published "New Utopia" ("Novaia Utopia")[16] to introduce Russian readers to the English Pre-Raphaelite William Morris, whose worship of the beautiful and desire to incarnate it in daily life led him to create the firm Morris, Marshal, Faulkner and Co., in 1861. Through the company's production of furniture and *objects d'art*, Morris applied Symbolist ideas to the domestic environment and formed the foundation of Art Nouveau.

When the Pre-Raphaelites were still barely known in Western

Europe, Vengerova introduced them to the Russian public, first by publishing "New Trends in English Art" ("Novye techeniia v angliiskom iskusstve")[17] in 1895. She followed this article with a lecture at the Neo-Philological Society in St. Petersburg, "Pre-Raphaelite Brotherhood," which she adapted for publication in 1897.

In 1896, Vengerova familiarized the Russian audience with one of the first representatives in the prose of French Decadence, J.-K. Huysmans; hers was the first critical description of Huysmans' work in Russian, and it appeared before any translations. She gave a thorough description and clear assessment of his life and works, classifying Huysmans as a Decadent and explaining the differences and similarities between Symbolism and Decadence.

In 1899, Vengerova was the first in Russia to write an article summarizing the life and work of the first representative of mystical Symbolism, Belgian playwright Maurice Maeterlinck, whose works in Russian translation appeared only six years after the publication of her article.[18] In 1897, Vengerova used her broad, sympathetic and universal vision of Symbolism to write and publish her first "Book on Symbolism" – the name she gave to her three volumes of *Literary Portraits* (*Literaturnye kharakteristiki)* in her private correspondence. She included in these books biographies and descriptions of the work of a variety of artists and writers who directly or indirectly were associated with the Symbolist movement. For instance, in her first volume of *Literary Portraits*, she included articles such as "The Pre-Raphaelite Brotherhood," "Dante Gabriel Rossetti," "William Morris," "Oscar Wilde and English Aestheticism," "Symbolist Poets in France," "Paul Verlaine," "J.K. Huysmans," "Henrik Ibsen," "Gerhard Hauptmann," "George Meredith," "Robert Browning and his Poetry," "William Blake," "Francis of Assisi," "The Meaning of Dante for Modernity," and "Sandro Botticelli." In her introduction to this volume she wrote:

> The purpose of this book is to emphasize the specific events of Modernist literature and art in Western Europe, to show the general ideological foundation in the creativity of contemporary poets

27

and painters in different European countries. . . . In Western Europe in the second part of the century, an art grew and prospered that created positive ideals and raised the level of the life of the spirit. Through studying poets and artists that stand in the forefront of this idealistic creativity, we will see how fruitful that type of art is from an artistic point of view. In addition, aesthetic and philosophical ideals, reflected in art, had a considerable impact on social life. In England, the development of the refined art and abstract poetry of the Pre-Raphaelites goes hand in hand with the liberation movement of the working class. One of the most outstanding poets who represents this movement is William Morris, a hero of popular meetings and the workers' movement. In Germany, the newest representative of the idealistic movement that recognizes in beauty the main principle of life is Gerhard Hauptmann, a passionate defender of the working class. An even more direct example of the idealist artist, who is at the same time a teacher of life, is Ibsen, who in his works began the fight against conventional morality in the name of deeper aesthetic attitude toward life. . . .

The literature and art of the last decades of the nineteenth century in Western Europe were called "the second Renaissance." Indeed, many things, among which is their idealistic nature and the discord between the striving for faith and the pessimism inherited from previous generations, remind one of the Italian Renaissance. We have tried to follow this connection between these two periods, separated by centuries, in a number of essays dedicated to the literature and art of the Italian Renaissance.[19]

Vengerova's selection of artists and writers for the first volume prompted controversy among Russian literary critics. They understood very little, despite Vengerova's explanatory introduction – particularly her distinction between Symbolism as a method and Symbolism as a trend – and attacked her with ferocity. No one agreed with Vengerova's belief that writers and artists who, in the opinion of the public, had nothing to do with Symbolism, could be viewed as representatives of that trend. In several anonymous essays, critics disagreed with Vengerova's opinion that Henrik Ibsen, Gerhard Hauptmann, and George Meredith were all

Symbolists. Reviewers objected, saying that it was strange that she saw features of Symbolism in works in which "real problems have been treated."[20] They also reproached Vengerova for the publication, under the same cover, of essays about artists who had, at first glance, nothing in common, and for proclaiming Symbolism as a "Second Renaissance."[21] "Why does Botticelli find himself among 'literary people?'" "What is the link between Verlaine, Ibsen and others on the one hand, and St. Francis on the other?" asks a perplexed A.K. in his review in *The Herald of History.*[22] Or, as a surprised A. Bogdanovich, the author of "Critical Notes" ("Kriticheskie zametki"), questions:

> Why is she trying to label such authors Symbolists, who in their very essence are not Symbolists, such as Meredith, that author of a fine novel? . . . Why Meredith has found himself in the company of the Symbolists, cheek-by-jowl with Wilde and Huysmans, is absolutely unclear to us. . . . His work does not present anything mystical, new or foggy . . . and is hardly suited to be included in the same category as that of Ibsen and Hauptmann.[23]

At that point, neither the Russian critics nor the uninformed Russian audience were ready for new ideas or the complexity and multi-sidedness of the Symbolist spirit, something that changed considerably with time. The majority of established Russian literary critics represented the Civic side of literature and based their judgements on prejudices that existed among them against Symbolism, without really knowing anything about this trend. In 1905, however, when Vengerova published her second volume[24] of *Literary Portraits*, positive reviews outnumbered the negative.[25] In 1910, when her last volume of *Literary Portraits* came out, and in 1913, when the first volume of *English Writers of the Nineteen Century (Angliiskie pisateli XIX veka),* of her *Collected Works* appeared,[26] all reviews were glorious,[27] and her selection of works to be considered under the category of Symbolism was perfectly understood and applauded, though the principle of her selections followed the same pattern as in 1897.

The knowledge that we have today about the artistic styles of many of the writers and artists that Vengerova included in her volumes of *Literary Portraits* reveals the ignorance of the Russian literary world and allows us to recognize the extent to which Vengerova's approach to the literature of the end of the century was ahead of its time. Her Russian critics did not know, or at least publicly recognize, the informed basis for her opinions; for example, that she was a friend of Dante Gabriel Rossetti's brother, W. M. Rossetti, from whom she learned a great deal about Dante Gabriel's life and his friends; or that she learned about Meredith through his friendship with Dante Gabriel Rossetti, with whom Meredith had shared a house, recognizing Rossetti later as "our Master."[28] In his article "Symbolism in Britain,"[29] Andrew Wilton quotes Meredith's poem, "The Day of the Daughter of Hades," to suggest that "Meredith's many-layered evocation of myth, allegory and religion, illustrates the ways in which Romantic iconography was enriched and transformed into Symbolism."[30] In 1899, two years after the appearance of Vengerova's book, which contained her article on Meredith, and four years after the article's appearance in *The Herald of Europe,* Arthur Symons, the poet and critic who, together with Aubrey Beardsley, edited the magazine of the Aesthetes, *Savoy,* published *The Symbolist Movement in Literature,*[31] in which he also included George Meredith as a Symbolist writer.

Vengerova's inclusion of William Blake among Symbolists was received with much surprise. Today, however, Blake's creativity and its influence on the spiritual and idealistic aspects of Symbolism are widely accepted, and he is often seen as the direct precursor of that movement. As Andrew Wilton notes:

> The most remarkable attempt to articulate spiritual values in the earlier part of the century had been that of William Blake, and all these men looked back to Blake with an admiration that was unusual for its time. Swinburne described Blake as though he were a Symbolist: "To him the veil of outer things seemed always to tremble with some breath behind it: seemed at times to be rent in

sunder with a clamor and sudden lightning. All the void of earth and air seemed to quiver with the passage of sentient wings and palpitate under the pressure of conscious feet. Flowers and weeds, stars and stones, spoke with articulate lips and gazed with living eyes. Hands were stretched towards him from beyond the darkness of material nature, to tempt or to support, to guide or to restrain."[32]

Blake had a strong influence on painters such as Burne-Jones, Spencer Stanhope, Simeon Solomon, and William Blake Richmond. Rossetti appreciated Blake, owned one of Blake's books and original engravings, and assisted Gilchrist in the compilation of his *Life of Blake.* In 1903, four years after Vengerova's inclusion of an article on Blake in her *"Literary Portraits,"* W.B. Yeats published a book on Symbolism, entitled *Ideas of Good and Evil,* in which he included two articles on Blake, "William Blake and the Imagination" and "William Blake and his Illustrations to the *Divine Comedy.*"[33] In 1910, Yeats also produced an edition of the *Poetical Works of William Blake* and included a long introduction, further establishing Blake's kinship with Symbolists. As for Russia, only in 1904 – seven years after the appearance of Vengerova's article – the Russian Symbolist poet, Konstantin Balmont, published an article about Blake entitled "Grandfather of Modern Symbolism." Contrary to Vengerova's article, which is rich in content and covers different aspects of Blake's life and creativity and also gives an interesting personal interpretation of his works, Balmont's article is narrow in content, and says practically nothing about Blake. His only addition to the knowledge of Blake in Russia is the description of his own "Symbolist" feelings awakened during the reading of Blake's works.

Vengerova's presentation of Botticelli and Dante, as the precursors of the Symbolist movement, is not surprising either, based on this section in her 1914 "Autobiographical Essay:"

At that time [the turn of the century] I was very much fascinated by the connection between poetry and the expressive arts, in particular the strange mystical kinship between the England of the end of

the XIX century and Florence of the XIV century, between
Rossetti and Botticelli. At that time I lived for long periods in
England, knew William Morris, Madox Brown and Burne-Jones
personally, heard a great deal about Rossetti from his brother W.M.
Rossetti, experienced, as live events [sic], the mystical moods of
Rossetti's paintings and the tender creations of Burne-Jones – the
spirit of the Pre-Raphaelites enveloped me as if it was my proper
element. From England, I went to Italy, and lived in Florence, the
place where I studied Dante and Botticelli. I reached the stage in
my passion [for this art] where, of all the paintings, . . . I clearly preferred the frescos for the complexity of their content. Modern
England and ancient Florence merged for me in such a strange way
that London, with its orange fogs seeming to come out from a fairy
tale, and Florence, with its bridges, buildings, and the gray foliage
of olive groves on the hills, remained forever alive in me and seemed to me the motherlands of my spirit."[34]

The Pre-Raphaelites, John Everett Millais, William Holman and
Dante Gabriel Rossetti created their Brotherhood in protest against
the pretensions of contemporary academic art. In their art, they
wanted to return to the simplicity of late medieval (or early
Renaissance) painting, before Raphael, such as painting by Sandro
Botticelli; however, they were also attracted to that period, and
especially to Botticelli, because of his unusual way of presenting the
image of woman – at once pure and sensual, simple and complex.

Symbolist painters and artists of all countries were fascinated
with woman because woman for Symbolists became a symbol of
the complexity of the human soul, of its contradictory nature,
depth, inaccessibility, and, to a degree, perversity. Symbolists painted woman as both pure and mystical, sensual and voluptuous – as
temptress who, following Judeo-Christian tradition, was at the origin of all evil and of all beauty, because she inspired in man, or man
wanted her to inspire in him, the destructive feelings of an all-
consuming, sensual passion. Vengerova understood and explained
in her article on Botticelli the kinship that existed between the divinely beautiful, complex, troubled, pure, inaccessible, and sensual

women of Botticelli and the women of the English Pre-Raphaelites
– Millais, Rossetti, Leighton, Sandys.

Dante played a determining role for Symbolists, especially in
their exploration of the subject of love. Symbolists were fascinated
with the idea of love, freed from all social conventions, and they
rebelled against society and its law. For them, the law represented
slavery, a barrier to the soul's aspirations. They objected to social
conventions on the grounds that they constrained individuals who
wished to unite with another on the basis of love rather than law.
Watts, John Flaxman, Rossetti and Symbolists in other countries
were especially captivated by Dante's vision of love, particularly his
love for Beatrice in *Vita Nuova,* and that of two lovers, Paolo and
Francesca in the fifth canto of his *Inferno.*[35]

In 1860, Rossetti painted his "Dantis Amor," inspired by *Vita
Nuova,* Dante's account of his unrequited love and mourning for
Beatrice Portinari. On the drawing made for the painting, Rossetti
inscribed the concluding line about love from Dante's *Divine
Comedy.* His fascination with Dante's love for Beatrice expressed
itself also in his beautiful painting of "Beata Beatrix." The story of
"Paolo and Francesca da Rimini" was a subject of Rossetti's and
Watts's "Paolo and Francesca da Rimini," painted in 1855 and in
1872-74, respectively. This story inspired several writers of the *fin
de siècle,* including the Italian modernist Gabriele D'Annunzio,
and was a topic of one of the Diaghilev's ballets.

VENGEROVA AND FEMINISM

It is impossible to talk about Vengerova without discussing her role
as a woman writer and a kind of "new" woman, a turn-of-the-century feminist. Vengerova was one of many such exceptional
Russian women, and in fact, can be considered one of the most cultured women of the late nineteenth century. She had an unusual
education for a woman of her time and was extremely independent,
traveling all over Europe alone. She was also a working woman.
Although she was in a profession from which she derived a great

deal of personal satisfaction, she worked to earn money. She was not married, and without working, could not have maintained a comfortable lifestyle.

Like many women writers of her time, Vengerova considered herself an artist; she was very much involved in the then-fashionable discussions about women and their places in modern society. Like other representatives of Russian Modernism, Vengerova believed in a woman's right to be an individual and fought against the idea that the function of a woman is only procreation. Although Vengerova never denied the importance of family and love relationships, for her, a woman was first of all a human being with all the complexities, talents, and aspirations of humanity, and she believed that for a woman, as for a man, love and family relationships should be only a part of life and not its fundamental or sole purpose.

Vengerova wrote two articles on that subject, "Russian Woman" ("La Femme russe")[36] and "Feminism and Woman's Freedom" ("Feminism i zhenskaia svoboda").[37] In both articles, she emphasizes the importance of the character and personality of a woman in her struggle to be recognized as an individual. Vengerova explains that the goal of a feminist movement, "equality" by law of economic and social rights of men and women, is not sufficient to improve the conditions of women's lives. For her, a woman first has to be freed in her own attitudes through education, to feel herself as an individual, rather than as an annex to a male as an object of pleasure. When she is psychologically ready, she will be able to benefit more from equality by law, for she will be seen as an individual by others only if she is herself convinced of her individuality. For Vengerova, social education is the means by which to change both men's and women's attitudes toward their respective roles. She hoped that men and women at the end of the century would perceive a working woman as a respectable member of society, and not as an unfortunate accident, who failed in her "career" as a married woman, obliged to make money instead of being supported.

VENGEROVA AND THE TWENTY-FIRST CENTURY

At the beginning of the 21st century, there is an undeniable interest in the period of the *fin de siècle*, and especially an interest in
Symbolism. In Paris, London, Chicago, Montreal and elsewhere,
fascinating exhibitions about the *fin de siècle* period have contributed to our understanding of that movement. In 1996, for example,
the Paris *Grand Palais* hosted an exhibition called "Paris –
Bruxelles," which presented the collaborative works of French and
Belgian Symbolist artists, writers, and musicians from the middle
to the end of the nineteenth century.

To celebrate the centenary of London's Tate Gallery founded in
1897, an impressive exhibit on English Symbolism, *The Age of
Rossetti, Burne-Jones and Watts*, took place. This exhibit acquainted
the general public with the thought of English Symbolists (the older
and younger generations of the Pre-Raphaelites), and how it
influenced the evolution of Symbolism in other countries. It presented paintings not only by Hunt, Millais, Rossetti, and Watts, but
also by Lord Leighton, Frederick Sandys, Albert Joseph Moore,
Simeon Solomon, Henry John Stock, Aubrey Beardsley, and the
sculptor, George Frampton.

In 1998, the *Grand Palais* mounted an exhibit entirely dedicated
to Gustave Moreau, who remained obscure during his life, but
today attracts great attention. His house-studio remains one of the
most attractive of small Parisian museums and is visited increasingly by Parisians and tourists alike. The same applies to Odilon
Redon, another French Symbolist, whose works were exhibited in
1995 in Chicago, and who is famous for his mystical, transparent
and unearthly motifs.[38]

A number of other important exhibits on Symbolist art have
taken place within the last fifteen years. *Le Symbolisme*, mounted in
1988-89, was based on Symbolist works located at the Museum of
Petit Palais in Paris. Another, *The Pre-Raphaelites*, took place in the
early 1990s in Chicago. Finally the most comprehensive of all was

Lost Paradise: Symbolist Europe, mounted in Montreal in 1995. In the 1980s, the Joffrey Ballet revived the Ballets Russes de Diaghilev, followed by another performance by the *Paris Opéra* in 1996. The Ballets' music, dance and décor are the embodiment of the ideas and creativity of the period. In recent years it was possible to see in Chicago, New York and Paris, ballets such as "Rite of Spring" ("Sacre du Printemps") and "Faun's After-Noon" ("L'Après-midi d'un faune"), as choreographed by Vaslav Nijinski; "The Wedding" ("Les Noces"), choreographed by Bronislava Nijinska, Vaslav's sister, and "Petrouchka," choreographed by Michel Fokine.

An understanding of Vengerova will help us appreciate this period. On the one hand, she was a critic, one who tried to understand and interpret, and on the other, she was also a practicing Symbolist herself: the Symbolist perception of the world, the Symbolist ideology, were hers, the values and credos in which she believed and by which she led her life and wrote her articles. As Valery Briusov wrote:

> The interpreter of art is a guide in new worlds. He is not interested in what is only typical of one's time, in what the artist has in common with his contemporaries, but he is captivated by the desire to understand the soul itself of the creator. The interpretation of works of art is a new creativity: by discovering the soul of the creator, the interpreter will recreate it, not merely in fleeting moods, but he will penetrate the essence that establishes the moods. The interpreter of the artist can only be a sage.[39]

Hence, learning about Vengerova as an artist and as a literary critic, "an interpreter of art," trying to understand her soul, her way of thinking about and perceiving art and literature as well as of propagating Western European Modernism in Russia and Russian literature in the West, will help us to learn more about the spirit of the *fin de siècle*, about its perception in the West and in the East and about its influence on 20th-century culture. Her life and her work will also serve as a window on Russian cultural history of the *fin de siècle* and the succeeding years – including the time after the revolution of 1917.

ORGANIZATION OF THE BOOK

Zinaida Afanasievna Vengerova provides the main focus of this book, but her life will also serve as a window on Russian cultural history of the *fin de siècle* and after, including after the revolution of 1917 when many left Russia forever, not necessarily realizing that their departure was final. The book consists of four chapters of different lengths and focus. Chapters I, II, and IV, although they treat some of Vengerova's works in passing, focus more on her life, and examine the intellectual milieu in which she lived. Chapter III is primarily a discussion of Vengerova's critical works and ideas and their importance for the evolution of turn of the century Russian Symbolist culture. The book is not organized chronologically, but generally according to the geographical location of the various intellectual milieu in which she lived from time to time; therefore, I hope that the biographical timeline following this introduction will help the reader to follow the thread of the book, Vengerova's life.

Figure 3. Zinaida Afanasievna Vengerova, around 1890.

BIOGRAPHICAL DATA

18 April 1867 (6th of April according to the old Russian calendar) Birth of Zinaida Vengerova in Sveborg.

1881 Graduated from the Gymnasium in Minsk.

1881-1883 Lived in Vienna.

1884-1887 Studied at Bestuzhev's Institute of Higher Learning for Women (Vysshie Bestuzhevskie kursy in St. Petersburg; during these years met Liubov Gurevich, the future editor of the Symbolist journal, *The Northern Herald (Severny Vestnik)*.

1888 Moved to Paris to study literature at the Sorbonne; met Sofia Grigorievna Balakhovskaia, a life-long friend.

1889-1914 Regularly contributed to *The Herald of Europe (Vestnik Evropy)*. In 1914, *The Herald of Europe* ceased its existence.

1893-1909 Was responsible for the section on *The News of Foreign Literature (Novosti Inostrannoi literatury)* in *The Herald of Europe*.

1892-1893 Traveled many times to London, and visited Italy and Switzerland.

1893 Returned to Russia.

1893-1899 Contributed to *The Northern Herald*. In 1899, *The Northern Herald* ceased its existence.

1893   Began theater activities which continued throughout all her life.

1894   Met Zinaida Hippius, poet, writer and literary critic.

1897   Published the first volume of *The Literary Portraits (Literaturnye Kharakteristiki)*.

1897-1899   Chaired the section "Lettres russes" ("Russian Letters") in the French journal, *Mercure de France.*

1902-1903   Was responsible for the section on Russian literature and literary events in the English journal *Saturday Review.*

1905   Published the second volume of *The Literary Portraits (Literaturnye Kharakteristiki)*.

1908   Moved to France to accompany Nikolai Minsky in his emigration.

1908-1912   Spent time in England, working in the British Museum.

1910   Published the third volume of *The Literary Portraits (Literaturnye Kharakteristiki)*.

1912   Returned to Russia after Nikolai Minsky's emigration.

1913   Published *English Writers of the Nineteen Century (Angliiskie pisateli XIX veka)*.

1921   Emigrated to Berlin.

1921-1923   Participated in foundation of *The House of the Arts (Dom Iskusstva)* in Berlin.

1923   Moved to London.

1924   Married Nikolai Minsky.

1923-1937   Lived in London and Paris.

1937   Moved to New York to live with her sister, Isabella Vengerova, after Minsky's death in 1937.

30 June 1941   Died of Parkinson's Disease in New York.

CHAPTER I

IN THE BEGINNING THERE WAS. . .[1]

"Even at a tender age I was aware that my family was a hotbed for geniuses, on both my maternal and paternal sides," writes Nicolas Slonimsky, a famous Russian-American musicologist, the nephew of Zinaida Vengerova on his maternal side. Although his comment lacks modesty, it is quite accurate, because, at least on his maternal side, his family did consist of many talented people, several of whom achieved considerable reputations and made an important contributions to Russian and world culture.

Nicolas Slonimsky's aunt, Zinaida Afanasievna Vengerova, our primary interest, was born on the 18th of April (6th of April according to the old Russian calendar) in 1867, in Sveborg,[2] to an intellectually gifted family of baptized Jews. Vengerova's maternal grandfather, Judah Epstein, was a rich merchant who is remembered only for his Talmudic scholarship. His daughter, Vengerova's mother, Paulina Iulievna Vengerova (1833-1916), was a writer. She published her first work in the early 1890s. This was a short essay of her reminiscences, written in German, in which she mentions her correspondence with Theodor Herzl (1860-1904), the founder of the Zionist movement. In a letter to Zinaida, she wrote about her epistolary relationship with Herzl:[3]

Nobody wrote to Dr. Herzl personally, and to nobody else he answered personally and with such a kindness; and nobody took such

41

lively interest in the Zionist movement from its beginning and acted
as I did. It is possible to see it in my article.[4]

When her article was accepted for publication, Paulina Iulievna
was filled with a great joy and wrote to Zinaida, her daughter, who
helped her place the article:

> With a hand trembling from joyful emotion I am writing with great
> thanks to announce the publication of my first essay; this first born
> of my works I would like to call . . . the Child of Old Age, that is why
> I love and cherish it so much. . . . For these moments of the highest
> delight, that I felt when I read your . . . letter, it is worthwhile to
> live.[5]

From 1908 to 1910 she achieved fame with her well-received book,
Memoirs of a Grandmother (Memoiren einer Grossmutter), written in
German and published in Berlin. Zinaida, encouraged her mother
and wrote to her younger sister, Isabelle, who disparaged her
mother's literary "mania:"

> About our "mother's memoirs," *mania* is a wrongful irony. The
> book has an enormous success. I was told in Russia that it is a
> monument to a disappearing style of life – and a book that will
> remain in literature. I read the long English articles about it – very
> enthusiastic. There is a heap of reviews and all are brilliant. The
> publisher is printing the second book at his own expense; the first
> volume sells excellently.[6]

Vengerova's mother played an important role in encouraging her
children, including her daughters, not only to develop their intellectual and artistic abilities and interests, but also to seek professional careers.

Vengerova's father, Afanasy Leontievich, "was a successful
contractor for taverns and real estate in Konotop, . . . who later
established himself as a banker in Minsk,"[7] and was very active in
the social and political life of the city. He died of a heart attack in

April, 1892, at a relatively young age, when Zinaida was only 25 years old. He was well loved and respected, and 15,000 people attended his funeral as a recognition of services that he performed for the community.[8]

Vengerova had three brothers – Semen, Mark and Vladimir – and four sisters – Elizaveta, Fanni, Maria, and Isabelle. The family was united,[9] extremely learned, and the children were gifted. Semen Afanasievich Vengerov (1855-1920), the oldest and probably the most famous of the brothers, was a literary critic and literary historian.[10] He taught at the University of St. Petersburg, the Bestuzhev's Institute of Higher Learning for Women (Vysshie zhenskie Bestuzhevskie kursy), and the Psychoneurological Institute. He was the author of many books about the history of literature[11] and of a number of historical biographies of Russian writers.[12]

Under the influence of Zinaida, Semen Vengerov assembled, edited, and published, *Russian Literature of the XX Century (1890-1910)*, which summarizes the Russian literary movements and writers of the *fin de siècle* of which Vengerov was quite suspicious. Nonetheless, this book, unique in its genre, is insightful. It has been useful for later scholars who study that period.

Nikolai Maksimovich Vilenkin-Minsky (1855-1938), a Russian Symbolist poet and one of the founders of Russian Symbolism, a friend of Vengerov and his sister, wrote in Vengerov's obituary about Semen Afanasievich's perception of Symbolism:

> It is easy to imagine Vengerov's confusion and his indignation, when toward the end of the 1890s, the gravitation toward Symbolism in our literature took the shape of a contagious illness. I remember our endless and, as often happened, fruitless arguments.[13]

Zinaida's youngest brother, Vladimir (Volodia), was a sensitive and artistically talented young man with whom Vengerova was emotionally and intellectually close. He died of consumption in 1900 in his early twenties. In Vengerova's and Minsky's archive in St. Petersburg, there is an extraordinary letter written by Volodia Vengerov. In that letter he expresses in a vivid way his Symbolist views of art, which stress the idea that the role of real art is not to imitate life, but to create its own life, life that is a mirror of an artist's inner world:

> Is it possible that in human activities there is nothing true? There is only one activity like that. It is art. It is a mirror of eternity. That is why art is a lie for those who believe that life is true. . . . The more the work of art is artistic, the more of that type of lie it contains. Indeed, is the painting created by an artist, novelist, dramatist, painter, reality? The idealist would represent the dream of his soul, but a realist would represent an aggregate that would contain the double of life.[14]

One of Zinaida Vengerova's older sisters, Fanni, was married to Ludwig Zinovievich Slonimsky (1850-1918),[15] who graduated in law from the University of Kiev, but was a journalist and man of literature. Beginning 1882, he was one of the editors of *The Herald of Europe (Vestnik Evropy)*, and was responsible for the section, "The Foreign Surveys." He wrote a number of articles about Marxism which were collected in his book, *Karl Marx's Teaching of Economy (Ekonomicheskoe uchenie Karla Marksa*, 1898). From 1892 until the end of *The Herald of Europe's* publication in 1914, Vengerova contributed a section "The News of Foreign Literature."

Fanni, in her own right, was a personality, although she did not fulfill herself in any other way than as a mother and a wife. In her letter to her son, Nicolas Slonimsky, written a few years before her death, we learn that she was an unusual young woman and, like Zinaida and their sister, Isabelle, certainly had talents and ambitious professional aspirations in her youth. She studied medicine and "planned to go into the country upon graduation to teach peasant women how not to be slaves."[16] She was also interested in chemistry and studied under Professor Borodin,[17] who, after her

44

graduation, offered her an appointment that she rejected. Her interests had changed. She decided to become a public speaker and enrolled in "the newly opened private college where women were admitted,"[18] where among the professors was the famous Russian philosopher and idealist, Vladimir Soloviev (1853-1900), who later became her friend and a godfather of Nicolas Slonimsky.

Isabelle (1877-1956), Zinaida's dearest sister and closest friend, became famous as a musician. In Russia, and later, after emigration to the USA, she was known as a wonderful pianist and outstanding teacher.[19] Her obituary in *The New York Times* on February 8, 1956 reads:

Although Mme. Vengerova has appeared in this country as a pianist, she was best known for her pedagogical work. As a professor of piano at the Curtis Institute of Music in Philadelphia and as a private teacher, she worked with many of the best-known musicians in the United States. Among her pupils were Samuel Barber, the composer; Leonard Bernstein, composer and pianist; Thomas Scherman, conductor; and Lukas Foss, composer. . . . Music critics often could, without being told, spot a pupil of Mme. Vengerova at a debut recital. Anybody who studied with her came to the concert stage fully prepared for the task in hand. Mme. Vengerova gave her pupils not only a firm technical background but also a musical one, instilling in them respect for the composer's intentions.

Zinaida and Isabelle lived together during different periods of their lives. Throughout Zinaida's correspondence with friends, we can follow Isabelle's evolution as a pianist. For instance, "Belochka is here – it is one of few light moments of my life," writes Zinaida Afanasievna. "Her musical career began very successfully. She has very good reviews, she is invited everywhere to participate in concerts, people treat her personally very well – she feels even giddy with unexpected success."[20] "Belka blossoms. . . . She is worried now about an important concert on Sunday; she refuses charity performances. In a month she will play with the Russian Symphonic Orchestra. Musicians say that she has 'her own style'

and she reminds them of Clara Schumann.[21] She works terribly –
she gives more and more lessons, and good lessons."[22] "Our Belka
is *molodets* [a brave girl]! Her music acquires more and more
friends and appreciation – but she is far from being satisfied with
herself. She works a lot."[23] "Belochka blossoms. Now she has a new
admirer – an old fellow Stasov.[24] He appreciates her music very

Figure 4. Isabelle Afanasievna Vengerova.

much, goes to listen to her – but he is known as a very severe judge and *connaisseur*."[25] "Belka . . . is very busy: she is preparing herself for her concert and maybe to the *tournée* with Tartakov.[26]"[27] "Belka is 'covered' with lessons. . . . In the spring she is going for a few weeks to Leshetitshki.[28]"[29]

Isabelle's nephew, Slonimsky, also gives an account of Isabelle's personality and the relationships she had with people, especially her students:

> Aunt Isabelle's personality and her teaching left a lasting impression on her students, famous and ordinary. Twenty years after her death, a music magazine conducted a survey of opinions among her former students, eliciting interesting responses. Here are some samples: "I feel that discipline was inseparable from Vengerova's musical and/or technical method." "Being 'Vengerova-ized' resulted in my becoming aware that it was my responsibility to understand and be able to control at will every physical activity related to technical mastery." "Intelligent, vital, sensitive, dedicated." But there were some negative reports. The dissenters were quite brutal in their criticism of Vengerova's teaching methods: "Autocratic, didactic, uninspiring, unsympathetic, frequently impatient, perhaps destructive.". . . "Tyrannical, dominant, relentless, awesome, authoritarian, uncompromising, demanding, overpowering."[30]

Nonetheless, Leonard Bernstein called her his "beloved Tyranna," and when she was diagnosed with cancer of the pancreas, he came and cooked a meal for her. Her other famous and less famous students were equally attentive to her. At her funeral, the Curtis Institute Quartet played a Barber's *Adagio,* the sign of Barber's special admiration for his beloved teacher.

Vengerova's two other sisters, the elder Elizaveta and the younger Marie, are not known for any accomplishments outside of marriage and children. However, Elizaveta (Liza) had a daughter, Liudmila Vilkina, who played a quite significant role in Zinaida's life. Liudmila and Zinaida had little difference in age, were both women of letters, and loved the same man, the poet Nikolai Vilenkin-

Minsky. While Minsky married Liudmila, he remained Vengerova's life-long love and friend, who despite the unhappiness and
disapproval of his wife, retained a close friendship with Vengerova
throughout his life. He married Vengerova in 1924, in emigration,
some time after Vilkina's death, who died in her forties of overall
misery and consumption.

Zinaida and Minsky first met when he studied in the Minsk
Lycée and lodged in the Vengerov family's house.[31] He was twenty
years older then Zinaida. At the time of his graduation from the
Lycée, in 1875, Zinaida was still a child. Their acquaintance
continued later, probably in 1884, when Zinaida moved to
St. Petersburg to study at Bestuzhev's Institute of Higher Learning
for Women. At that time Minsky was in his first marriage to the
writer Iulia Iakovleva, who published under the name of Iulia
Bezrodnaia. In 1887, when Vengerova graduated from the
Institute, Minsky had already separated from Iakovleva.

When in 1892, Vengerova's niece, Liza's nineteen-year-old
daughter, Liudmila, came to St. Petersburg, Vengerova wrote:
"Bella Vilkina came from Moscow, where she was getting ready to
become Sarah Bernhard. She is divinely beautiful and is happy
knowing the impact that she has on people."[32] In 1896, Minsky and
Vilkina began their life together, and in 1904, he married her.
However, their marriage had little intimacy, because the third person, Zinaida Afanasievna, was always present in their lives.

Vilkina's diaries and Vengerova's letters to Vilkina and Minsky describe a great ambivalence in the relationships of these three people.
Vilkina did not trust Minsky, did not trust Vengerova, and justifiably
did not trust Minsky's and Vengerova's "friendship." These excerpts
from Vilkina's diary reflect the turmoil of her soul. In the first one she
records a quote from Minsky; the others are her thoughts:

N[ikolai].M[aksimovich]:[33] You make me laugh when you reproach
me Zina.[34] If you only knew how she is repulsive to me. I only feel
myself guilty in front of her. That is why I do not break it off. It is
still okay when she speaks about books. But at the moment when

she becomes silent or shows tenderness on her face. . . .[35]
What I foresaw occurred. Z. Vengerova who never wrote to
Iunia,[36] suddenly wrote her a letter dated July 2. In this letter she
told Iunia that she spent two days in St. Petersburg. These are the
exact two days that N.M. spent there. It means that she had to
come deliberately from Elizavetino;[37] it means that she knew that he
lives alone, and I am here. Perhaps Hippius came with her; consequently these three days they spent all together. Z[inaida] V[enge-
rova] informed me of that; it means she has a reason to triumph, in
general . . . lies, lies. Oh, my God, how to remove the dirt of life. In
any case the second dirty intermission will not take place in my life.
I swear by my honor. Why, why does he contaminate my soul with
evil suspicions?[38]

I am again alone in my soul . . . as it turns out he made a gift to
Z[inaida] V[engerova] of a book by Dostoevsky and did not tell me
about it. In that there is a lie. Lies separate.[39]

In the evening I found pieces of a torn envelope with an address
written by Z[inaida]'s hand. But N. M. told me in the morning that
there were not any letters, except from the bank. I knew in the morning that there was a letter but allowed him to think that I did not
know that. It is essential that he be happy. . . . My God, my God,
how exhausted I am. To live without having the possibility to be
close with someone, is so desperately difficult.[40]

Probably to avoid constant worries and suspicions that would, as
she states, "contaminate her soul with dirt," and to avoid constant
concealments and lies, Vilkina preferred to accept the then fashionable view in the artistic *milieu* of Symbolists, of a *marriage à trois*.
From 1904 to 1906, the three of them, Minsky, Vilkina and
Vengerova lived together in the Minskys' apartment at Angliiskaia
naberezhnaia in St. Petersburg. Though Vilkina obviously did not
enjoy the arrangement, Vengerova perceived it differently. Her letter to Vilkina indicates that she was convinced of her right to be
close to Minsky and erroneously believed in Vilkina's acceptance.
She wrote to Liudmila Vilkina in November 1904, just before
moving to the Minskys' apartment:

Dear Bela! I am afraid that the first visit to Semen[41] will discourage you in the meaning of my moving to you. He does not understand the motives and that is why he is upset. But *I will live at your place for sure* – be sure. I am sending you a letter for Semen, and if you go to his house now, he will see it differently. In any case, know that our mutual decision is completely firm, and do not worry ... N. M. is still in Bern. . . . It is cold here. But tomorrow we all will move to Lake Geneva, where it is marvelous, warm and pleasant. I will find him a place somewhere in a small village. We will be near Lausanne (Montreux or Ouchy). Write to him in the meantime to Lausanne Poste Restante, to my name. Today I received your post card from Vienna, which I will give to N.M. tomorrow in Bern, where I shall go to meet him. In Bern, he is in good health – I spoke with him on the telephone. The solitude probably is beneficial for work. I hope that three weeks in Switzerland will have good results for his work. I will set him up in good condition – then he can live alone and work.

Visit Semen, become friends with him, ask him to give you work. . . . Semen thinks I imposed myself upon you as a roommate (that is why he tears me to pieces) and you do not feel comfortable refusing. Convince him that you are less than any of us against me moving to your place; the personal conversation will convince him.

But in any case, do not doubt that I will move in. I will convince even Semen, and will arrange everything. Be calm, count on me in all these matters. . . . Talk to Masha and organize everything for all of us in relation to our working comfort. I am taking care of the rest as much as I can.

In Bern, when I took the train, I ran into Berdiaev, who was going to the same place as me, Beatenberg, and now he will go with us to Lake Geneva. I introduced him to N. M., only very briefly, but they will meet again. . . . Be calm regarding the future. I take responsibility for everything. Only come meet our train and be healthy. . . . How cold it is here! . . . I am happy that N.M. is down there, in Bern.

P.S. Here is another suggestion for you: if you have money prob-

lems, . . . write to me about it. I will take care of it. The most important thing is for N. M. temporarily to forget the financial difficulties.
But do not refuse anything necessary to yourself: you must eat very
well and not refuse yourself other things and do not think of yourself as "poor." Everything will come at the right time.[42]

To better understand the relationship between Minsky and
Vengerova and what kept him close to her, I reprint here two letters
that Vengerova wrote to Minsky. Reading these letters, it is hard
not to be impressed by Vengerova's feelings for Minsky, and by her
readiness, almost to the point of humiliation, to do anything for
him; but at the same time one can see her selfishness and her perhaps unconscious manipulation to make him feel both guilty and
seduced. Vilkina's acceptance of the mutual life together gave
Vengerova a chance to live with Minsky, something she believed
was her right, whereas it gave Vilkina (perhaps) the illusion of
being in control of the situation.

As a Symbolist (which became almost a religion at that time),
and influenced by the ideas of extreme individualism, Vengerova
believed in the importance of free love and the power of love outside marriage. Vengerova of the *fin de siècle* did not respect marriage because it was a social institution, not necessarily associated
with the feeling of love. For her, love was a feeling apart from all
social impositions and rules. Moreover, she believed that real love is
possible only outside of marriage. That attitude, typical in the
milieu of Symbolists, may strike us with its similarities to Plato's
description of love in antiquity in his *The Symposium* and *The
Phaedrus*, works that were translated into Russian by the Symbolist
writers and were influential in shaping Russian Symbolist ideas.
Vengerova's attitude toward marriage also explains her offer to
Vilkina in one of her letters[43] "to arrange" her marriage with
Minsky.

Here are the two letters that Vengerova wrote to Minsky, that
picture their relationship:

Thursday

I do not know why you are angry with me. Is it because it hurts me when you go away? Can it be possible that you are insulted by my love for you, love of which you are as sure as I, myself? Can I be joyful when you hurry to leave, that you do not love me? Whereas in me, as the years pass, my incurable and joyless love for you is deeper. . . . To demand friendly indifference from me, is unfair and cruel.

All my life is a reflection of your acts. I only do what I believe is your will, obvious or hidden. That is why it is not fair to be angry at me and silently reproach me. You may dispose of me, even out of caprice, and even then you are constantly humiliating me, making my life a hell, treating me as a victim . . . it does not matter. One should not have loved me in order to make me suffer – here reasoning won't help. The grief is in the fact that in my soul there is only one feeling. I do not reproach you for anything, and there is not a drop of anger in me. I only regret not being, for instance, beautiful. Then how easily all psychological problems could be resolved.

Is it possible that you will leave without seeing me? I will be in the city on Tuesday 10:30 in the morning, but I can come any time you call, whenever you like. Send a telegram to Elizavetino, if you will leave on Tuesday and wish to see me. Should I repeat that I always, always wait for your call – but never hear it. . . .

If you wanted me to make your life richer, I would give all my life for it. But I am powerless and useless for you and in that is the whole nightmare.

I will be writing to you every day. . . . If it is *necessary* for you to leave, tell me, call me. Whatever will be in your telegram, it will be a sign for me to come by the first train and wait for you or the news from you at home. But call me only if it is desirable to you, without charity.

If you end up here, try to finish the *feuilleton*[44] by Tuesday and read it to me still in manuscript or in the corrections. Yours Zina.[45]

§

Village of Nebyvaly
Saturday

Forgive me for my commotion in front of you. I work so much on myself to be worthy of your "friendship" and if it raises a thirst in me, then what to do? Have pity for me, but do not get angry. I am not yet used to the despair. It is only very recently that I completely understood your attitude toward me, and I need time to get used to it and strangle the feelings that I have. But it will happen. I promise. Then you will entirely possess my soul, which will no longer desire. It hurts so much, when you leave and detach your life from mine, because there are excruciating desires, like a nightmare. . . .

Everything I know in you seems to me absolute truth and there is no movement, no act, no word that awakes in me inner revolt. I feel in you the Divine so clearly and so obviously, and I do not understand how it is possible to see something else, something that is not you, but simply life. It is strange to me that you sometimes think me capable of judging and reproaching you. It is instinct that speaks in me, the desire to be closer to you, since I am the only one to whom is given the gift of loving you completely. I have a torturous feeling of anger against those who are close to you – I consider that place to be mine. But you as a person and even the fact that you do not love me and are unable to love me, I understand and accept, including all the sufferings associated with it, and, would you not agree, there are quite a few.

None of the other relationships in my life have any similarity to my feelings toward you. I am terribly cold and empty precisely because you are so irrevocably distant from me, and I am happy for any kind of *mutual* attachment, that encourages me and gives me an opportunity to feel that I am someone whose presence is desirable. Then I even work better. Here in the silence, sitting under the wind which howls, watching the pale colors of undying ill dawn, I think of you with endless pain and endless love. I feel some harmony in these thoughts. I know that I am not as good as you, endlessly worse than you are and that I am only capable of loving you. If I were strong and worthy, I would have been able to lighten your life. Otherwise I can only fulfill your will as much as I am able to – and that is so little.

Forgive me, my dearest friend. Until Tuesday, yes?
Have you received my letter (yesterday)? With love,
Your Zina
Please, make sure that the *feuilleton* is finished. I would have liked to
read it.[46]

These letters show Vengerova emotionally in a vulnerable position toward Minsky, but at the same time they definitely reflect the right, she believes, she has over him and his life, although she understands that she is not loved the way she wishes. The letters create an impression of unrequited love. In life, however, it is unusual that one person would write love letters to another when the recipient feels a complete indifference toward that person. It would be reasonable to assume that Minsky, contrary to his assurances to his wife and the impression of being indifferent, perhaps at different points of his life, gave to Vengerova the sense that he had some kind of interest in her, and she was aware that, at some level, he needed her. In this, she was not mistaken.

Their large correspondence, located in archives in St. Petersburg, and the further development of their relationship prove this premise. Vengerova was an important professional support for Minsky. Often she was his first reader and critic. Because she had an incredible number of literary connections in a variety of international journals and newspapers, she was very helpful to Minsky in placing his works and promoting them, as well as organizing lectures for him in Russia and abroad, especially in England and Scotland. They were also literary partners throughout their lives, working together on a number of ventures including the publication of two newspapers, *New Life* (*Novaia zhizn'*), in St. Petersburg, and of the Russian language, *Word* (*Slovo*), in Paris, and the establishment of the Berlin House of the Arts (Dom Iskusstva), an important Russian cultural center. In St. Petersburg, for a number of years, Vengerova shared an apartment with Minsky and his wife, Liudmila Vilkina. When in 1906, after the trial related to the complication with the newspaper, *New Life*, Minsky was forced to escape to

France, Vengerova, who was not persecuted and could continue to live in Russia, chose to leave her life in St. Petersburg and follow Minsky to be near him in Paris.[47] Probably if Minsky resisted Vengerova's "impositions," they would not have taken place. Not only did he not resist them, he encouraged them, but maybe not in a very obvious way to the outside observer. And the proof of his "disinterest" in Vengerova would be his marriage to her in 1924, a few years after Vilkina's death. Minsky had a reputation as a womanizer, but women he was in love with, such as Hippius for instance, were not interested in him. He was able, however, to keep feminine love directed toward him. He never rejected Vengerova and kept her love and her in his life until his death.

EDUCATION

Vengerova received an unusually good education for a woman of the nineteenth century. From her childhood, she studied literature and foreign languages, learning French and German at home. German and Russian were Vengerova's mother's native tongues and became Zinaida's. French was the language of all educated families. In 1883, Vengerova began to study English during her *sejour* in Vienna. She also learned Italian, beginning in 1894, during her first visit to Italy, and then continued to study it in 1895 on her return to St. Petersburg. Vengerova was also fluent in Spanish, a language she studied in Spain during her visit there in 1900 with Minsky and Liudmila.[48]

While still a child, Zinaida studied piano, but probably stopped playing at the age of sixteen during her stay in Vienna. In a letter from Minsk, written on 11 October 1883, her mother, Paulina Iulievna, writes to her: "Music would have entertained you as I already told you; play at least one hour a day to not forget it completely: I will be very upset if you do not and you will be sorry about it, but then it will be too late."[49] However, her sister, Isabelle kept on with her practice and went on to become a distinguished performer and teacher.

Figure 5. Zinaida Afanasievna Vengerova with Nikolai Maksimovich Minsky, 1890.

Vengerova spent the first part of her childhood in St. Petersburg and the second in Minsk where she graduated from the Gymnasium (*lycée*) in 1881. She became interested in literature and philosophy very early, and had accomplished serious studies in them. Her 1881 notebook contains notes about Spinoza and Daudet; her 1882 notebook goes into the history of literature; while her notebook of 1883 is dedicated to philosophy, particularly to her study of Aristotle's and Plato's texts.

At approximately the same time, she began to write fiction. In her archive in Russia, there is a manuscript of her unpublished short story, written in French, "*The Young Man with Blue Eyebrows*" ("Le jeune homme aux cils bleus"), and some poetry written in Russian and English. Some of the poems in the archive represent exercises in translation.

For two years after her graduation from the Gymnasium, Vengerova lived in Vienna, where she "studied foreign languages and literatures."[50] Then, from 1884 to 1887, she entered Bestuzhev's Institute of Higher Learning for Women (*Vysshie Zhenskie Bestuzhevskie kursy*), in St. Petersburg. There she met Liubov Iakovlevna Gurevich, who later became the editor of the Symbolist journal, *The Northern Herald (Severny Vestnik)*, and Vengerova's friend.

Vengerova retained strong memories of the studies at *Bestuzhevskie kursy*. In her "Autobiographical Essay," she wrote:

The main subject of my studies was history (under the direction of Prof. V.G. Vasilevsky) and history of literature. I went to Prof. A.N. Veselovsky's lectures and studied under his direction, after I chose History of Western Literatures to be my specialty. The influence of these two professors determined my future activities. . . . I was most interested in English literature, stimulated mainly by very engaging lectures on Anglo-Saxon Literature and on the literature of XVI century, especially the precursors of Shakespeare, by Professor A.N. Veselovsky.[51]

In 1888, Vengerova moved to Paris to continue studying literature at the Sorbonne.[52] Between 1892 and 1893, she traveled many times to London, and visited Italy and Switzerland. In Paris, at the boarding house where she lived, she met and became a life-long friend of Sofia Grigorievna Balakhovskaia (1870-1966). Balakhovskaia was the daughter of Grigory Balakhovsky, a sugar factory owner in Kiev and a merchant of the highest rank, who was also the future father-in-law of the Russian philosopher, Lev Shestov.

Balakhovskaia came to Paris to study law and graduated in 1900. She was the first woman in France to be accepted to the lawyers' bar, to which women were not allowed until that year. She did not try many cases, mainly because she decided to dedicate the major part of her time to the development of cultural relationships between France and Russia. At her home, 6 rue Alboni, she had a literary salon where she received a great number of Russian and French writers, poets, and artists. She was interested in literature and wrote a number of plays and a few short stories. The most famous of her plays, "Phantoms of Life or Mirra" ("Prizraki zhizni ili Mirra"), was performed in the early years of the twentieth century by the theater of Gaideburov,[53] but without any particular success. She met Eugène Petit (1871-1938), who graduated from the same law school, at one of the school's balls and married him in the early 1890s. Petit was very much interested in Russian culture and spoke fluent Russian. In the first part of the twentieth century, he became an influential politician and worked very closely in the 1920s with French President Millerand. After the revolution of 1917, Balakhovskaia and her husband were instrumental in obtaining visas and organizing the emigration of many Russian writers and artists to France, whom they had met through Vengerova.

Given the fact that Russia had a harshly controlling monarchy, the bulk of Russian intellectuals, including Vengerova, were political liberals. As students in Paris, Vengerova and Balakhovskaia became close friends with Petr Lavrovich Lavrov (1823-1900), a Russian revolutionary, philosopher, literary critic, and journalist. At

Figure 6. Sofia Grigorievna Balakhovskaia-Petit, 1900.

his house they met Karl Marx's middle daughter, Laura (1845-1911), and her husband, Paul Laforgue (1842-1911). Vengerova's father, Afanasy Leontievich, worried a great deal about the political unreliability (*neblagonadezhnost'*) of Vengerova's Parisian friends. In a letter, he tried to convince his daughter to ask for an audience at the Russian Embassy in order to explain to the Russian ambassador that she had learned that there were doubts about her reliability *(blagonadezhnost')*; that she was a daughter of the director of a bank, and that she had been from childhood dedicated to sciences; that she was [in Paris] only for this purpose, was not taking part in any political events, and was not interested in politics.[54] He added in his letter that if she felt uncomfortable talking to the ambassador, he was ready to write a letter to him. He begged her to stop all relationships with people whom he calls "even slightly unreliable."[55] In response, Vengerova called her farther "dishonest" *(beschestnyi)*, and he, justifying himself to her, said: "I do not suggest that you be a spy."[56]

In spite of the insistence of her father, Vengerova did not see the ambassador and did not stop her friendships with the representatives of the radical intelligentsia living in Paris. Moreover, she continued her acquaintance with the radical intelligentsia in London, the city that she visited for the first time in November of 1891, the last year of her professional preparation, when she graduated from the Sorbonne. London became "the home of her soul."

The education Vengerova received helped her follow her aspirations, but her accomplishments, her courage, and dedication, should be entirely attributed to her tenacity and determination. At a time when travel was difficult, when women almost never traveled alone and rarely worked, Vengerova – who established her base in St. Petersburg – regularly visited France, England, Germany, Austria, and Italy, building and maintaining literary contacts in each country and finding ingenious ways to obtain the books and manuscripts, hot off press or pen, which she needed for her work.

Figure 7. Eugène Petit.

CHAPTER II

SAINT PETERSBURG

"She had a soft and tender voice – a great beauty in a
woman," – said King Lear regarding Cordelia. I think of these
words every time, when I read the articles written by Zinaida
Vengerova. Men do not know how to write in that way. In their
case, literature and art are often located in the background,
whereas in front they usually put their convictions. But when
convictions are involved, it is important to defend them. It leads
to screaming, curses, and even worse than that, battles. You will
encounter nothing of that in the book of Madame Vengerova.
Certainly she has her own preferences: there are writers she
likes more, there are other writers she likes less. But most of all,
she likes art, talent, and for that reason her soul likes everything
that is a reflection of talent and beauty."[1]

LEV SHESTOV

We lead a very Saint Petersburg type of life, which means an endless commotion. We go to bed at 3:00 or 4:00 in the morning – right
now it is about 1pm and I only now begin to work. Yesterday there
was an interesting evening at *The Northern Herald*, at L. Gurevich.
In the debates and discussions time passed unnoticed. Boborykin,[2]
used to the European customs, was exasperated by the Russian
manner of starting endless debates in the middle of the night.

Yet I work zealously, despite the fact that the bulk of the evenings
are lost. I have a bottomless supply of work; toward the spring I

expect to have to write endlessly, in order to have a moral right to rest.[3]

This excerpt from Vengerova's letter to her sister Isabelle in 1895 reflects the style of life of writers and artists in St. Petersburg at the turn of the century. Vengerova returned to St. Petersburg from her time of study in London and Paris in 1893 and became actively involved in the literary life of the city, which was based around newly formed Symbolist and non-Symbolist publishing houses, literary reviews and circles.

Those literary circles played a critical role in the life of Russian society. The reactionary Russian government perceived all of them as dangerously revolutionary. For intellectuals who never went along with these types of governments and revolted against them, these circles represented a breath of fresh air, and having them signified for the Russian intellectuals a near revolutionary action aimed at changing a society through discussions and education. Symbolist circles were especially important for the cultural, artistic and intellectual revolution of Russian society at the turn of the century. Writers and artists who became their members established new cultural and artistic standards that they hoped would ennoble and enrich the social life of Russia.

Many members of these circles believed that they could improve society without resorting to brutality of revolutionary methods, but rather through the peaceful means of education. Each group played its own role to enhance and innovate art and culture which later, because of the First World War and the Russian Revolution, were lost in Russia. They were, however, adopted in Europe and influenced the evolution of Western European art and style of the early 20th century.

An important number of Russian women were involved in these endeavors. These women were as successful as men due to their energy and determination, and because gender in upper class Russian society was not an issue. In the Russian political, cultural and literary tradition, women were perceived as individuals. They were gifted and active, and brought a unique energy and style in shaping intellectual life of literary and artistic circles.[4] Vengerova was one of these women.

THE NORTHERN HERALD

Immediately after her arrival in St. Petersburg, Vengerova frequented the literary circle of Aleksandra Arkadievna Davydova (1848-1902), a founder of the literary journal, *The World of God* (*Mir Bozhii*), to which Vengerova contributed an article on Richard Sheridan[5] in 1893.[6] Prior to 1890, Davydova worked as a secretary for *The Northern Herald* which, at that time, belonged to Anna Mikhailovna Evreinova.[7] Davydova's gatherings included a relatively large group of the younger generation of writers and poets, such as Zinaida Hippius, her husband Dmitry Merezhkovsky, Nikolai Minsky, and Akim Flekser-Volynsky.

Lubov Gurevich, Vengerova's classmate at Bestuzhev's Institute of Higher Learning for Women, first heard of *The Northern Herald* at Davydova's. In 1890, she became an editor at the journal – the first dedicated to Symbolism – and determined its focus as an introduction of Russian and Western European authors who represented new trends in literature. For instance, *The Northern Herald* was the first journal to publish in Russian the works of Henrik Ibsen, previously unknown to Russia. Ibsen's "Heather Gabler" appeared in *The Northern Herald* in 1890.

In 1895, Vengerova began to study the works of Ibsen and saw his play, "The Doll House," also called "Nora" for the name of the main female character, at the newly formed Symbolist theater in St. Petersburg, *Théâtre Libre*. She described her perception of the play in one of her letters to Sonia Balakhovskaia-Petit, emphasizing the play's Symbolist nature:

The event of the day is the opening of our *Théâtre Libre* with the presentation of Ibsen's *Nora*. Do you realize the degree to which this play is filled with genius? . . . I was burning, feeling in each

65

word its great Symbolic meaning, sensing how the earthly truth becomes dispelled in confrontation with the superior truth of the soul. Nora seemed to me to be a soul of mankind, thirsty for a miracle, yearning to be understood by, felt by, and fused with the earthly common man in the mutual search of the divine. . . . But a human being, chained to his eternal banality – embodied in the drama by Nora's husband – does not understand her. The miracle does not take place, and the soul, insulted in its great expectations, goes into the night, without a sense of direction, to be as far away as possible from people and feelings. . . . But the public is sitting passively and the words are falling on deaf ears, while thoughtful men of literature are involved in discussions about an immoral mother who gives up her children. How terrible it is to create a world filled with genius for such spectators.[8]

Subsequently in 1896, in the journal, *Education (Obrazovanie)*, Vengerova published "H. Ibsen," one of the most important articles about Ibsen's life and work. In that article, she stresses the issue of revolt in Ibsen's dramas, which she perceives as one of the features of Symbolism:

Ibsen comes as a destroyer of the fundamentals of the social life of his time. He looks in depth and shows the falsity and illusiveness of the interior motives and moral principles that guide people's actions. . . . Only the presence of a few outstanding protagonists in his otherwise sad dramas gives one a reason to believe the ideal of and the eventual triumph of the absolute truth, which has nothing in common with the truth upheld till then by society.[9]

Vengerova was well acquainted with the editorial board of *The Northern Herald* before her final return to Russia in 1893. She visited *The Northern Herald* publishing house, which was also a cultural center, a number of times during her seasonal visit to St. Petersburg in 1892.[10] She liked Gurevich and in 1892, wrote that Gurevich "is wonderfully kind and pure."[11]

The Northern Herald was interested in Vengerova's work. The journal was in need of people who were familiar with contemporary

Western European literature. In the early 1890s in Russia, there were a very few people with that knowledge. Gurevich described the situation of 1893 in her *Memoirs*:

Nobody in our new young literature of that period really followed up on what was happening then in the literary world in France and Germany. . . . Some people, who were not professionals in the domain of letters, brought to us in 1893-94 the first translations of Maeterlinck, Hauptmann, D'Annuncio and some other contemporary Europeans.[12]

Very early in her career, Vengerova began to publish in Russia, and in Russian, articles about Western European writers and poets of the second half of the 19th century, as well as about writers and poets who influenced the literature of the late 1880s. Her first article, "John Keats and His Poetry," appeared in *The Herald of Europe* in 1889[13] and influenced such poets[14] as Afanasy Fet, Aleksei Apuchtin, Innokenty Annensky, and Valery Briusov. In 1892, also in *The Herald of Europe*, Vengerova published an enlightening article, "Symbolist Poets in France (Verlaine, Mallarmé, Rimbeau, Laforgue, Moréas)."[15] This article was a revelation for the future Russian Symbolist poet, Valery Briusov.[16] In 1893, Vengerova started her sixteen year tenure as a foreign correspondent for the section, "The News of Foreign Literature," for *The Herald of Europe*. There she published many book reviews and essays about the latest literary works of English, French, German and Austrian writers.

In 1893, Vengerova, who already had a reputation in Russia as one of the most knowledgeable people in the affairs of contemporary Western European literature, began her collaboration with *The Northern Herald* and published an article, "New Utopia: William Morris and His Last Book."[17] Gurevich commented on it in her *Memoirs*:

We began to publish articles about particularly interesting events and phenomena of Western European literature, written by Zinaida Vengerova, who at that time came back to Russia.[18]

67

One of Vengerova's letters to a French friend (whose full name is unknown) after her return to Russia in 1893, reveals that she continued to be professionally well-informed about new works in Western European literature. In 1893, she wrote in French:

> By the way, Bibi, you could do me a great favor by communicating to me the literary news from Paris. I am asked by "Novosti"[19] to write one literary *feuilleton* every fifteen days (foreign literature certainly), and I also write in *The Herald of Europe* detailed articles about the recent publications abroad. Thus, I am especially interested in literary movements. I have at my disposal *Les Débats, Le Temps, Revue Bleue, Revue de Deux Mondes*. However, if you see interesting critics in other journals, which are not as *bourgeois*, send me excerpts. If you hear by any chance of a new book that has value, or excites the public attention, give me the title, so I will be able to ask my bookstore to order it for me. But especially, if you have literary relations, talk to me about the gossip of that *milieu*. I am very interested in the movements among the "youth." Write to me if you know something about the young novelist M. Jekwabb and others. Does criticism about them exist? [20]

In the winter of 1895, Liubov Gurevich started the Saturday literary circle and Vengerova became one of its permanent guests. Gurevich describes its atmosphere in her *Memoirs*:

> Around the winter of 1895-96 many new "contemporary" figures appeared in my environment and changed its atmosphere. Starting in the autumn, Minsky became the secretary of the publishing house, and Liadov constantly appeared there, sometimes in the very late hours of the night, to help with the preparatory publishing work, and at the same time, pour out his thoughts regarding the new trends in literature. At that time, I began to feel the need for interaction with people. I decided to open *zhurfiksy* (gatherings) at home. On Saturdays many people gathered at my house. The first to come exactly at 9 pm was always Sologub, who talked little before the arrival of other guests, and who would later silently sit in the corner to contemplate and to listen. Then, the indefatigable,

lively Boborykin, who would come either from Moscow or from
abroad, would show up. He had a tendency to start talking by
catching someone by the button of the waistcoat or by tapping his
heels and slapping his hands. He would talk, talk, would tell stories
and then would argue. . . . The appearance of Dobroliubov, permanently in black leather gloves with furs, which for some reason
he would never take off the whole evening, would attract the avid
attention of Boborykin . . . and would improve the mood of our
Symbolists. Minsky looked at him amorously. Liadov buzzed like a
bumble-bee, repeating that he was drunk even without any wine.
Toward midnight at a fast and daring gait would enter Iavorskaia,
followed by . . . bold and a little bit slightly languorous Shchepkina-
Kupernik – both the stars of the then famous currently running
play "Princess Greuze," which captured the attention even of
Minsky and Vengerova. During the second part of the season, we
met Minsky's wife, the very young L. Vilkina, who just began to
write poetry. It would be possible to name here many more guests
of these gatherings, young and old, and to recollect the spicy
episodes. We would usually sit up until 5-6 in the morning, would
debate, and the poets would read their works. I remember Minsky's
weak and melancholic voice, as he, standing and looking up in an
absent minded way, would read his long poem.

   The same winter, Lou Andreas Salomé [21] came to St. Petersburg
and became known to us. She, at one time, was very close to
Nietzsche and had written an insightful book about him. This
book, [22] in Vengerova's translation, we published the same year in
The Northern Herald. [23]

Vengerova was actively involved in the life of *The Northern Herald*
throughout its existence until 1899, contributing literary essays and
translations of contemporary Western European authors. In the
article "Illness or Publicity," Boris Glinsky, the journal's short-term
editor in the 1890s, writes derisively about the publishing house,
including Vengerova's role as an active member:

   We know all these faces. Here is the forty-year-old poet,
   Mr. Minsky; Mme. Zinaida Vengerova is seated next to him. Sitting

uneasily is Mr. Merezhkovsky, raving on about either the German philosopher, Nietzsche, or declaiming beautiful yet crazy Symbolist poetry. Next to him sits Mme. Hippius (Merezhkovskaia), proclaiming herself to be "a new human being" and repeating the following phrase with no regard to Mr. Volynsky's address: "You and I are surrounded by enemies. . . ." There presiding over the chaos of the household is the landlady of the establishment, L. Ia. Gurevich.[24]

In her letter to Isabelle, written in 1896, after the publication of Glinsky's article, Vengerova laughingly comments:

By the way, together with the latest issues of *The Northern Herald* I will send you the issue of *The Herald of History* which contains a curious article about *The Northern Herald* written by B. Glinsky. Glinsky calls Luba [Gurevich] the landlady of the establishment for mentally sick; all of us are the interns; the most hopeless is Minsky because he proclaims the publication of my book. I can be cured, if I let myself be rescued from Minsky's, Volynsky's company; if my decadent articles are not published and I am handed over to my respectable brother, Semen Afanasievich. Isn't it good? Now we call the publishing house "establishment," and each other psychopaths.[25]

Despite Gurevich's tenacity and the contributors' enthusiasm, the journal ceased its existence in 1898 because of a lack of funds. It was a painful loss for Gurevich. The journal was a milestone of the Russian Symbolist movement. However, when it ended its publication, the Symbolist movement was on its way toward recognition, and the number of new Symbolist ventures between the two capitals, Moscow and St. Petersburg, were exponentially growing.

ZINAIDA NIKOLAEVNA HIPPIUS

Vengerova became close with some people who visited Gurevich's circle and published in *The Northern Herald,* and collaborated on a number of Symbolist projects. One of her contributors was Zinaida Nikolaevna Hippius-Merezhkovskaia, a poet, critic and prose writer, who at the time when Vengerova met her, in 1894, had already manifested great talent. In her *Memoirs*, Gurevich describes her first impression of Hippius, whom she met for the first time in 1889, when Hippius arrived in St. Petersburg after marrying Dimitry Merezhkovsky:

I did not record at that time my first impression of Z.N. Hippius, who was destined to occupy in the 1890s one of the most visible places in the young literature. However, this impression is very vivid in my memory. Thin, narrow, with a figure that later was perceived as decadent, dressed in a half short dress, she had a sharp and tender face, as if she had consumption. Her face was framed in the aureole of fluffy golden hair. . . . She had light, half-opened eyes, which held something inviting and mocking. It was impossible not to pay attention to her; although she looked seductive to some, she made others feel uncomfortable, and yet irritated others. She had a brittle, screaming, childish and cheeky voice. She behaved in an affected manner, like a spoiled girl. . . . She soon began to publish, but I doubted still for a long time the importance of her talent, thinking that significant people cannot be so affected, so artificially naive in their manner and writings. In any case, her original poetical talent, as well as her caustic spirit and her charm developed much later. . . . Her image, though, was kindred to the "newly discovered" (in the 1890s) feminine figures in Botticelli's paintings.[26]

Vengerova met Hippius in 1894. "Recently I spent a pleasant evening at the house of some friends," she wrote to Sonia Balakhovskaia. "The soirée was nice because of the presence of Merezhkovskaia. I liked her very much. She seemed to me intelligent, interesting – the only person I have met for whom the question of aesthetics is not a boring one."[27] Vengerova and Hippius soon became close. In the next letter to Sonia, Vengerova added:

I study Italian together with Merezhkovskaia, with whom I am becoming increasingly intimate. It is strange to what degree I feel close to this woman. She is completely different from one's general perception of her. Although our natures contrast, I feel in her the mirror of my soul. There are so few such people. Her beauty is amazing. Recently she participated in the reading of Griboedov's comedy at the soirée of the literary foundation, and she seemed to look like a being from a fairy tale. But do not be jealous, Sonichka, I speak of her so much because she left me an hour ago, and the sounds of her poetry and her special way of talking, still reverberate in me. Read in the February issue of *The Northern Herald* her poem, "Grizelda.[28]" [29]

A little later Vengerova wrote to Balakhovskaia:

At the end of January they [Merezhkovskys] leave for Italy. . . . I cannot think about her departure – during these last months I have become inseparably close to her and started to love her *d'amour*. It is such a nightmare that she has to escape at the beginning of spring. From outside she seems to be even better looking – at least that is what is said. . . . Read her new book, *Zerkala*.[30]

In 1896 however, the relationship began to change. Hippius became close, at least in appearance – and there were even rumors she had a love affair – with one of the editors of *The Northern Herald*, Akim Flekser-Volynsky, a person Vengerova disliked intensely.[31] Although Hippius ended the relationship at the end of the 1890s, her letters in 1896 still indicate some intimacy with him.[32] That intimacy negatively affected Vengerova's and Hippius' relationship, and the following letter from Vengerova reflects the change:

I see Merezhkovskaia only in public though I love her as much as before – but a third person has come between us, whom she likes, and whom I cannot bear. I saw her today in the theater and there afterwards followed a drinking bout, and my heart still aches. It was hard for me to look at her sick and emaciated face. She is ill and it is said that she has consumption. In a month, she is leaving for Sicily. Her book, *New People,* was published. Her stories and poems truly reflect her talent. She is such a whole and beautiful human being, in spite of certain things that are incomprehensible to me.[33]

Nonetheless, in 1898 they spent the summer together in the country near St. Petersburg, in the village of Elizavetino, a summer stay that Vengerova recorded in a number of her letters:

I live between the city and Elizavetino. It is still very pleasant at the *dacha,* and Zinaida Nikolaevna, who decided to stay here all of September to finish an important novel, wishes me to stay with her. But I already have many threads in Petersburg, which begins its damned season, so that I come to Elizavetino only in snatches. It is divine to work in the country – we are completely alone, surrounded by . . . the trees – and because of that, at midnight, when the working day ends and the discussion begins, the words become especially sincere. The house in which we live was built at the time of Elizaveta Petrovna,[34] and the furniture is a leftover of the old luxury. . . . The words that are said here are very new, but what is behind them is as sad as at the times of Elizaveta Petrovna – and before her.[35]

Religious and Philosophical Gatherings

Hippius became not only a person of literature and arts, but also a religious and social activist. In his essay, "Z. N. Hippius," Russian poet Valery Briusov divides Hippius's creativity into three periods: "the first, when her world view was limited by pure aesthetics; the second, when she became interested in questions of religion, and the third, when she developed an interest in social questions."[36] Hippius' interest in religion was inseparable from the basic ideas of the Russian Symbolists as they evolved toward the end of the 1890s. At that time, she started to include a great number of people in her endeavors. Vengerova was one of many participants and

Figure 8. Zinaida Nikolaevna Hippius, around 1900.
To "straightforward" Sofia Grigorievna from artless Hippius.

supporters of Hippius.

To better understand the importance of social and religious enterprises in Russia at the end of the 1890s, it is important to understand the philosophy of the Russian Symbolists which established itself by the end of the century. Among all movements of European Symbolism, the Russian Symbolist movement came last. It was born out of a variety of influences, such as the rebellious poetry of Baudelaire and of French Symbolist poets, as well as the perception of beauty of the English Pre-Raphaelites. Russian Symbolists, especially Hippius, were fascinated with individualism and its connection to mysticism. They based their world view on a mixture of Nietzsche's idea of superman and Vladimir Soloviev's philosophy of the soul.[37]

Like French Symbolists, Russian Symbolists revolted against the conventional social environment and what had been fashionable in the main literary and artistic stream before them. In poetry they began to experiment with free verse, with sounds that would not follow the established metrical canons, but would express the music of their souls. In painting they experimented with unconventional images, colors, and interpretations of stories. Instead of believing that art can be objective and imitate life, the Symbolists created as an expression of their inner world, a world parallel to "real." Believing it was not art that imitated life, but life that imitated art, art became an expression of inner life, and a world in itself. Like the English Pre-Raphaelites, the Symbolists were searching for an earthly beauty that would be an expression of the divine. To them, beauty was not purely aesthetic; it was inseparable from ethical values.[38]

Vengerova's interest in ethical beauty is related to the importance that Russian Symbolists attributed to the idea of beauty as a whole – spiritual, ethical and aesthetic – which they perceived as the manifestation of divine reality on earth. Russian Symbolists saw the human soul as a divine, ennobling force on earth. But, at the same time, the soul was also human. Thus, Symbolists believed that to realize the divine will, or reach the stage of Nietzsche's superman, required enough inner spiritual power to improve the world. One must be faithful to the soul's aspirations and follow its inclinations. Under the guise of being faithful to God, the Symbolists aspired to be faithful to themselves, which, in extreme cases, has the potential for a great many aberrations. But, being idealists and hoping for the best, Russian Symbolists saw only the positive side of this extreme mystic individualism. They expressed these ideas not only in poetry, prose, literary criticism, and painting, but also in social activities.

Hippius was one of the most active Symbolists. Ideas not leading to social change in Russia did not satisfy her. She wanted to have the Kingdom of God on earth. And in 1901, she began to act upon it. With her husband, Dmitry Merezhkovsky, and their friend, Dmitry Filosofov, she founded Religious and Philosophical Gatherings. The group came together to improve Russian society by bringing peace and understanding between the two leading social groups: the quite varied Russian intelligentsia, and the representatives of the Russian Church.

At that time, the Russian Orthodox Church had a great deal of power. The Church was not separate from the state. To be Russian was inseparable from being Orthodox. The Russian tsar was crowned by the Church, and, as its figurehead, served as the representative of Christ in Russian society – a great responsibility for a mortal. In theory, the Russian Orthodox Church was supposed to be the ambassador of the spiritual within the society; in reality, it was one of many corrupted social institutions.

Partly because of this negative image, Russian intellectuals who were against the monarchy were also against the Church. The Merezhkovskys hoped that, through open discussions, it would be possible to find among those who represented the Church, people who were willing to change the institution and, among the intelligentsia, those who would be willing to open their hearts to faith. The Merezhkovskys hoped that by eliminating misunderstandings, the two groups would come together to found a reformed church that would save the Russian people.

These gatherings took place for two years. In total there were twenty-two of them. Eleven of them took place between 1901 and 1902, and eleven more between 1902 and 1903. The paranoid Russian government decided to discontinue them because it found them dangerously revolutionary, seductively attractive to the different classes of the Russian population, and overly influential.

During the time of their existence, the gatherings had a structure. The meetings always included lectures, which were followed by passionate debates. The first gathering was opened by the Church representative, V. Ternavtsev,[39] who emphasized his understanding of the intelligentsia. He talked about the faith of the intelligentsia, its aspirations to relieve human suffering. He talked about its rejection of the Church as being directly related to the Church's lack of spirituality, its selfishness and rigidity. He believed that the Church and the intelligentsia might have different understandings of happiness and the ways it could be achieved, but should strive to collaborate.

Vengerova was an active participant in Religious and Philosophical Gatherings. At the time gatherings began, she was very much taken by the movement. Through her correspondence it is possible to follow the thread of the meetings. In 1901, Vengerova wrote:

What do I do? All of us here are taken by the passionate aspiration "to enter into action," not only to write, but to feel the power of our words on people, to become united in the common search with people, independently of their camps. If we talk sincerely about our truth, unification will be possible, and it will take people away from their passivity. From that point of view, the new Religious and Philosophical Society[40] is interesting. The philosophers, poets . . . and the representatives of the Church participate in that society. They want a lot, act with passion, but we will see what will come out of that.[41]

In January of 1903, Vengerova explains her understanding of the role of the gatherings for Russian society in a letter to Sonia:

All of us are now taken by the new Philosophical and Religious Gatherings, where it seems an important cause is really treated – a cause which brings something significant to Russian self-consciousness. . . . The upper clergy and the best writers and radicals participate in the gatherings. The total freedom and the variety of speeches – everybody's passion about the search for the truth – is something exceptional in the history of Russian society.[42]

In February of 1903, Vengerova added: "The Philosophical Gatherings are very alive – and all of them together create very enriching ideological perspectives. Are we going toward the truth?"[43] In one of her letters, she gives a particulary thorough account of one of the gatherings:

I write you at night after an interesting religious gathering, which lasted until one o'clock in the morning. Prince Volkonsky[44] gave a presentation about faith, tolerance and the persecution of sects. The poor popes got what they deserved. The main orators were Nikolai Maksimovich, Merezhkovsky, and Rozanov. It was very interesting and the courage of the speeches was inconceivable given our conditions of life. It is the only place where thought is alive.[45]

The New Path

In the summer of 1902, Hippius and Merezhkovsky began to publish a literary journal, *The New Path (Novy Put')*. The journal's title implied that a new path should be taken so that society would change for the better. Like the Gatherings, the journal concentrated its efforts on uniting the intelligentsia and the clergy. Nonetheless, in its spirit the journal evolved more as a literary endeavor than a philosophical and religious one. It opened its pages to the representatives of the new Russian literature, publishing the first works of Alexandre Blok, who later became known as one of the most gifted Russian poets. It also published the works of Fedor Sologub, the Symbolist writer and poet; Viacheslav Ivanov, poet and one of the best Russian specialists in classics; and Vasily Rozanov, the Russian thinker.

Hippius invited Vengerova to contribute articles on the Western European literary trends to the journal. "*The New Path* gave me some work – right now I am preparing an article for the March issue, and Zinaida Nikolaevna will not let me breathe until I finish,"[46] writes Vengerova. She contributed two articles, "The Singer of the Time: Henri de Régnier" ("Pevets vremeni. Henri de Régnier")[47] and "The Mystics of Godlessness. Emile Verhaeren." ("Mistiki bezbozhiia. Emile Verhaeren").[48]

In the article, "The Singer of the Time: Henri de Régnier," Vengerova gives an overview of de Régnier's life and works. She stresses de Régnier's cult of the momentary, his worship of sensations and feelings awakened by strong but passing impressions; however, her commentaries extend beyond a description of de Régnier's works to include the pertinent issues of French Decadence, the movement with which she associates him. She also offers a mystical interpretation of the spirit of de Régnier's works, which allows her to classify him as potentially a Symbolist, and not only a Decadent poet.

In her discussion of French Decadence, it becomes clear that the worship of momentary, fleeting pleasures is associated with the worship of the inner world. The inner world, as opposed to the world of physical reality is the only "real" world and the only one which deserves worship. Thus, anything that might enhance the life of the inner existence – pleasures, smells, emotions – is beautiful and is worth being worshiped. Vengerova sees these features in the poetry of Henri de Régnier. But she also sees some other moods in his poetry – moods that she believes classify him as a Symbolist poet.

She stresses the presence of a feeling of longing and unhappiness in his works and puts a mystical value on his feeling of longing. Symbolism, like Decadence, worshiped the importance of the inner world, but for a different reason. For Symbolists, especially the Russian Symbolists, the inner world, or soul, reflected the world of a perfected outer reality. Thus, Vengerova wants to believe that the

worship of pleasures and the spirit of longing, present in de
Régnier's works, results from his awareness of the existence of
some other perfect reality and his recognition of his inablity to
reach it, while on earth. The poem, "Angel," by nineteenth century
Russian Romantic poet, Michail Lermontov, beautifully reflects
this sentiment, and was uniquely influential among the Russian
Symbolists:

> The angel of Heaven was flying at night
> And softly he sang in his flight.
> The flickering stars and the cloud and the moon
> Were wrapped in his beautiful tune.
>
> He sang of the innocent spirits above,
> Of blissful existence and love.
> He sang of the Lord, of His will, and His ways,
> And pure was the worshiper's praise.
>
> He flew, and he tenderly carried a soul
> For misery destined and dole.
> It did not remember his singing, and yet –
> That tune it could never forget.
>
> It languished on earth, and by sufferings burned,
> For things unattainable yearned;
> But nothing it heard could destroy or replace
> The music of heavenly grace.[49]

Vengerova endeavors to convince the reader that de Régnier understands how useless and vain the earthly pleasures are and that he
wishes to see beyond them. She admits, however, that he does not
offer solutions and does not struggle for change. Her hope is that
his poetry implies that life as it is, is not sufficient for happiness
and, thus, one should look for a *new path*, which would open the
way for a more harmonious and satisfactory existence.

Vengerova's second article, "The Mystics of Godlessness; Emile
Verhaeren," published in *The New Path*, is very instructive. Belgian

Symbolism was quite different from French Symbolist thought. It was an overtly mystical, spiritual, almost religious movement, which questioned the relationship between the human soul and God. Thus, if Vengerova does not find in de Régnier's poetry the mysticism and spirituality she seeks, she does find it in Verhaeren's. Following her usual analytical strategy, she gives a thorough introduction to Verhaeren's life and works, emphasizing the spiritual way that should unveil *the new path* for mankind. We learn that Verhaeren's poetry is filled with despair and disappointment and that is not accidental, because Verhaeren is consciously dissatisfied with life and is aware of human unhappiness. He sees human unhappiness in the fact that mankind cannot live without God, because mankind needs something to believe in; but despite this longing, mankind has rejected God and faith in God. Humanity lives, carrying within a deep longing for the lost God and for its dead faith. At the same time, humanity did not create either new values or a new God. As a result, the human soul is empty and suffers. Verhaeren's poetry maintains that something should be done and offers a solution: he appeals to the internal revival that will give birth to the new faith, to a new God, whose function will be different from the traditional one. God will embody the presence of mysterious universal forces that govern the world, but will also reflect its higher reality in the soul of each human being. Hence, contrary to the religion, faith will not be a social institution. It will become the divine path of the human soul, while leading to a better understanding of the universe, and humanity's place within it, creating an overall universal harmony. This new vision should resurrect the human soul and God for mankind and will ennoble and improve the earthly world.

It is interesting to note that both articles, "Henri de Régnier" and "Emile Verhaeren," emphasize the search for *the new path*, so prominent in the works of the western European poets and so essential for the representatives of the new Russian literature and art. For the Russian Symbolists, an individualistic search was closely linked to the social and religious reformation of society. Merezhkovskys' Gatherings and their *New Path* were prominent examples of the active form of that search.

The last issue of *The New Path* appeared in December 1904. "We have this year an inert season without literary events, without religious gatherings, and with a dying *New Path* (if 20,000 rubles do not fall from the sky, it will cease its existence around January),"[50] writes Vengerova.

Although during the existence of The Religious and Philosophical Gatherings and *The New Path*, Vengerova collaborated with the Merezhkovskys, actively supported and contributed to their projects, and continued to admire Hippius, her relationship with Hippius continued to undergo changes, partly due to the different ways the two worshiped the "religion" of Symbolism. Hippius searched for an active expression of her "Symbolist" views, of her new religion, whereas Vengerova was interested mainly in its literary application. Active people are often quite intolerant of those who talk but do not act. As a result, quite early in their relationship, their "ideological" differences began to create a tension between them and later led to a complete and final breakup after twenty-five years of friendship. Already in 1901, Vengerova mentions their differences in the letter to Sonia:

In my soul at this time is a strange high mood of detachment from everyday life. . . . Is it possible that it is because I went to Merezhkovskaia and she was beautiful beyond expression? . . . There were strangers present. Merezhkovskaia played the fool and said many nasty words to me (but the truth was not in them). I also laughed, flirted with Bakst (only because I dislike him more than anybody else). . . . Merezhkovskaia is right in her accusation that I do not know how to "act"and do not want, but am merely content with moods. In itself my attitude is unfruitful – I know that. She says that through this "meonism"[51] it is impossible to discover ecstasy, to be able to feel oneself in unison with eternity. What do you think, where is the way toward ecstasy, in action or by denying action? When you come here, you will probably start to think about the attractive theory of Zinaida Nikolaevna – the unification of the spirit and of the flesh, the cognition of eternity in the flesh, the resurrection in the flesh. Read the articles of Merezhkovsky in *The World of Art (Mir Iskusstva)*, . . . the articles of Zinaida Nikolaevna and Rozanov go deep into and become acquainted with their new religion. I do not profess it, but recognize the beauty and the essence of that doctrine.[52]

Vengerova's letter written several months later reveals that Hippius' unyielding views of Vengerova had increased tension between them:

I and Zin. Nik. mainly argue. We call her *her Holiness*, because she has endless discussions with priests and laces her conversation with quotations from *The Acts of the Apostles*. Yesterday until 2am, I was embroiled in discussion with her and I lost control in arguing with her. *N'empêche*, that she is the most talented and intelligent person among all those here and writes poetry of unsurpassed beauty and depth. She reproaches me for my inaction and Aestheticism. She reproaches me for searching for salvation in literature.[53]

Hippius was right. At that stage of her life, Vengerova was more a person who contemplated life than acted upon it. She was a revolutionary in spirit, however, and hoped to enhance the society by changing its tastes and world view through the written word and education. Although at that time she was not an initiator of any new social endeavors, she actively participated in many significant enterprises available in St. Petersburg by bringing her expertise, talent, idealism and a striving for beauty and harmony.

Hippius' works in France and England

Vengerova's appreciation of Hippius' works led her to write two articles about Hippius. The first of these was published in French in 1898, in the then well known literary journal, *Mercure de France*, which supported the new literary movements. Vengerova contributed articles on new Russian literature to its section, *Russian Letters (Lettres russes)*, between 1897 and 1899. The second article appeared in 1903, in English, in *The Saturday Review*, when Vengerova worked as a Russian correspondent for that magazine. She was the first literary critic to write about Hippius and to introduce her, as well as Russian Symbolism, to Western European readers.

In an article in *Mercure de France*, she initiates the French audience to Hippius' *Mirrors (Zerkala)*, a collection of short stories and poems that had just appeared in Russia. In her review of Hippius' short stories – "Mirrors," "Witch," "Living and Dead," "The Motherland," "The Dawn of Days," and "The Moon" – Vengerova explains the foundation and the major influences on the first generation of the Russian Symbolists of which she and Hippius were a part. She asserts that Hippius' works were strongly affected by the individualism of Nietzsche, by the revolt of the French Symbolists, the perception of feminine beauty of the English Pre-Raphaelites, and also by Tiutchev[54] and Baratynsky,[55] who were then forgotten Russian poets whose works had been revived by the Russian Symbolists.

Vengerova also delineates the major themes of Hippius' work: divine love; a faithfulness to one's own soul, through which the individual could potentially achieve perfection and become one with the universe; and love-pity, a banal, earthly love, through which an individual betrays his own soul by pleasing another. As Vengerova states, Hippius' love in *Mirrors* is "love that reflects divine truth, rigid and pitiless, love that abides in the depths of the human soul, but which the will does not always have the strength to obey. This love . . . teaches 'the grand and difficult love for God.'"[56] Vengerova examines as well the typical decadent and symbolist relationships between life and death, in which death is praised as a path leading to eternal, perfect reality, and life is blamed as an embodiment of the earthly reality, governed and controlled by the *demon*, the prince of the earthly world.

Vengerova also mentions the importance of nature for Hippius, especially the image of the moon, a symbolism common in the works of European Symbolists which is often perceived as an interlocutor of one's soul and its reflection. An integral part of Hippius' *Mirrors,* the moon both judges and reflects characters' souls. Vengerova is aware, however, of the weakness in Hippius' prose and discusses these in her conclusion to the article:

> She [Hippius] seeks especially to show the subtle links that unite man to the universe, to represent the human soul mixing in a subconscious manner with mysterious life. . . . And this soft and musical pantheism is the most prominent feature in Mme. Hippius' works. She is much weaker in her analysis of characters. The psychological side of her stories is weak in general, encumbered with reasoning theories. Mainly the characters are lacking in life and seem to be abstract ideas, disguised in human puppets. In sum, Mme. Hippius represents, with an incontestable talent, a very particular literary genre that expresses an entirely abstract morality shaped in a very precise way. She is a moralist who seeks to overthrow current ideas, to replace kindness with beauty, and to fight human virtues by what is above them – the divine ideal. She does it in witnessing poetic and artistic qualities.[57]

Vengerova gives a more sympathetic overview of Hippius' recently published works in the article, "Zinaida Hippius," in *The Saturday Review*.[58] She asserts "Zinaida Hippius-Merezhkovskaia is one of the best known Russian writers of the younger generation," an author who has evolved greatly since she began to write ten years earlier. "She began by being entirely aesthetic – and has developed now into a passionate teacher of a religious truth of her own." Vengerova explains:

> In Mme. Hippius' Aesthetic conception of life, beauty, considered as a symbol of the soul's highest aspirations, plays a destructive part; the work of true beauty and true love are only to destroy the ugliness of commonplace feelings and thus to clear the way for the advent of a higher power, which will change the whole aspect of life. The revelation of a new aesthetic ideal, of a beauty which shows the insufficiency of the ordinary joys and interests of life,

must lead to the development of a higher moral ideal.

Hippius was also a very talented poet; and, according to Vengerova, her poetry was without doubt superior to her prose: "Her [Hippius] verses are intensely passionate and exquisite in form and melody. They also express in lyric form a longing for things eternal, weariness of life as it is." The relationship between Hippius and Vengerova ended in 1917 with the Russian revolution.[59]

LITERARY CIRCLES

The World of Art

1898 was an important year for the Russian aesthetic renaissance. "Now many events take place: the new decadent journal, *The World of Art*; the Mondays at the publishing house: painters, Symbolists, youth," Vengerova wrote in November.[60] *The World of Art* was founded in 1898 by Sergei Pavlovich Diaghilev.[61]

The birth of the journal was the product of a group of talented and artistically innovative young people who studied together at the Gymnasium. Diaghilev, who arrived from the provincial city of Perm to attend the University at St. Petersburg, was introduced to this group by his cousin, Dmitry Filosofov, one of its members. Diaghilev, together with Filosofov (who later became a friend of Hippius and Merezhkovsky), became editors of *The World of Art*. At that time, Diaghilev had a great interest in painting. Therefore, one of the purposes of the journal's creation was to initiate the audience to the new trends in Western European art; to the forgotten but important Russian painters of the past; and to the avant-garde, the Symbolist and Decadent Russian art and literature of the present. The journal was divided into two main sections. The first reproduced the paintings and the second was entirely literary. It published the works of literary critic and philosopher, Vasily Rozanov; a new Russian philosopher, Lev Shestov;[62] and the first Russian philosopher, Vladimir Soloviev. It also published Nikolai

Minsky, Zinaida Hippius, Dmitry Merezhkovsky, as well as other Symbolist and Decadent writers. In addition, the journal was interested in literary works written in Western Europe about the trends of the new Western European art. Vengerova was a good resource, and she collaborated with the journal as a translator. She was invited to translate *The History of Painting of the Nineteenth Century,* written by the German art historian, Muther Richardt,[63] which, according to Alexander Benois,[64] a member of *The World of Art* who later became a famous painter and illustrator, was the first to introduce readers to the new trends in painting.[65] Before starting the translation, Vengerova visited Muther. She described this meeting in her letter to Minsky written from Berlin in July of 1899:

> I went to Breslav to visit Muther. He is an extremely pleasant person. . . . In conversation, he is attentive and "new," the complete opposite of the German Professor. He is surrounded by pupils, with whom he constantly spends time as if they were his comrades. . . . In Breslav, there is a whole school of Muther, which despises the spirit of academia and is preoccupied with the creation of the new Kunstkritik als Kunst.[66] All that is young, interesting and sympathetic.[67]

In September of that year, Vengerova wrote to her sister Isabelle: "I translate Muther."[68] Nonetheless, because of some disagreement with *The World of Art,* Vengerova's translation of Muther's *The History of Painting* never appeared in *The World of Art,* but was published in full by the publishing house, «Znanie.»

One of the most important of Vengerova's contributions to the journal's success was her 1899 publication, "The World of Art," in the section, "Lettres russes" of *Mercure de France.*[69] The article's basis was the celebration in Russia of Pushkin's centennial, organized by the Russian government. In her article, Vengerova introduced the journal's position regarding this celebration, which corresponded with her own. She discusses four articles, written by

Minsky, Rozanov,[70] Sologub[71] and Merezhkovsky. All four writers condemned the government's way of celebrating Pushkin's centennial for its vulgarity and lack of respect for Pushkin's precious wish for privacy. As Vengerova explains in her article, using the example of Pushkin's poem, "Poet and the Crowd" ("Poet i tolpa"), Pushkin was full of contempt for the crowd and reviled its ignorance and vulgarity. She notes that the position of the journal is not in agreement with the official position of the government, which neglected the poet's disdain for the crowd and made him its target. She, together with the authors of *The World of Art*, believed that only those few who are truly able to understand the art of Pushkin and respect his views have a right to celebrate his centennial birthday. The celebration organized by the government to entertain the masses was an insult to the poet's memory.[72]

When the journal was founded, the contributors and potential contributors gathered at the publishing house of *The World of Art* on Mondays. Later, the journal held a salon on Wednesdays. The regulars of the salon were the writers, poets, and artists who contributed to the journal and shared its views and its ideas. Vengerova wrote to her friend, Sonia: "If we have in Russia in some places a movement of *real* thought – strong and original, it exists just in a small circle of *The World of Art*, where people, instead of playing the liberals, *think*."[73] The activities of the salon centered around discussions and lectures given by the participants. In the same letter, Vengerova added:

Recently Merezhkovsky gave a lecture, in the spirit of his new Christianity, about Tolstoy and inveighed against him for his lack of understanding of Christ. The lecture was incredibly powerful, showed great talent and burst on the public like a bomb. The public almost tore the lecturer to pieces. Several priests defended Tolstoy, a number of critics attacked Merezhkovsky – he was the one who was right, however, and the crowd merely abused its right to ignorance, did not understand the meaning of the lecture, and just heard the "strong words" describing its idol.[74]

Princess M. K. Tenesheva,[75] who had subsidized *The World of Art's* publication, was not able to continue, whereas S. I. Mamontov,[76] also involved in the publication, had already stopped its financing in 1900. The years 1903 and 1904 were very difficult for the journal, and it had an impact on the Wednesday salons as well, which stopped entirely in 1904. In January 1905, the journal published its last issue and ceased to exist.

Fridays at Sluchevsky

Between 1890 and 1914, the literary life in St. Petersburg blossomed and gave birth to many literary circles that met at the publishing houses as well as in private homes and literary associations. Vengerova actively participated in all of them.

The circle of poet Konstantin Sluchevsky (1837-1904) gathered many representatives of the new trends, and became known as "Fridays at Sluchevsky." These Fridays were the continuation of Fridays at the home of poet, Iakov Petrovich Polonsky (1819-1898). Polonsky had begun to welcome a literary and a musical circle to his home when he came back from Paris in the 1860s, and continued until his death. At Polonsky's funeral, Sluchevsky suggested carrying on the tradition by gathering at his house.

"Fridays at Sluchevsky" was not an open salon. Similar to other salons, the guests were invited. But in order to become a part of the group, it was necessary to have a published collection of poetry or literary works and three letters of recommendation from three established members of the salon. Thus, Sluchevsky's circle was open only to the writers and poets who already had some literary reputation. The Symbolist poets and writers, N. Minsky, V. Briusov, D. Merezhkovsky, M. Lokhvitskaia, Z. Hippius, F. Sologub and K. Balmont, were among the members and frequent visitors. Vengerova was one of them, and at numerous occasions she mentions "Fridays at Sluchevsky" in her private correspondence.

After Sluchevsky's death in 1904, his salon continued at the home of a different member each Friday. After 1906, salon members included poets such as Viacheslav Ivanov and Alexandre Blok; and after 1908, the poets Nikolai Gumilev and Anna Akhmatova. The salon lasted until 1917.

Pierre Weinberg

The representatives of the new literature also gathered at the house of a famous writer and one of the best translators of Western European literature, Pierre Weinberg.[77] In her third volume of *Literary Portraits*, appearing after Weinberg's death in 1908, Vengerova published an article on him. In it she gives an overview of his creative life and praises his receptiveness to new literary trends and ideas, as well as his support of Symbolism – although by that time he was at the end of his literary career and did not belong to the new generation of writers and poets. Vengerova wrote about him:

> I remember at the moment of the birth of so called "Decadence" in Western European literature, at the time when an interest in French Symbolists – Verlaine, Maeterlinck – appeared in Russia, Petr Isaevich at first was surprised at the unusual forms of poetry. I vividly remember the debates about it in different literary associations. Petr Isaevich was the first to provoke them, since he was always very interested in new trends, which he did not criticize, as many did, but tried to understand the creativity of the new poets. Later he began to like it. . . . During the last years of his life he had an opportunity to observe the new trend in the newest Russian literature. He had quite an interest in it. Even when we talked to him about the talented poets and prose writers among the most courageous youth, he was happy to recognize a talent. In literature . . . he was free of fanatical ideas and prejudices.[78]

The gatherings at Weinberg's home lasted until his death.

Baronessa Varvara Ivanovna Ixkul

Another important literary salon of the turn of the century took place at the house of Baronessa Varvara Ivanovna Ixkul.[79] From the end of the 1880s until the 1900s she held the salon, which was open to a very mixed group. Among those who came were people involved in various political movements and representatives of different literary trends, including Symbolist writers and poets of St. Petersburg. Vengerova wrote in her letter to Balakhovskaia that Ixkul's salon "gathered the *fine fleur* of literature and art." Her guests included the Russian philosopher, Vl. Soloviev, who had a strong impact on the idealistic branch of Russian Symbolists; Merezhkovsky, who dedicated to her a cycle of poems published in 1886 and 1887; as well as Zinaida Hippius, Fedor Sologub, and Anton Chekhov. New writers and philosophers read at each gathering. In the first decade of the twentieth century, the popularity lay with Chekhov and Sologub, whose works were featured there. Vengerova often mentions Ixkul's salon in her correspondence.[80]

Viacheslav Ivanov's Tower

Other literary gatherings Vengerova attended included those of the poet Mirra Lokhvitskaia, who moved from Moscow to St. Petersburg in 1898 and who received at her house the representatives of the new literature almost until her death in 1905. In early 1900, Vasily Rozanov was famous for his Sundays, which competed with Sundays at Fedor Sologub's.

One of the most influential literary salons in which Vengerova participated took place at the "Tower" of the Hellinist poet Viacheslav Ivanov. The Tower circle at Ivanov's was extremely famous among Russian intellectuals and artists. Some even called it the most colorful Russian salon. Ivanov started it in the fall of 1905 at his apartment at Tavrisheskaia ulitsa 25, in St. Petersburg. The gatherings at Ivanov's house, the *zhurfiks*, took place on Wednesdays, and were open to all artists, writers, and poets interested in new art and literature. These meetings lasted only for a short time. However, until 1912, the year Ivanov went to Italy, his house was a literary and artistic colony for many of his friends who lived in his house.

All of literary and artistic St. Petersburg was present at Ivanov's early gatherings. There, individual ideas were exchanged and new ideas were born. The Russian philosopher, Nikolai Berdiaev, who was one of the members of that circle, remembers:

On the "Tower" of V. Ivanov – the name of the apartment on the 7th floor across the street from the Tavricheski garden – the most talented and remarkable people of that epoch, poets, philosophers, scientists, painters, actors, and sometimes the men of politics gathered every Wednesday. The most refined discussions on literary, philosophical, mystical, occult, and religious themes occurred there. . . . When I think about "Wednesday," I am stunned by the contrast. On the top of the Tower the refined discussions of the most gifted cultural elite took place, but at the bottom of the Tower the revolution was taking place. These were two non-converging worlds.[81]

Ivanov himself was a fascinating personality. Berdiaev describes him:

Viacheslav Ivanov was one of the most remarkable people of that epoch, rich in talent. There was something unexpected in the fact that such a refined man, who had such universal culture, was born in Russia. The Russian 19th century did not know people like him. . . . V. Ivanov was the best Russian Classicist. He was a universal man: poet, scientist, philologist, specialist in Greek religion, philosopher, theologist, occultist, publicist. He also intervened in politics. He was the most remarkable, the most aristocratic discussant . . . and a real charmer. He belonged to people who have an aesthetic need to be in harmony and in correspondence with the milieu and the surrounding people. He gave the impression of a person who always adapted himself and constantly changed his views. . . . But in the end, I think, he always remained himself. . . . He was everything: the preservationist, the anarchist, the occultist, and the defender of the Orthodox religion; he was a mystic and a positivist scientist. His talent was enormous. As a poet, he was scholastic and difficult. . . . First he was a brilliant essayist. He was the most interested in seducing souls.[82]

In a letter from 1906, Vengerova depicts an episode that took place at Ivanov's Tower, related to the 1905 Revolution. That episode not only gives a picture of gatherings at the Tower, but demonstrates the degree to which the government was suspicious of and even persecuted the intellectual circles of St. Petersburg, especially after the Revolution of 1905. The "tradition" of being suspicious of intellectuals and their circles and of persecuting intellectuals continued in Soviet times. The Soviet government was in name revolutionary, but in reality was harsher than the pre-revolutionary Russian government. The dictatorship of the proletarians brought more harm, more destruction, more death and persecution – not only to the intelligentsia, but also to the whole populace – than did the Russian monarchy. However, at the time Vengerova wrote a letter about the incident at Ivanov's tower, Russian intellectuals did not know what the future would hold for them and could not imagine that the Soviet government to come would be a terror and nightmare for the Russian people. In 1906, they all wanted change and struggled against the government of the time. Vengerova wrote:

You cannot imagine the present atmosphere of life. The reaction reached its top. . . . About two weeks ago we gathered at Viach. Ivanov's Tower to discuss religion and mysticism. The police showed up, soldiers with arms were searching all of us until morning. A lot has been written about this incident in the newspapers; Merezhkovsky's "open letter to Vitte," entitled "Where is my hat?" (the police stole his hat during the search) made a lot of noise. . . . There are constant arrests, destruction, repression – and . . . the complete absence of the cultural life. I feel in myself something savage – it is true that the tension of the political moment is so intense that everything else is colorless. For us, the people of thought and spirit, it is not the right place to be at this moment.[83]

Although there was not any literary press associated with the Tower, it was an important center of intellectual life and very influential in the development and evolution of art, literature, philosophy, and social ideas of the early twentieth century.

Turn-of-the-century literary meetings also took place at literary associations such as the Neo-Philological Society of St. Petersburg University, the Shakespeare Circle, and the Women's Society, though in these associations the government was less intrusive.

FEDOR SOLOGUB

At all these places Vengerova often met Fedor Sologub, who in the 1890s had already become one of the important figures of Russian Decadence. To launch his literary career, Sologub had moved to St. Petersburg from Vitega in 1892, where he worked as a school teacher. Sologub was a member of the same literary and artistic circles, as Vengerova, and like her, wrote critical essays for a St. Petersburg newspaper, *News (Novosti)*. Vengerova had a great appreciation of Sologub's talent and wrote about him in 1896:

[Sologub] is an amazingly interesting and special person. Yesterday he was proving that everything which can be derided and repeated is funny and showing why in life everything is funny, sad and joyful. The only thing which is not funny is death, because the "ocean of death" cannot be repeated at will.[84]

Then later, in 1898, she added in a letter to Sonia:

The lion of the season is Sologub. He began to write poems of unreal beauty. Nikolai Maksimovich [Minsky] and Merezhkovsky became the heralds of his glory. . . . I call Sologub . . . *cher maître,* but he is convinced that everybody praises him only because of his respect for "poets and critics." I shall send you some of his new poems – you will see yourself how beautiful they are.[85]

Vengerova's appreciation of Sologub went further than the mere expression of her impressions of him in her private correspondence. In 1899, in "Lettres russes" of *Mercure de France*, she published an article about Sologub.[86] Here she introduced Sologub to the French audience; using him as an example, she explains the specificity and novelty of the ideas of Russian Symbolism and suggests that his works encompass two main levels typical of the movement. On the first level, his works represent his perception of physical reality, which he depicts as an embodiment of ugliness. On the second level, he shows that in this ugly reality there is always beauty, and it symbolizes the beauty of the outer world here on earth. The role of that beauty, as it became for Russian Symbolists and Decadents, is to ennoble the ugly physical world of every day life and to make us aspire for the better.

Vengerova also explains the symbolic role of the inner world of Sologub's protagonists as well as the role of love in his works. In her view, the world of the protagonists' dreams is more real and more powerful than the physical reality surrounding them. For instance, in Sologub's short story, "Shadows," the little boy, Volodia, and his beautiful mother liberate themselves from the boredom and meaninglessness of life only when they focus on the world of their imaginations. Sologub portrays this inner world with strange images of shadows on the wall, the creation of which becomes Volodia's and his mother's main occupation.

Vengerova also emphasizes the importance of love in Sologub's works. She demonstrates that for him, love is not a test, as in Hippius' works, but rather an initiation to the world of Beauty through the path of self-knowledge. These ideas were inspired by Plato's famous *The Symposium*, to which Russian Symbolists were drawn. For instance, in Sologub's novel, *Heavy Dreams,* a precursor to his masterpiece, *The Petty Demon*, Vengerova sees three types of love. The first type of love is typical for the majority of people, who are absorbed in everyday banality and pettiness of existence. In Sologub's novels the majority of the protagonists experience this type of love. Usually born out of revolt against the world and relationships, the second type is filled with many negative emotions. Here, everything is questioned. The characters who experience this type of love usually search for something beyond the world they live in and strive to break through it. The third type reflects a certain intimacy with a higher reality, or at least an aspiration toward it. In *Heavy Dreams,* that higher reality is a love between the teacher, Login, and Anna-Niuta Ermolina, his fiancée. To emphasize the purity of this love and the union that it builds through the return to the freedom from original sin, Vengerova describes it in the following terms:

> To bring out the intensity of the feelings of these lovers thirsty for an ideal, Sologub imagines an original scene. Niuta appears entirely naked in front of Login, who is her fiancé at that moment. The beauty of the beloved, whom Login respects like a saint, inspires a new ardor of his striving for moral perfection. At the end of this scene, Niuta and her fiancé feel regenerated and are ready to live a life of beauty.[87]

Vengerova was the first to introduce Sologub to the French audience, while he was still little known and accepted in Russia. As with Hippius, this introduction was instrumental in initiating the French public to the specificity and novelty of Russian Symbolism.

ANTON CHEKHOV

Vengerova met Anton Chekhov at the salon of Baroness Ixkull. In 1900 she described him in her letter to Sonia as the *"Clou* of the evening, . . . the lion of the present season,"[88] and "an amazingly pleasant, intelligent and simple"[89] person. In 1899, Vengerova wrote about him in "Lettres Russes" of *Mercure de France,* as a writer whose works were lying on the cusp between Russian realist literature and Russian literature created by Symbolists, whom Vengerova depicts as "a very small group that has a more elevated and more disinterested idea of art, and seeks to realize pure beauty."[90]

In that article, Vengerova discusses Chekhov's three short stories, "Heartache," ("Toska," 1886), "Ward 6" ("Palata 6," 1892) and "Peasants" ("Muzhiki," 1897). She explains that his description of hideous physical reality, although it resembles the style of Russian Realists, is very Symbolistic. Like Symbolists, he describes the ugliness of life not for the sake of some political or ideological cause, as the Realists do, but rather to convey its effect on the spiritual aspects of human existence, on his protagonists' moods and the overall state of their souls.

In her view, Chekhov's works did not have the mystical dimension found in Symbolism: he neither perceives reality as a vehicle for another, higher existence, nor the inner life as a symbol of that existence. However, in Chekhov like in Symbolist works, the souls of his characters often strive to break through everyday existence for the sake of creating a new and better life, one more congenial with the aspirations of the soul. Vengerova believes that Chekhov's skill at painting the darkness of life, the nuances of his characters' inner worlds, as well as the atmosphere he creates around them by reflecting the aura of their inner life, had a strong impact on Russian Symbolists. She sees Chekhov as a precursor of Russian Symbolism.

Vengerova's article about Chekhov was the first written about him in French. It played a seminal role in introducing him to the Western reader, and in having his works translated and published in French, and later in other European languages.

THEATER

When Vengerova returned to St. Petersburg in 1893, her activities in St. Petersburg became closely associated with theater life. As her

correspondence indicates, she wrote reviews of foreign theater performances, including performances of great Western European
actors and actresses in plays representing the new western
European trends which Vengerova had translated into Russian –
often from manuscripts. While translating the plays, she worked
with the Russian theaters to stage the performances. In 1893, she
wrote in one of her letters to Sonia:

> I wrote to you in my previous letter that I am covered with literary
> work and am very happy about it. I am less happy about the other
> type of work. I wrote to you that at one point I published the
> reviews about the English theater, which came here. The English
> left, but my reviews for some reason were liked by the *gens du
> métier*, and I was given the same assignment regarding the German
> theater – for *The News*. It is less amusing, although the company is
> excellent. The theater takes three evenings a week, and it is quite
> upsetting. *Enfin, il faut passer par là.*[91]

Later on in a letter to her sister, Isabelle, Zinaida Afanasievna wrote:

> I am writing an article about "The City of External Culture
> (Berlin)," translating Muther, preparing articles for publication. I
> even dream about a book that I hope will be ready in two years. In
> the intervals I will be writing, starting next week, about the foreign
> theaters for *The News*. Rejan, Duse, and Mune-Sully are coming.
> They will be the subjects of my articles. I decided to write about
> these actors because they do not come as often. To write about the
> theater occasionally is not that bad. This year theater somehow
> became the inseparable part of life. The new theater director,
> Volkonsky, is in touch with *The World of Art*. Starting in January, a
> new journal, *The Pantheon of the Theaters*, will be published.
> Probably "Alma"[92] will be published in it. I will be a constant con-
> tributor to that journal. In addition, I plan to present on the
> Imperial stage, "The Green Parrot," by Schnitzler.[93] I translate the
> part in prose, and Chumina[94] translates the part in poetry. Now to
> stage that play will be easy for me.[95]

One of the most interesting of Vengerova's articles written on the theater is "About the Abstract in the Theater" ("Ob otvlechennom v teatre").[96] As a real Symbolist, faithful to her convictions, she asserts that the only great theater can be that which does not imitate or depict life, but conveys the inner lives of the characters, the spirit and essence of their inner worlds. For her, "Theater . . . which imitates life, without using the interior spirit of life, is dead theater."[97]

In the article, "Stanislavsky,"[98] Vengerova offers an engaging interpretation of plays staged by the famed Russian actor and theater director whose innovative acting method was later used all over the world.[99] She asserts that his performances represent a symbol of the inner life and of a spiritual mood of the characters. She stresses that, although Stanislavsky uses details to describe external reality, his purpose is to emphasize the internal. He uses the details of the external to create a mood, through which he can introduce the invisible but always present reality of the inner existence:

Stanislavsky . . . is an artist who keenly understands the symbolism of everyday details, expressing for the eyes and for the ear the conditions of the human soul. It is not important that he gives many details. What is important is that he emphasizes what is the most important among them and through that carries the spectator to imaginary worlds. He surpasses the limits of realistic theater and creates the intimate theater of moods.[100]

Vengerova was closely associated with Stanislavsky's theater, Moscow Art Theater (MHAT – Moskovskyi Khudozhestvennyi Teatr), and was well acquainted with the actors. In one of her letters to her sister, Isabelle, Vengerova described an intimate and interesting evening she spent with the MHAT actors, "in the company of *moskvichi*," as she called it:

At the end, the most pleasant event took place: Kachalov[101] took me . . . to a separate room. Stanislavsky, Moskvin,[102] Knipper[103] and a few others followed, and in an intimate circle we drank only

Cordon Rouge. Kachalov told me that the dry champagne is good for one's heart and we had a very interesting conversation until 6 am. There were not any taxis anymore and in some kind of child car, which had a narrow bench, Stanislavsky and Knipper drove me home. . . .
During the drinking party, I had a serious discussion with him [Stanislavsky]. Schnitzler's play . . . is not good *for them*. He says that it does not touch any "nerve." If they had had in repertory ten plays, they would have staged this one without hesitation. Whereas for one among three it is a little bit weak . . . Stanislavsky, however, comforted me by other promises: he wants very much to stage D'Annunzio[104] and B. Shaw.[105, 106]

Her intimate acquaintance with MHAT and some other Moscow theaters for which she supplied the plays she translated, gave birth, in 1912, to the article "Moscow Theater" ("Moskovskie teatry"),[107] one of the most interesting pieces on the theater published in various Russian newspapers. Here Vengerova describes Moscow theaters as more progressive than those in St. Petersburg; the former city, she believed, staged plays representing new artistic trends and ideas. She discusses three plays: Ibsen's "Peer Gynt," staged by the Moscow Art Theater; Minsky's "A Small Temptation" ("Maly soblazn"), staged by the Korsh Theater; and Schnitzler's "The Broad Field" ("Das weite Land"), staged by two theaters – Maly and Nezlobinsky – under two different translations of the title. Her article analyzes, from a literary point of view, the difference, between how the plays had been written and staged. In all three cases she emphasizes the Symbolist ideas of the turn of the century. In "Peer Gynt," she finds that the title character lives a life of fantasy that becomes his reality, a circumstance not accepted by those around him:

Peer Gynt is an embodiment of a fantasy, which is a reality opposed to the world, and in which this fantasy seems to be false. . . . Peer Gynt also embodies the search of the desired in life and the . . . desired in death.[108]

In Minsky's play, "A Small Temptation," Vengerova stresses the danger of "small things." The outside world can enslave the inner world by imposing rules in human existence, thus killing the soul. Vengerova writes:

> The idea of "A Small Temptation" is that the objects are beautiful. And the guilty one is the one who made out of beautiful objects the signs of what serves vanity.[109]

Analyzing Schnitzler's play, "The Broad Field," Vengerova asserts that the essence of the play is that "people . . . in a fatal way become slaves, or . . . victims of emotions, against which their conscious will most of all rebels."[110] Being a Symbolist, Vengerova shows the power of the unconscious world and implies the importance of finding harmony between the conscious and unconscious worlds so that the two can co-exist. All three plays belong to a new trend in theater and literature, because their main subject is the inner world of an individual or the inner life of humanity as a whole. They are not preoccupied by the external; they emphasize, in one way or another, only the internal.

Among the theater people, Vengerova was quite close with the actress Lidia Borisovna Iavorskaia (1871-1921), who in 1901 founded and directed The New Theater in St. Petersburg. Although their relationship, at least in the early stages of their acquaintance, was quite rocky, throughout life it greatly changed and became very warm. In 1914, when Vengerova found herself in London on the brink of the First World War, sick and unable to return to Russia, she, after almost twenty years of acquaintance with Iavorskaia, wrote to her sister Isabelle about her for the first time:

> I have here a real friend – Lida [Lidia Iavorskaia]. In this difficult time she showed herself to be a stunningly warm and giving person; . . . I suddenly found myself completely alone in the world and without her would have perished from all points of view, and she, with an endless tenderness, took care of me . . . in the darkest

moments and overall tried to make my life happy. If she did not always succeed, it is not her fault. But the fact that I am alive and healthy is only thanks to her.[111]

Vengerova was also well acquainted with Iavorskaia's friend, the poet and playwright Tatiana Lvovna Shchepkina-Kupernik,[112] whom she did not appreciate as a person though she was aware of her literary talents, and worked with her on a number of projects.[113]

NEW LIFE (NOVIA ZHIZN)

Although Vengerova was an integral part of the St. Petersburgeois literary milieu and played a role in shaping the Russian culture of the turn of the century until the First World War, she spent many years before 1893, and again in the decade that preceded the War, in Western Europe. In the Winter of 1908, she left Russia to live in Paris and London. Her decision resulted from the circumstances that forced her friend, Nikolai Minsky, to depart from Russia as a political emigrant in the Spring of 1906.

Vengerova's and Minsky's hope was to have their own publishing venture. In 1904, Minsky tried to obtain permission to publish a newspaper, *The New Life (Novaia Zhizn)*, and in 1905, the year of the first Russian revolution, he received it. During the Revolution, Vengerova wrote about the events and the newspaper:

We are not cut off from the world any more. The post is more or less reestablished. . . . It is unthinkable to describe what we are going through. We are in the *middle of the ferocious Revolution*[114] – which will end only when "the document about freedom" will be guaranteed. In the meantime the struggle is getting worse and worse and the senseless horrors are still to come. The anarchy already on its way – fierceness of the *chernaia sotnia*,[115] murders of intellegentsia. . . .

Here everything is boiling. We live by facts, which distanced us from our "love for the distant, abstract." The first sign of it is Nik. Mask.'s newspaper, *New Life*, which is a part of the press of the political and economical section of the Social Democrat party,[116] headed by Gorky. Do you remember our negotiations with Gorky, who still in the summer seemed to us to be extreme? Our views now changed, because of the changes in the Russian reality.[117]

Although officially Minsky was the editor-in-chief of *New Life*, in reality he did not have any power. The power was in the hands of the Social Democrats. In a biographical essay[118] about Minsky, Semen Afanasievich Vengerov explains the reasons for Minsky's collaboration with the Social Democrats, and how it happened that Minsky, an enemy of the party a few months before the creation of the newspaper, became, unexpectedly for himself, a victim of that collaboration:

It was not possible for the Social Democrats to have their own press, and it is on that ground that the God searcher, Minsky, united with the Bolsheviks, although still six months before in his book, *The Religion of the Future,* he called the Social Democrats the representatives of banality and of spiritual pettiness. Later, trying to justify himself against attacks coming from all the sides, . . . Minsky explained that he considered this union purely mechanical. The newspaper was strictly divided; the editor did not intervene in the Social and Political section, but had full autonomy in the Literary and Philosophical section.

The naive belief in this type of cohabitation ended up in all respects in a tragic way. Already in the first issues, . . . without asking the publisher-editor, Gorky published an article where "aesthetics" was treated *en canaille,* and all writers, including Leo Tolstoy, were called the petty bourgeois.

In addition to all that, in the first issue, the Social Democrats placed their full program, including the ideas about creation of the Democratic republic. Although it happened in the midst of the "days of freedom," that same day there was a call for a trial and Minsky was arrested. After he spent a few days in prison, he was released and was required to pay a large ransom that he neglected to pay. Instead he soon moved abroad. . . .

Minsky's speedy passage from the struggle for mysticism to the struggle for "the organized social proletariat" cannot be explained by Minsky's complete lack of understanding. . . . The editor [Minsky] . . . did not repudiate in any decisive manner his belonging to "the political section" of his newspaper. He, for a short time, although in an entirely uncertain way, was in agreement with the intolerance of that "political section." Here appeared the fatal shortcoming. . . . That shortcoming manifested itself in the absence of depth and in the fast transitions from one type of feeling to another, which is the nastiest feature for the organic growth of talents. . . . The three-day love affair with the Socialists took place not only with Minsky the editor, but also with Minsky the poet, as exemplified by his poem, "The Hymn of Workers."[119]

Zinaida Hippius also describes, quite ironically, the situation related to Minsky's departure from Russia:

S.D. [Social Democrats], as soon as it did not smell right, packed their suitcases and cleverly slipped away in emigration, with Lenin at the head. Almost all members of the "new" Lenin's "life" disappeared in that way. Whereas Minsky . . . before Lenin clearly told him "no," was arrested. He was scared, although in vain. Nothing would have happened to him. This kind was usually peacefully released. His admirers, however, bought him out (took him to freedom until the "end of the trial" under the condition of ransom), but he immediately ran away abroad, and became a free but useless emigrant.[120]

Zinaida Vengerova, who lived in a *menage à trois* with Minsky and his wife at that time,[121] was personally concerned and records these events:

The New Life ended its existence with the publication of the Revolutionary Manifest, because of which it is stopped until the trial, and Nik. Maks. is arrested. He spent a week in a prison, in conditions horrible for his health. Then he was not accused of one crime, but of seven, for different issues of the newspaper, including article 103 (the insult of His Majesty), for which one is condemned to penal servitude. The government became furious, especially against the press of the extreme parties; that is why the trial on the first accusation (for which the lawyer Grusenberg expected an acquittal) was, in a completely unlawful way, dismissed the day before the trial – and all seven accusations for the trial were put together in their totality. In the best case, the prosecutor and the procurator told us that he would be condemned to two years at the fortress. . . . Do you imagine it for N.M.! And before the trial it was necessary either to pay 10,000 for each accusation (total of 70 thousand), or to sit in prison. Given the situation, the editorial board and friends helped, . . . and N.M. is now abroad.[122]

After his departure, Vengerova and Vilkina rented their apartment, and in the winter of 1908 Vengerova left Russia to be closer to Minsky. She went first to Paris, where Minsky lived in exile, and then to London. She felt at home in London, loved its spirit, and cherished the group of friends and colleagues she kept there throughout her life. She felt at home in the British Museum Library, where she always enjoyed working. London for her, unlike Paris where she never felt entirely at ease, was the city of her heart.

CHAPTER III

HOMELESS AND AT HOME: ACROSS EUROPE

In 1908, Zinaida Afanasievna moved to Europe, where she lived principally in England and France. If previously her base was in Russia, now her base became Europe as a whole. She traveled, lectured, and wrote extensively on the topics of her interest: French, English, German, and Italian literature and art. She was truly a "European" person; comfortable with western European languages and cultures, she wrote in great depth on art as well as literature, on the past as well as the present. But it was for Russia, for the Russian audience, for the Russian journals and newspapers, that she continued to work. Living in France, despite the hardship of Minsky's emigration, was a positive experience. She was able to follow closely the literary and artistic news of the countries she was interested in and write about them in her essays.

FRANCE

I hate Paris as much as I love England. I am here in Paris only because of N.M. There, in England, there are people, there is comfort and it is a pleasure to work there. I even get too many literary assignments. I have finished the English translation of Tolstoy, and a few other things for the English magazines. I just avoided the publication of Chekhov in English, under my editorship. Everything I need for my Russian works is there in the British

Museum. Whereas here, in this illiterate Paris, besides rugs and hats there is nothing. I think it is the reason why Sonia[1] lost her sensibility. She "swims" among rugs and hats, which, unfortunately for her, are accessible to her in the quantity she wishes.[2]

Vengerova wrote this letter to her sister Isabelle in 1911. Zinaida Afanasievna's attitude toward Paris, however, was not always the one she expressed in this letter. At the time she wrote it, she did not recall the pleasant years (1888-1891) she spent in her youth in Paris. Neither did she know at that time that she would seek to establish herself there after the Revolution. Many years of her life and work were associated with Paris. These years can be divided into two major periods. The first, from 1888 to 1893, corresponds to her first years in Paris as a student of literature. Although she returned to Russia in 1893, she visited France every year until 1900. During her visits, she collected important information that she used to write articles for Russian periodicals about literary and social phenomena that took place in France. She also used her visits to build contacts with a variety of newspapers and journals in which she published articles about the literary and social events in Russia.

The second period corresponds to her life in Paris between 1908 and 1912, when she decided to establish herself in Europe to be closer to her friend, N. M. Minsky.[3] Although she spent considerable time in London during that period, she had a base in Paris and was always coming back to check on Minsky and help him with the publication of the Russian language newspaper, *Word (Slovo)*.

Finally, she visited Paris occasionally after her definitive departure from Russia that followed the 1917 Revolution, when the Soviets came to power. Vengerova left Russia in 1921. She first lived in Berlin, then moved to London and periodically stayed in Paris for extended periods, collecting the material for some of her articles in libraries and museums, especially in the Musée Carnavalet.

French Symbolism and Decadence

Vengerova arrived in Paris for the first time in 1888, at an important moment in French literary history: Decadence, though still viable, began to decline, and the new movement of French Symbolism, an idealistic variation of Decadence, came to life. Although in name Symbolism and Decadence were different, between French Symbolism and Decadence there were many similarities, because both movements sprang from the same root. Both were born from the introduction of Théophile Gautier's novel *Mademoiselle de Maupin*, which "might be called the very manifesto of '*l'art pour l'art*,'"[4] from Charles Baudelaire's *Les Fleurs du mal* and Gautier's "Notice" to the second edition of *Les Fleurs du mal* in 1868, which appeared after Baudelaire's death. The Decadence and Symbolist movements in France emerged from a revolt against "bourgeois" life and the desire to shock by unconventional ways of thinking. This attitude manifested itself in the poets' and artists' beliefs and claims that the artificial in all its forms is superior to nature, "a sign of the human will correcting to its liking the forms and colours furnished by matter."[5] This attitude is also evident in the contempt for physical and material life, in the desire to escape to a world created by imagination and expressed in art. This "new" world was reflected in the artwork's form, choice of words, and musicality; and through the artist's emotions and sensations, the wealth of his or her inner world – the part of human existence that survives decaying physicality.

These basic ideas took the shape of a "movement" among the young artists of the 1880s, a few years before Vengerova's arrival in Paris. Max Nordau, a committed positivist, summarized the history of literature and art of the *fin de siècle* in biting but still quite instructive terms, and described the birth of the French Decadent-Symbolist movement in his book, *Degeneration* (1895):

We see a number of young men assembled for the purpose of founding a school. . . . Shortly after 1880 there was, in the Quartier

Latin in Paris, a group of literary aspirants, all about the same age, who used to meet in an underground café at the Quai St. Michel, and, while drinking beer, smoking and quibbling late into the night, or in the early hours of the morning, abused in a scurrilous manner the well-known and successful authors of the day, while boasting of their own capacity, as yet unrevealed to the world.[6]

When Vengerova arrived in Paris in the late 1880s, the distinction between the movements of Decadence and Symbolism in the minds of the general public, and even in the minds of the representatives of both movements, was confused. The differences between them were not articulated for a long time. Today, however, it is possible to see that French Symbolism came into existence not to replace the basic ideas of French Decadence, but to supplement them, and to elevate the essence of the movement in the 1880s and 1890s because these two movements were still perceived as one. One of Vengerova's major contributions was not only in introducing the French Symbolist and Decadent poets, writers, and artists to the Russian public, but in seeking to understand the differences between them and to articulate these differences in her articles.

At first, in the 1880s and 1890s, Vengerova was attracted to French Decadence and Symbolism because of the rebellious nature of these movements. She wrote in her "Autobiographical Essay" (1914):

In French Decadence I sharply felt its liberating element, its striking individualism, that breaks down the moral code of dead social interdictions in the name of the creation of new spiritual values. This revolt in the name of aesthetic ideals captivated me in the poetry of Baudelaire and in the creativity of his immediate followers, Verlaine, Rimbeau, Moréas, and others. In my articles about these best representatives of French Decadence, published in *The Herald of Europe*, I tried, as much as I could, to emphasize that particular meaning of the French poets, the renovating influence of their tempestuous individualism. They seemed to me to be fighters in the area of spirituality, fighters for beauty, which was the essence of the freedom of individuality. In that element, their creativity had an importance for a certain part of Russian literature and influenced the young generation in Russia.[7]

But later, in her articles about French and Belgian Decadent and Symbolist poets, she made a subtle distinction between the two movements. The result of her stay in Paris in the late 1880s and early 1890s, "at the time of the blossoming in France of Decadence and of Symbolism,"[8] was the publication of her article, "The Symbolist Poets in France" ("Poety Symvolisty vo Frantsii"). This article appeared in 1892 in *The Herald of Europe,* and is considered to be seminal for the introduction of Symbolism into Russia.

The article is dense with information. Vengerova included the Poets-Decadents under the category of Poets-Symbolists, because between the two bodies of poetry there is little distinction, both having the same root and eventually merging into each other. In this article she traces the origins of Symbolism in poetry and describes the major works, ideas, and styles of French Symbolist poets. She discusses the works of Verlaine, about whom in 1896, after his death, she wrote a separate article.[9] She initiates the readers into the works of Mallarmé, Rimbaud, Laforgue, Vicaire, Baudelaire, Moréas, and mentions Tristan Corbière and Gustave Kahn.[10] She also writes about Morris Rollin, George Rodenbach, and Henri de Régnier, one of the most popular Symbolists to whom she devoted an article in 1904. In "The Symbolist Poets in France," she introduces readers to several important Decadent and Symbolist periodicals of the time – *Revue Contemporaine, Revue Indépendante, La Vogue,* and *Revue Wagnerienne.*

As noted earlier, the article greatly impressed Valery Briusov, the future Russian poet and creator of the "Decadent" branch of Russian Symbolism. Today Vengerova's article is mentioned in many encyclopedias – Western European and American – as the piece which introduced French Symbolism to Russia.

In her next article, "The New Trends in the French Novel: J.K.

Huysmans" ("Novye techeniia vo Frantsuskom romane. J.K. Huysmans"), published in 1896 in *The Northern Herald,* she discusses the differences between Decadence and Symbolism and expresses her own attitude toward these movements. Joris Carl Huysmans published his first novel, *Against Nature (À Rebours),* in 1884, a few years before Vengerova's arrival in Paris. That work was classified as one of the first Decadent novels, in which the main character, Jean Floressas des Esseintes, turns away from life to create his own "superior" world – an extension of his imagination and the wealth of his inner life.

In 1891, when Vengerova had already lived in France for two years, Huysmans' second novel, *Là Bas,* was published. In this novel, Decadent in its spirit but naturalistic and graphic stylistically in its description of the world of black magic, Huysmans also deals with the search for impressions and strong feelings, which this time are provoked by the escape from the reality of life to the reality of that magic. As in *Against Nature,* Huysmans recognizes the failure of such an escape and, unlike *Against Nature,* suggests a solution: the main character finds the answer and harmony in his conversion to Catholicism.

Vengerova was fascinated by Huysmans, and her initiation of the Russian reader to this unusual writer was thorough and detailed. In her article, she narrates Huysmans' life and retells all his novels written up to that time. The most interesting part of the article, however, is Vengerova's conclusion regarding the nature of Huysmans' novels, a conclusion that demonstrates her own attitude toward Decadence, as opposed to Symbolism, and one that makes a clear and novel distinction between these two movements:

> Huysmans is a brilliant representative of the positive side of Decadence. His creativity is filled with noble pessimism; he mercilessly prosecutes the values of earthly life, and, during his interest in naturalism, he paints, with special pleasure, the ugliness of life, and in later novels, the abyss of vice. . . . He has a natural disgust for bourgeois ideals. From this pessimistic approach toward reality comes

the destructive role of Huysmans in general and of Decadence in particular toward the previous formulation of art: by humiliating life, by showing that its every phenomenon is insulting to the superior side of the human spirit, Huysmans demonstrates the illusory quality of art imitating nature in a servile way.

Another artistically valuable quality of Huysmans is the exceptional refinement and susceptibility of his aesthetic sense. . . . A further feature of Huysmans goes hand-in-hand with the Decadent ideal. Together with his negation of life's banality and with the exceptionally refined development of his taste, we notice his complete lack of categorical conclusions. . . . Huysmans is not a fanatic of his aesthetic ideals. Always, when he develops his schemas, he gives the impression of someone who consistently supposes the possibility of schemas completely opposite and equally illusionary to his own. Scepticism . . . is one of the strongest sides of Decadence, that moderates by its aesthetic intuition all extremes of dogmatic ideologies.

Behind all the negations of Huysmans, behind his pessimistic attitude toward reality, there is not any kind of aspiration of the idealistic nature. Beauty that seems to replace, for Huysmans, any kind of other sacred object, attracts Huysmans purely by its exterior manner: a certain artificial way of combining the words, colors, sounds that are agreeable to his exhausted nerves and to his refined taste, but he does not attach to it any symbolistic meaning, he does not see in it the reflection of a truth inaccessible to reason, he does not see in the Beauty its mystery, its divine beginning. As a result, Huysmans' moods, in spite of all their originality and artistry, are not profound. In them, there is no reflection of the creative nostalgia of the soul yearning for an unreachable attraction toward the mysterious and divine; in them he paints only the psychology of disappointment and boredom of a person who is searching for a solution in the novelty of his impressions, like the neurasthenic . . . searches for oblivion in opium and hashish. All Huysmans' creativity is endowed with ill nature; it does not open new horizons to the fatigued soul . . . it only lulls to sleep ill humanity by telling strange fairy tales and by caressing the sense of smell with the perfume of poisoned flowers that speak about the decay.[11]

Vengerova sees in Huysmans a Decadent because his perceptions of the attributes of Decadence and Symbolism, such as Beauty, creativity, soul's moods, are superficial. He is unsatisfied with life and revolts against it; he sees some kind of salvation in Beauty, creativity, and the wealth of one's inner life; but contrary to the Symbolists, he does not offer any kind of superior meaning to these notions. They are here, but they lead nowhere. Whereas for Symbolists, these things have almost a religious meaning; they are a path to superior reality, to the mystery and the transcendental, to salvation.

In articles about Symbolist poets and writers, as opposed to Decadents, Vengerova often emphasized the importance of their mystical ideals and the correlation that can exist between these ideas and the embellishment of one's life on earth. In her view, the harmony between contemplation and activity often manifested itself in the aspiration of some of these writers and poets to embody their spiritual ideal into a social form. For instance, when she writes about Gustave Kahn, one of the champions of the "vers libres," she emphasizes the union between Kahn's literary and social activities. After she gives a list of all his literary merits, she asserts:

> Recently his active nature pushed him to the path of practical activity. . . . Gustave Kahn participated in the organization of the first open universities and continues to give lectures to workers and fight in print against racist and class persecution in France. Gustave Kahn's social activity merges with his purely artistic interests. He believes in immediate connection between art and life, in the necessity to raise the free self-consciousness in people in order to engender in them an artistic receptivity and to develop their tastes. Combining Aestheticism with democratic propaganda, Gustave Kahn follows the steps of English writers, Ruskin and Morris, and in France, Anatole France, the advocates of "art for everybody."[12]

If we follow the main thread of her articles about French Symbolist and Decadent poets and writers, we will notice that, for her, Symbolism is a movement which worships Beauty. This Beauty consists of a harmony between the ability to contemplate, to enjoy different pleasures related to the senses, and to cultivate an inner world of activity and mysticism. She regards Decadence, on the other hand, as a movement which, although it also worships Beauty and embraces some features of Symbolism, does not seek any superior mystical meaning and avoids any tendency toward action to change the world.

Belgian Symbolism

In Paris, during her first stay between 1888 and 1893, Vengerova discovered and was fascinated by another kind of Symbolism – Belgian Symbolism – that manifested itself through mysticism and spiritual quest. At the same time she came to France in 1888, Belgian Symbolist literature and art had begun to establish themselves. The names of Maurice Maeterlinck, Georges Rodenbach, and Emile Verhaeren were already known as fervent Symbolist poets.

In 1889, Maeterlinck published his collection of poetry, *Serres chaudes,* and staged his play, *La Princesse Maleine.* In *Le Figaro* of 24 August 1890, Octave Mirbeau published his famous article about Maeterlinck's play, comparing Maeterlinck's talent to Shakespeare's. By that time, Emile Verhaeren was already known for his collections of poetry: *Les Flamandes* (1883), *Les Moines* (1886), *Les Soirs* (1887), *Les Débâcle* (1888), and *Les Flambeaux noirs* (1890).

Georges Rodenbach became famous between 1881 and 1891, when his literary career was at its most intense. He lived in Paris and represented "young Belgium" in France. During this time, he published his well-known books, *La Mer élegante, L'Hiver mondain, La Jeunesse blanche, Le Règne du silence,* and in 1892, his most famous novel, *Bruges-la-morte.* He was especially appreciated by his fellow

115

poets. Verhaeren was the first to call him "the poet of dreams," and put him next to his friends, Edmond de Goncourt and Stéphane Mallarmé.

These three poets-writers, Maeterlinck, Verhaeren, and Rodenbach, fascinated Vengerova. She followed their works from the moment of their first discovery in the late 1880s until the late 1890s and early 1900s, when she wrote richly informative articles about them. Vengerova was especially attracted by the mystical and dream-like spirit of their writings, by the atmosphere they created, and by their originality.

Her article about Maeterlinck appeared in 1899, six years before the first translations of his works were published in Russian.[13] Although Vengerova was not the first to mention Maeterlinck's name to the Russian audience, she was the first to write a detailed and thorough article about him and to awaken a great interest in him by relating his biography, retelling his works, and explaining his ideas. She was familiar with Maeterlinck's works because she had read them in France, and in French, long before they were translated into Russian. She also spends a considerable part of her article discussing his philosophy, and symbolism, and how both are related to life and social issues. Vengerova's articles on Verhaeren[14] and Rodenbach[15] pioneered Flemish culture, introducing these poets-writers and their ideas to Russia. They reveal her understanding of the influence of Belgian writers on their French counterparts at the time.

Although Vengerova returned to Russia in 1893, she continued to be closely associated with France and interested in the literary life of Paris. She visited France every year either in the summer or in the winter. Moreover, she wished to have a position in France and work for one of the French journals. Her wish came true in 1897, when she began an extensive collaboration with *Mercure de France*'s section, "Lettres russes," where she published, in French, articles dedicated to Russian contemporary literature. Here, as discussed earlier, she introduced to the French audience Russian writers such as Chekhov, Hippius, Sologub, as well as the Russian art journal, *The World of Art*, and its reaction to Russia's celebration of Pushkin's centennial.[16]

Symbolism and Feminism

Zinaida Afanasievna was very much taken by the feminist movement of the turn of the century. As a woman, and a professionally active one, she was interested in the role and the place of women within society, and wrote two articles. One, "The Russian Woman" ("La Femme russe"), was written in French and published in *Revue mondiale* in 1897.[17] A second, "Feminism and Woman's Freedom" ("Feminizm i zhenskaia svoboda"), was written in Russian, published in 1898 in the Russian journal, *Education (Obrazovanie)*,[18] and dedicated to the place and role of French women within society. Following the philosophy of Symbolism, both articles emphasize the importance of the individual and individuality, which has as a center: the will and the soul. In the article, "La Femme russe," Vengerova familiarizes the French public with the history of women in Russian society, introducing it from the Symbolist point of view. She shows how the Russian woman is able to overcome difficulties in life and make a contribution to the development of society using her will and the power of her inner world and soul.

The article, "Feminism and Woman's Freedom," familiarizes the Russian public with important French social issues of the turn of the century. In it, Vengerova demonstrates how the French woman – as a product of French society which dulled in her any desire to develop an inner strength and personality, and made out of her a comfortable annex to a man – is not only incapable of making a contribution to society, but represents a destructive element. Vengerova uses examples from French history and literature of the 19th century to support her ideas. In "Feminism and Woman's Freedom," she asserts that Feminism, the equality of a woman with a man by the intermediary of the law, is not a sufficient guarantee for a woman's liberation, because the first step for freedom is not legal but psychological: to create in women feelings of individual spirit that will demand equality as a birthright. A law not backed by feminine conviction and confidence in this moral imperative will be ineffectual. This article shows Vengerova's exceptional familiarity with French society and her ability in perceiving the hidden aspects of its social life.

Vengerova was interested in exceptional women, even, or perhaps especially, if they did not have a good reputation. They represented the example of her philosophy. Thus, she wrote several articles on various women writers. For instance, Georges Sand, a French woman, who had enough courage to leave her family in order to start her independent life in Paris and become a writer, was a subject of Vengerova's interest.

In 1892, after the death of Helena Blavatskaia in 1891, Vengerova wrote an article about Blavatskaia's activities, which was published in the *Bibliographical Dictionary*.[19] Her interest in Blavatskaia was mainly related to Blavatskaia's striking personality, independent spirit, abilities, and fame she achieved as the founder of the Theosophical Society. Although Vengerova gives a thorough account of the disclosure of Madame Blavatskaia as a charlatan, her article shows her appreciation of the strong and unusual woman.

Annie Besant's *An Autobiography*, came out in England in 1893. Vengerova translated it into Russian and it appeared in 1895, in six books of *The Northern Herald*.[20] Vengerova took a special interest in the woman who had the courage to take an anti-Christian position in the 1870s, and to publish in Victorian England in 1877 the book by Charles Bladlaugh, *The Fruits of Philosophy*, which advocated birth control. Later in life, Besant entered the Theosophical Society of Madame Blavatskaia and never stopped searching for meaning in life. Vengerova believed that these various women could serve as examples for societies which establish feminist laws, but still have far to go to prepare their citizens to incorporate these laws into their ways of thinking.

Although Vengerova was not interested in theosophy, her article on Blavatskaia and her translation of Annie Besant's *An Autobiography* into Russian were instrumental in introducing theosophy and its ideas to the Russian general public – especially to the younger generation of Russian Symbolists, such as Andrei Bely, who pursued his growing interests in theosophy by going to see Rudolph Steiner[21] in Germany.

Russian Novel and French Culture

In 1899, in *The Herald of Europe,* Vengerova published another instructive article about French culture, "Russian Novel in France" ("Russky roman vo Frantsii"). This article discusses the integration of the Russian novel within French culture, but also examines and stresses the inner differences between French and Russian mentalities, which in Vengerova's view limits the ability of the French reader to appreciate the multi-sided complexity of the Russian novel. Despite the differences, she believes that bringing the two cultures closer together through literature will make them more intimately acquainted and help them achieve a better mutual understanding. In closing, she expresses hope in the ability of time to erase in French readers the present lack of understanding of the Russian novel.

Life in Paris and Minsky's Emigration

The period between 1888 and 1899 was the most prolific and positive in Vengerova's relationship with France. At that time, she was attracted to France and to French culture, and it was a joyful exprience for her to return to France every year. That was not the case during her second stay in France, when she moved to Europe to be closer to Minsky. During that period (1908-1912), when Minsky was in exile, although Vengerova had her "base" in France, she spent a great deal of time in London, traveled to Germany and Austria, and often visited St. Petersburg. She continued to write for Russian periodicals, to translate from different European languages, and to expose trends in western European literature that seemed new to her. She wrote very little about French

119

culture. Her letters from France are filled with bitterness and dissatisfaction.

When Vengerova moved to France in 1908, she had to free up the apartment she had occupied with Minsky and his wife, Liudmila. The departure from that apartment was painful. Liudmila somehow burned both of her hands with petroleum, and Zinaida Afanasievna had to take care of her and the apartment at the same time. She writes about it in a letter to Isabelle:

> I spent the last six days in completely unpredictable and difficult circumstances. Bela [Liudmila Vilkina] burned both her hands. What torture it was and what kind of screams. It is impossible to imagine. It is lucky that only her hands were burned. She could have burned herself entirely. Now she feels better, although . . . the pains in her hands are still horrible. The burns are horrible. Now the wounds are getting dry, but because of the shock Bela is completely sick; she is unable to get up from her bed, looks like a corpse and every second she passes out. . . . We have to go. N.M. does not understand why Bela and I are still here. To write to him about what happened is unthinkable. During Bela's illness, it was necessary to liquidate the apartment . . . In short, that is how everything is organized: books and clothes are packed in 17 boxes, 1 basket and one trunk. [22]

While in France, she wrote "we live in Paris as in a desert, seeing no one."[23] Vengerova organized her work from Paris. She wrote to Isabelle asking her to transmit important professional messages to her friends and colleagues:

> Please tell Chumina, that (1) I want *very much* the Mikhailovsky theater for *Slovo* [Russian newspaper that she and Minsky published in Paris]; (2)Tell everybody that I will participate with pleasure in all periodicals; and that (3) I will bring plays for all theaters. [24]

Describing Minsky's life in Paris and how it affected her, Vengerova wrote to her sister:

I did not have enough courage to write to you from Paris, because of the affect that N.M.'s situation had on me. The newspaper, that gives the minimum for survival, kills him. [25]

In August 1911, Vengerova wrote to Isabelle that she hated Paris with all the fibers of her soul and especially Parisian luxury, but that she deeply loved England. "Oh, my lovely England! How much I love it, because it is not Paris,"[26] she wrote. That attitude toward Paris was not accidental. When Vengerova came to Paris the first time, she was a student. She met many people who had interests and backgrounds similar to hers. One of them was Sonia Balakhovskaia. She easily became integrated within the milieu she lived in and it gave her a feeling of belonging. Later, when she returned to Paris, she was involved in Parisian literary activities. Thus, she was never an idle tourist. Paris had a meaning for her.

When she moved to Paris in 1908, her situation was different. She came because of Minsky and she did not feel that she had a moral freedom to live her life in Paris as she would have done had she been alone. She felt that she was there to help Minsky. As a result, her life was mainly centered on his interests that she made for a time to be hers, which at some level went against her independent nature. Since he was mainly interested in Russian affairs and wanted to publish a Parisian newspaper but in Russian, it separated Vengerova from her natural involvement with France and French culture.

Vengerova's closest friend in Paris, who lived there permanently, was Sonia Balakhovskaia-Petit. With her, Vengerova had complicated and at times rough relations. Balakhovskaia came from a wealthy family. Her husband, Eugène Petit, who practiced law and was involved in French politics, was also wealthy. Although Balakhovskaia was trained as a lawyer like her husband, she had chosen not to practice law and to become involved in the establishment of Franco-Russian relations. In a way she became a patron to her Russian friends involved in arts and literature, and she periodically helped Vengerova, a freelance writer, by giving her money. Though Vengerova and Balakhovskaia originally came from a similar background, their lives evolved differently. Balakhovskaia was a patron, interested in arts and literature, but not involved in them professionally; Vengerova, however, was involved in arts and literature professionally. She worked partly for pleasure, but also to make a living, and often did not have enough to live on. That difference between the two friends created a certain imbalance, and that imbalance grew through the years, especially because Balakhovskaia did not have an easy character. She liked to be appreciated. The tensions between her and Vengerova were often created by their financial relations, in which Balakhovskaia appeared to Vengerova as a person more interested in money than in literature, and as one who regularly reminded her friend that Zinaida owed her for her support. Because Vengerova's stay in Paris was associated with Minsky's emigration, and with financial difficulties, Vengerova did not feel comfortable in having a close interaction with Balakhovskaia at that time. She did not want to feel herself a poor relative, dependent on her friend's favors. Since the bulk of Vengerova's connections with French intellectuals took place through Balakhovskaia and their interactions were quite limited at that time, Vengerova was cut off from French society and did not interact with the French intellectuals as she would have in better circumstances. Not having a library of a caliber sufficient for her work exacerbated the situation, and Paris appeared to her as an unfulfilling place to be.

ENGLAND

Vengerova passionately loved England, especially London: "London has a refreshing effect on me. It is a fact . . . the conditions of work are excellent, and I begin to believe in myself and in my work."[27] For Vengerova, London's landscape was the embodiment of the new understanding of beauty and of the incarnation of "the essence of art of our times."[28] She liked to spend extensive periods of time in London working in the British Museum, walking the London streets, visiting museums. For her,

England was a country of great opportunities and fruitful begin-nings . . . in England and only in England the new word about 'beauty as a foundation of life' was able to find its place in life and to turn the country, which was earlier known for its lack of taste, into the motherland of contemporary Aestheticism, unique in its kind realization of harmony between the teaching of Beauty and the teaching of life in beauty.[29]

Vengerova was especially captivated by English art and literature of the second part of the 19th century. She wrote:

I was personally very much attracted toward the trend in literature and art that was developing in parallel with French Decadence: the English Pre-Raphaelites. I was captivated by its idealistic meaning, the presence of spiritual values. Decadents negated tradition in the name of a Beauty that has not yet been acquired, whereas the ide-alistically tuned Pre-Raphaelites confirmed it – that was their supe-riority. When I speak about these trends at this point from a biographical point of view, how they reflected on my spiritual world, I underline my profound emotional experience, related to the study of Rossetti and other poets and artists of English *fin de siècle*, idealistic, contrary to the amorality of French Decadents.[30]

Oscar Wilde

Vengerova spent many years of her life in London. Her first stay there from 1890 to 1896 was by short periods but gave birth to many important articles about the emerging English culture of the turn of the century. When she first came to London in the early 1890s, English Aestheticism was blooming. This movement, espe-cially associated with Oscar Wilde, was partly derived from French Symbolism and Decadence and partly from the English Pre-Raphaelite movement. Wilde and his followers worshiped Beauty.

In 1897 and in 1913, Vengerova wrote two articles about Wilde, "Oscar Wilde and English Aestheticism," and "Oscar Wilde." She described for the Russian reader the essence of English Aestheticism and Wilde's role in it, as well as the details of Wilde's life and the role he played in turn-of-the-century English culture.[31]

Wilde's dandyism was very popular among Russian Decadents and Symbolists at the turn of the century. To pose as a dandy signified a revolt against bourgeois morality and, often, an effort to shock public opinion. Betsy F. Moeller-Sally defined the phenomenon:

> Historically, dandyism at its best was an individual's response to society's demand for conformity in the 19th century, to the homogenizing tendencies of bourgeois society and morals. Dandyism confronted bourgeois morality and ideology with its refusal to glorify labor, to idealize the natural, its rejection of utility, its scorn for the sacred cow of progress, and the scepticism with which it greeted the great liberal ideals of democracy and equality. The dandy felt himself set apart from society, or above it; his life's task therefore, was to *manifest* the distance he felt. He resisted society by amazing it, shocking it, testing its tolerance, by persistently going "too far" in his dress, gestures, actions, and opinions.[32]

In Russia, Wilde represented the model of dandyism, which explains why Vengerova's article, "Oscar Wilde," centers more on his life than on his works; even so, she discusses his works as well and stresses that "the main feature of Oscar Wilde's works is his audacity,"[33] his ability to overthrow the established rules and morals and to create his own. In her discussion of Wilde's works, Vengerova drew attention to his article, "Critic as Artist," in which he formulated the idea that literary and art criticism are forms of art no less important than the work of art.[34]

Vengerova suggests that the central idea of the article, "Critic as Artist," is at the foundation of Wilde's Aestheticism, because the critic is the one who creates the new world, using as his material different forms of the world surrounding him, including literature and art. She asserts that all Wilde's creative works use this idea as their basis. They often do not have a story. Their main focus is on impressions, and the impressions are a form of criticism, the creation of a new world through one's own perception using different types of material. She also emphasizes another *fin de siècle* feature in Wilde's works: his creation of characters, such as Salomé, who "are beautiful because of their feelings of inner freedom, which replace in them the moral principles."[35] For Russian Symbolists and Decadents, the idea of freedom was inseparable from the idea of individualism.[36]

Vengerova's articles on Wilde contributed to his popularity and to the acceptance of his style of dandyism by Russian intellectuals. His influence was immense and expressed itself in different ways: the way people dressed, decorated their houses, and even talked.[37] One of the most interesting effects of Wilde on turn-of-the-century Russian culture came from his perception of literary and art criticism as an expression of a view of life. Vladimir Soloviev, Vasily Rozanov, Lev Shestov, and especially Zinaida Vengerova, used literary works and literary criticism to express their own philosophies of existence, their own "souls and minds."

The English Pre-Raphaelites

Despite her recognition of Wilde's importance, Vengerova's primary interest did not lie with the movement of English Aesthetes. She was more attracted to the English Pre-Raphaelites, especially to Dante Gabriel Rossetti and Edward Burne-Jones, whom she considered the first European Symbolists, despite the fact that the movement of the Pre-Raphaelites started in early 1850, twenty years before the appearance of French Decadence and Symbolism, and thirty years before Moréas published his manifesto on Symbolism. At the time of Vengerova's arrival in London, a number of representatives of that movement or of those who were inspired by it – John Everett Millais, Holman Hunt, Edward Burne-Jones, William Morris – were still alive and active, and their works were exhibited in English art galleries that Vengerova visited often. She describes one of her visits in her letter from London in 1893:

> This week flew by as in a dream, because of the intensive work in the Museum and of the mass of different impressions. Imagine, we saw "Angels of Creation" by Burne-Jones in the original and his "Hope and Fides." Mme. de Morgan sent us the owner's business card, and we went to see his gallery. . . . You cannot imagine how charming the colors of clothes, wings, etc. In the original, it appears that the fifth day of the Creation is quite weak in its mood – faces are a little banal. But to the contrary, how beautiful is Hope.[38]

In her "Autobiographical Essay," she shares more of her attitudes toward the Pre-Raphaelites and the role they played in her life and literary career:

> The Pre-Raphaelites created a cult of beauty and applied it to life. . . I knew personally W. Morris, Maddock Brown, Burne-Jones, and I heard a lot about Rossetti from his brother, B.M. Rossetti; I lived through . . . the mystical moods of Rossetti's paintings and the tender creations of Burne-Jones. The spirit of the Pre-Raphelite paintings conquered my soul.[39]

In November 1894, Vengerova gave a lecture about the Pre-Raphaelites to the Neo-Philological Society in St. Petersburg. That lecture, "The New Trends in English Art," later took the shape of an article and appeared in 1895 in *The Herald of Europe,* and in 1897, became a part of Vengerova's first volume of *Literary Portraits.*[40] She was the first to introduce this movement to Russia and one of the first in Europe to see it as part of the larger Symbolist movement.[41]

Dante Gabriel Rossetti

In the second part of her article on "The New Trends in Symbolist Art," Vengerova focused on Dante Gabriel Rossetti, his duality and her impressions of his paintings and poetry. She was the first in Russia to suggest that Rossetti had created "a new type of a madonna," a woman who reflects the great complexity of the human soul, both its divinity and its downfall. Using the examples of Rossetti's "madonnas," she concentrates on the aspect most real for her: the importance of the inner world of Rossetti's characters. The inner world represents the essence of the Symbolist movement as it evolved throughout Europe. She discusses Rossetti's attempt to express the intensity of the invisible world within each human being and the plurality of the soul's states: the conflict between the soul's aspiration towards heaven and the body's attachment to earth.

She argues that Rossetti successfully represented the duality of human nature. He portrayed human nature's course by showing its eternal struggle for internal peace, and its ability to achieve it only when the earthly shell falls away and the divine part of the human being, the soul, is liberated and returns to the world of its origin, the world of invisible reality. As one example, she cites his famous "Beata Beatrix," in which Rossetti paints the face of his dead wife, Elizabeth Siddal, incarnated as the image of Dante's Beatrice, who finds peace at the moment when she enters eternity. Vengerova calls Rossetti's beauty "anxious (uneasy) beauty,"[42] because his beautiful faces represent a yearning for an unattainable eternity and a dissatisfaction with present reality. She emphasizes the importance of colors that create an unusual light in Rossetti's works, because it is through the light that he is able to bring out the contrasts in individual moods and to convey his mystical message.

An example of Vengerova's ability to capture the complex and contradictory spirit in Rossetti's paintings is her discussion of "Venus Astarte" ("Astarte Syriaca"). She believes that Rossetti succeeds in portraying in Astarte's face the conflicting aspects of the inner world of the individual and, at the same time, the mystery of universe:

Astarte isthe creation of uneasy transports, in which the elements
of the divine and the sensual do not combine, but exist independently and simultaneously as symbols of the highest religious
ecstasy and of the deepest depression, equally possible for the
human being, and understood in him. And simultaneously with
this modern psychology, . . . Rossetti's Astarte symbolizes the unresolved mystery of existence. She seems to be the living embodiment of the poignant enigma.[43]

In her description of Astarte, Vengerova also stresses her sensuality
as a symbol of earthly life. At the same time, she sees in Astarte's
dimmed, passionless eyes the reflection of her exhaustion from
drinking deeply of the vanity of her earthly existence and in her
"absolute eyes, eyes looking into eternity" – a sign of a profound
desire to reconcile herself to the peace of the eternal, harmonious
world of God.[44]

William Morris

Between 1893 and 1896, during her early stay in England,
Vengerova produced several articles, such as "The New Utopia:
William Morris and His Last Book" (1893), "Browning and his
Poetry" (1893), "George Meredith" (1895), and "The Precursor
of English Symbolism: William Blake" (1896). In 1897, these articles, as well as "The New Trends in English Art," and "Oscar
Wilde," became a significant part of Vengerova's first volume of the
collection, *Literary Portraits (Literaturnye kharakteristiki, 1897).*[45] In
the second volume, published in 1905, she included an article on the
English art critic Walter Pater, who was already becoming known
for creating the new canons of beauty and art criticism in England.

Before the First World War, Vengerova was offered a contract to
prepare a collection to be called *Western European Writers of the
Nineteenth Century*. Unfortunately, because of the war, only the
first volume, *English Writers of the Nineteenth Century,*[46] was pub-

lished. It came out in 1913. All her previous articles on English artists, poets, and writers, except for the article on Pater, were included. She added to this volume one more article, "John Ruskin: The Apostle of Beauty," because Ruskin was the admirer of the Pre-Raphaelites to whom they largely owe their fame and recognition. The article on Ruskin was originally published in 1900 in *The Herald of Europe*.[47] [48] Each of the articles has an interest and function of its own. Taken together, they introduce Russians to those English writers, poets, and artists who were influencing new trends in Western European literature, art, and society of the time.

Through her articles and her books, Vengerova made an important contribution to the evolution and complexity of Russian Symbolism, as well as to the shaping of tastes in the Russian public. For instance, her presentation of William Morris and his ideas in her article, "The New Utopia: William Morris and his Last Book," was an important event for Russian society. In the early 1890s, when Vengerova came to London, William Morris was already a well known artist. He had an interesting and tumultuous career. He was one of the followers of the Pre-Raphaelites, a painter, writer, poet, and an idealist who endeavored to apply his idealistic view of beauty to contribute a richness to the daily lives of people at all levels of society. In 1862, he created the firm, "Morris, Marshall, Faulkner and Co." Its goal was to introduce the general public to beautiful and accessible objects of functional and decorative art that might ennoble their tastes and make their environment more beautiful and pleasing to the soul as well as to the eye. He believed in the beauty of the human soul, in the necessity for individuals to be surrounded by beauty and to have time to develop the best features of their inner lives. For this reason, he advocated the shorter working day, better wages, and the significance of beautiful objects accessible to working people at low prices. His hope was that a life surrounded by beauty would allow people to develop spiritually, artistically, and intellectually during the free time unoccupied by work.

Vengerova's article, although entitled "Morris's Last Book," covers much more, providing her Russian readers an introduction to

Morris's philosophy of existence. As a Symbolist, Vengerova believed that any real change can only come from inside, through education. It is not sufficient to change the society and its rules without changing the mentality and inner structure of the individual. She found just such an approach in Morris's utopia, *News from Nowhere*, and explained that Morris himself was convinced of the importance of changing the mentality of society through education and the ways people occupied their time.

Vengerova's introduction of William Morris and his ideas to Russia proved to be one of her most effective educational efforts. This article played a double role: on the one hand, it announced the idea of the ennoblement of everyday life without resort to the brutalities of revolution, but by means of developing industry and changing lifestyles. In a country like Russia this was a novel idea, because it was an agricultural society with very little developed industry. Her article also aimed to shape the sensibility of Russians by explaining how beauty can be accessed by everyone's willingness to be initiated. At the same time, she was showing those who represented the school of civic literature and criticism – the social movement in literature – that ideas of social equality were not foreign to a Symbolist like Morris. Contrary to the existing prejudice against Symbolism, Symbolism was not only a movement of withdrawal, but also a movement concerned with people and a search for ways to improve their existence. Of course, in the case of Symbolism, this social dimension was united with a strong mystical foundation that governed the actions of its representatives, but, as Vengerova notes, the result was the same: the motives of social actions are less impotant than the results. Thus, although Morris' ideas might have a mystical background and his aspiration was to create a paradise on earth, the results of his ideas and of their application to life were socially positive and helped bring many improvements, including a decrease in the hours of the work week. Vengerova suggested that Morris's example and philosophy of existence might play an instrumental role in bringing positive changes to Russian society.

З.А. ВЕНГЕРОВА.

СОБРАНІЕ СОЧИНЕНІЙ

Т. I.

АНГЛІЙСКІЕ ПИСАТЕЛИ XIX ВѢКА.

КН-ВО -ПРОМЕТЕЙ-
Н.Н. МИХАЙЛОВА

Figure 9. Cover for *Angliiskie pisateli XIX veka*
(English Writers of the Nineteenth Century), 1913.

Robert Browning

Vengerova's article, "Browning and His Poetry," made another important contribution to the ideas of Russian Symbolism. Although it was not as globally important as the article on Morris, it certainly influenced some of the Russian Symbolist writers and poets including Zinaida Hippius. One who has only a superficial knowledge of Robert Browning's poetry and life might be surprised at Vengerova's interest in him. Nonetheless, he was seen as a precursor to Symbolism by the English Pre-Raphaelites and later by the representatives of the English aesthetic movement. Dante Gabriel Rossetti was fascinated by Browning. "Confronted with Browning," he wrote, "all else seemed pale and in neutral tint."[49] Rossetti considered Browning's "knowledge of early Italian art beyond that of anyone I ever met - encyclopedically beyond that of Ruskin himself."[50] Browning's poetry inspired some of Rossetti's paintings and poetry. In 1851, young Rossetti selected a passage from one of Browning's poems, "Pippa Passes," as a subject of his oil painting "Hist! - said Kate the Queen." He chose the incident in that poem, which describes the Queen with "a maiden, binding her tresses." That image became a frequent subject of many Symbolist paintings: a maiden combing or tending her hair. As Andrew Wilton points out, "Long hair, specifically hair that is touched and handled as a surrogate for the woman's body itself, is closely associated with the Symbolist image of woman."[51]

In 1845, Browning wrote a short poem, "Porphyria's Lover." This poem tells the story of the strangling of Porphyria by her lover, who used her long hair and then admired the act with a morbid eroticism.[52] Another Browning poem is known as an inspiration for Rossetti's sonnet, "Lilith."[53] That sonnet in its turn, together with some of Rossetti's other works, infused the atmosphere of Swinburne's writings, who considered himself a follower of Rossetti and Baudelaire. Arthur Symons, author of the book, *The Symbolist Movement in Literature,* and a friend of Aubrey Beardsley with whom he was editing the journal, *Savoy,* was also fascinated by

Browning's poetry. He became a member of Browning's society and for a while was in correspondence with Browning.

Vengerova was probably aware of Rossetti's interest in Browning and of the influence Browning had on Rossetti; but in the case of Browning, her interest focused on the mixture of psychological and mystical aspects in his protagonists' inner worlds. She calls Browning a painter of the human soul, "whose poetic goal, starting with his poem, 'Pauline,' was to create an entire range of poems in which interest would be concentrated exclusively on the moods of the human soul, on the permanent capture of feelings and ideas which provoke outside actions."[54] In Vengerova's view, through Browning's description of different states of the soul, he attempts to discover the meaning of its existence on earth and endeavors to show that its different states are proof of its aspiration to find "the truth." The truth lies in the individual's fidelity to the inner aspirations of the soul, or to how each individual "conceives his soul."

This idea became important in the evolution of Russian Symbolism. When Vengerova wrote her article, "Browning and His Poetry," Russian Symbolism with its complex mystical ideas was in the early stages of development, although, in the minds of many, the seed of this development had already been sown. In the mid-1890s, we can see these ideas appearing in Zinaida Hippius' poems, such as "Love," and later in her short stories, *Mirrors*. These emphasize the importance of the search for inner truth and fidelity to it, which, in the view of Russian Symbolists, especially Hippius, became inseparable from fidelity to one's own soul, because the soul was perceived as the divine on earth and its function was to ennoble the human life. Paradoxically, these ideas derived from Friedrich Nietzsche's revolt and the mysticism of a Russian philosopher, Vladimir Soloviev.

William Blake

Among the many articles that Vengerova wrote on English writers and artists, the most prominent is her article on William Blake. It is important not only because it was the first article to introduce Blake to Russians, but also because it helped shape the direction of art at the turn of the century in Russia, including the philosophy of Diaghilev's *The World of Art*. In addition, this article is interesting as an example of Vengerova's ability to introduce the Russian public to the complexity of the origins of Symbolism. Blake, who was underappreciated by his contemporaries, is introduced by her as a precursor to the English Pre-Raphaelites.[55] The English Pre-Raphaelites, of course, were the first to claim Blake. Dante Gabriel Rossetti, for example, owned one of Blake's hand-illuminated originals, and assisted Blake's first biographer, Alexander Gilchrist, in the compilation of his book, *Life of William Blake* (1863). Rossetti's enthusiasm in turn inspired the poet Swinburne to write his book, *William Blake, a Critical Essay* (1868).[56]

Vengerova published her article on Blake in Russian in 1897, at the same time when Yeats published "William Blake and the Imagination," in England. As the first Russian critic to bring Blake to the attention of the Russian public, she thoroughly describes Blake's works and emphasizes two features of his creativity explaining why his overall vision and use of these features can be considered Symbolist. The first feature is his spirituality, "denied of dogmatism," – that is, Blake perceives the world as a mysterious creation of God whose manifestation on earth can be sensed through different sign-symbols. The second feature is the central role of imagination, which Blake perceives as a force that brings spirit into nature. In his view, imagination is an enlightened consciousness and raises humans above their dependence on nature.

Vengerova describes the contrast between Blake's uneventful life and his gigantic imaginative world, expressed in his artistic creations. She depicts his poetry and his paintings in detail and explains how his allegorical works are different from his symbolic ones. In her conclusion, she asserts that Blake created a new understanding of beauty, based on contrasts, that is a struggle between the limitations of visible nature and the initiation of the human into the eternal. "His poetry serves as a pointed example of the true

Symbolism, one that combines life with the depth of philosophical thinking. . . . Blake-painter is equal to Blake-poet."[57]

This article demonstrates the inseparable connection that exists between literature and visual art. Dante Gabriel Rossetti certainly inherited that idea from Blake, although Blake first wrote poetry and later illustrated it. For the Russian journal *The World of Art*, the idea of the connection between poetry and painting was fundamental. The journal tried to incorporate literature and painting, and sometimes used paintings as illustrations for the poetry.[58]

Social Life in London

During her first stay in England, Vengerova's closest friends were the Russian writer, translator, publicist, and revolutionary, Sergei Stepniak and his wife Fanny. Stepniak died in 1895 at the age of 44 in a train accident. Stepniak had introduced Vengerova to his circle of friends, which included a number of English liberal intellectuals. She became close with the literary family of the Garnetts. Constance Garnett was a translator of Russian literature, whose first translation was I.A. Goncharov's book, *The Banal Story*. Throughout her career, she translated into English a number of nineteenth-century Russian classics. Her husband, Edward, was a literary critic known especially for being the first to appreciate and to write about the works of Joseph Conrad and D.H. Lawrence. Later in life, they were instrumental in inviting Vengerova to collaborate with a variety of English publishing houses, especially those involved in the publication of Russian literature in English.

Vengerova also met the artistic family of Felix Moscheles.[59] He and his wife were well-known English painters. She became acquainted with a playwright who was also an art and literature critic, Monkhouse Allan,[60] and with a young writer, Isabelle Ormiston Ford,[61] whose interests and tastes appeared to be similar to her own. Vengerova was often a guest at the home of the Hambourgs, a family of Russian musicians.[62] They were established in London and later moved to Canada, where the father of the family, Michail, together with his youngest son, Boris, a violon-cellist, founded the Hambourg Conservatory of Music.

Among all her new acquaintances the person who probably most strongly influenced Vengerova's life was Eleonore Aveling, the youngest daughter of Karl Marx. To her, Vengerova later dedicated a sketch, "My Encounters with Eleonora Aveling." Aveling worked in the British Museum and collaborated with the Shakespearean scholar, Dr. Fanival. She also studied the works of Browning, and other English writers. Thus, she and Vengerova had many common literary interests. Vengerova's sketch on Aveling was written in 1933 and sent to Russia to the Institute of K. Marx and F. Engels for publication. The publication, however, never took place during Vengerova's life. It was only in 1963 that some parts of this work were released from Soviet censorship, but it has never been published in full.[63]

Vengerova's first letters from London offer a vivid picture of the life she led there, the ways she perceived English society, and the people who surrounded her:

I slowly begin to feel at home in London, and I would be happy if the weather were better. Today from early morning there is a thick fog. . . . I limit myself by going to the Museum twice a day. I study a great deal, resting only after lunch and dinner, chatting with my English friends. Here the *boarding houses* are organized in a cosy way; it is easy to run into the guests and during the dinner there are endless conversations, which makes me very happy for the sake of the language. . . .

Yesterday, Sunday, I spent a very interesting day, which, how-ever, made me very tired, since I inhaled a great deal of steam in the underground railways. . . . I went to the *afternoon tea* of one young English writer, Miss Ford, who happens to be very kind and very welcoming. I will probably become closer acquainted with her, because it appears that we have a lot in common in our studies and tastes. It is impossible to imagine, without being present, what the English *afternoon tea* is. There is a small society that gathers together, by the fire place. Any new arriver is obliged, before he would be allowed to speak, to drink a cup of a bitter *burda* of a black color, which they call tea, then you are introduced to your closest neighbor, who is obliged to entertain you. . . .

From there we went to the secretary of *Free Russia*. . . .[64] Yesterday, together with her, we went to the meeting of Polish socialists, organized by Mendelsons. . . .[65] At the meeting, I met Mrs. Aveling, whom I will visit one of these days.

You can imagine how tired I became of all these adventures. But the first impression of the English is very pleasant - they are very sincere; . . . it is very pleasant after France.[66]

Fortnightly Review

Vengerova's association with England also included a two-year collaboration, from 1902 to 1903, with a famous English magazine, *Fortnightly Review*. As with *Mercure de France*, she was responsible for the section dedicated to the new trends in Russian literature. There she published an essay on Hippius (discussed above) and two essays dedicated to the works of a Russian modernist writer, Leonid Andreev, and to the Russian writer, Maxim Gorky, who, after the Revolution, became the founder of the Soviet ideological movement in art and literature, Social Realism. At that time, although Vengerova never perceived Andreev and Gorky as Symbolists, she saw in them representatives of Russian Modernism. In both Gorky's and Andreev's works, she emphasizes the importance of the thread which runs throughout all of their writings: the idea of the superman, that she believes they inherited from Nietzsche.

"Tolstoy's Last Days"

Although Vengerova visited London for a few months in 1906, her second important stay in England took place during Minsky's emigration in Paris, between 1908-1912. Once again, that stay was in short periods. Vengerova's base was in Paris, near Minsky, but very often she went to England to work in the British Museum, to breathe

the English air that she liked so much, and to visit her literary friends. Her stays in London during that time were marked by two major events: her lectures, organized by her Russian friends, Prince Bariatynsky and his wife, the actress Lidia Iavorskaia; and the publication of her article, "Tolstoy's Last Days," in *Fortnightly Review.*[67]

Iavorskaia and her husband were part of the Russian upper class and were acquainted with many of the influential people from upperclass English society. They had known Vengerova and her work for many years, and they had great respect for her. Bariatynsky and Iavorskaia were able to organize lectures on literature for Vengerova and then for Minsky, which they gave in 1910 and 1911. These lectures were critically successful but also financially important for both Vengerova and Minsky. In the middle of July 1910, Vengerova wrote of the project:

> I have been in London since yesterday. I am here for about ten days. Iavorskaia convinced me that she would organize lectures for me for the fall . . . if I come only for 8-10 days. . . . I shall try to organize lectures for him [Minsky] as well. He has two extremely interesting lectures. . . . I will have to read them for him – he could be present as an author and participate in the discussions. For my part, I would read my own lectures. . . . Baratynskys and I do the necessary visits – everybody is receptive to the idea of lectures and promises to help. I often have lunches and dinners with the "influential" English people.[68]

At the end of August 1910, the lectures were organized, and she wrote about them in one of her letters to her friend Sonia, who at this time was supporting her financially:

> I gave a so-called experimental lecture, *"On the Russian Soul,"* at Baratynskys' house to an invited society, partly worldly people, partly press etc. It seems that what I read was very much liked. I was asked to give my *"paper"* to *The Fortnightly Review.* I was praised for my excellent English, etc. I was really convinced that I made a good impression. . . . The practical results are that in the fall (at the end of September), there will be a series of lectures: 1) *The*

Russian Drama and its Tendencies, 2) *Maupassant and Chekhov*,
3) *Religious Thought in Modern Russia* at the house of the Duchess
of Southerland. The conditions are excellent and I also received
many invitations to clubs, societies, etc. This is for me. There will
also be lectures for N.M. . . . Baratynskys, touchingly, having been
helping me. Lidia Borisovna forgot about her own goals and really
mobilized all London for my lectures.[69]

The results of the lectures were very successful and Vengerova
wrote to her sister Isabelle:

I am writing to you after the lecture, which was a wild success; it is
really a madness, these lectures. So many people came today that
people were standing on the windows and I, because of the lack of
air, even began to cough. I will be here until Saturday, then I will be
traveling to the north of Scotland . . . where I will give a lecture – by
an invitation of a literary society – on Monday. From there, I will go
back to Edinburgh, where next week I will give three lectures: one
is at the university, one (in French) on Franco-Scottish Society, . . .
one – at the wish of the public – a public lecture. . . . I had more
invitations to give lectures, but I refused. I will tell you all details of
the lectures when I see you. The only thing I can say is that I could
not have anticipated such a success.[70]

In 1911, Vengerova published an article on Tolstoy in the prestigious English journal, *Fortnightly Review*, in which she tried to
prove that Tolstoy had an important influence on the trend of
Russian modernists. She supported her position by explaining the
importance Tolstoy attributes to the hidden inner world of an individual, often subjugated by society and social laws. She pointed out
that in Tolstoy's works, the inner world of an individual eventually
rebels against the constraints and laws of the outer, social world.
Tolstoy, she argues, proclaims the importance of being faithful to
one's own soul, to one's own consciousness, and urges the individual to have the courage to confront society, and to follow the call of
his inner, often deeply hidden, self.

After the revolution of 1917, Vengerova emigrated to London, but once again did not live there permanently and visited her beloved city only occasionally.

ITALY

In Vengerova's life, besides England, there was one more country that played an important role in her creativity and in her understanding of the new trends in England; that country was Italy.

My God, how beautiful Florence is! The feeling of that beauty does not come right away. One has to become consumed by the spiritual atmosphere, spread in the old buildings; to become intimate with the walls, so tenderly painted by the brush of pious, naive artists. Then one would stop perceiving the city as a huge museum, in which are collected the monuments of art, but would see the organic growth of a great culture, its first inspirational impulses, and would hear the victorious chords of its most important cultural period. Here, Art is not an invention of single, outstanding geniuses, but is the life of the nation. . . . It cannot be explained with words. It can only be felt, as when you are standing on the Cathedral square, in front of the ancient octagonal Baptistery with its strange marble mosaics. In modern-day Florence this pristine monument is one of the smallest chefs-d'oeuvres of art but that was the only one that Dante was able to visit before his exile, and while he praised his beloved motherland, he was yearning, with his entire soul, for San Giovanni, which embodied for him the ideal of beauty. . . .

Here, nothing but art comes to mind. Life seems to be poor comparing it with its reflection in paintings, sculptures, etc. And now it seems to me that love, suffering, and passions are needed because only they create the great artists. [71]

Vengerova wrote this letter to her friend Sonia during her first visit to Italy in May 1894. In a letter sent a few days later, Zinaida Afanasievna added:

I lead a strange life in Florence, such that I would never live elsewhere. There are in me positively two souls: one entirely immersed
in the past, and it feels good, peaceful when in imaginative interaction with the creators of Florence, departed long ago from the
earthly struggle. Without any fatigue I visit churches, galleries,
streets, where each corner brings up the phantoms of the past; at
home I read a great deal; I begin to feel a lot tangibly, which was
earlier in a fog. But this is not all: together with constantly satisfied
curiosity, there is the damned self that also wants something. . . . I
madly want to stand in the middle of the ancient piazza della
Lignoria, the place where four hundred years ago the fire was lit for
Savanarola; I want to scream, to shake the walls of the centuries-old
buildings, and to abandon my soul in my scream. [72]

Italy was, of course, for many writers and artists, the country of
dreams and inspirations, the motherland of the Renaissance, the
place where the new belief in the dignity and worth of the individual, known as humanism, was born. The Italian Renaissance
changed people's images of themselves and the vision of the world
around them, and touched every aspect of human life. For centuries that followed, many writers and artists went to Italy to study
and to perfect their art. In the second part of the nineteenth century, at the time when academic art was stifled and deprived of
spirit, these trips helped stimulate the birth of European
Symbolism. It is no accident that many called it the Second
Renaissance, because, although on a much smaller scale, the movement artistically drew its inspiration from the complexity of the
ideas of the Renaissance.

Russian Symbolists, like the English and French, were captivated
and bewitched by Italy and drew a great deal of their inspiration
from its art, history, and culture. Many Russian artists and writers
traveled to Italy at this time and wrote books in which they endeavored to connect the artistic ideas of the Italian Renaissance with the
vision of the art that they believed constituted this "second"

Renaissance, which represented their times. Vengerova was one of them:

> I was captivated . . . by the strange mystical kinship of the England of the end of the nineteenth century and Florence of the sixteenth, between Rossetti and Botticelli. . . . From England I traveled to Italy, lived in Florence, where I studied Dante and Botticelli and where I developed a passion for ancient painting; at moments it seemed to me that I was able to see the frescoes . . . being painted on the naked walls. In a strange way I felt a merging in me of the new England with ancient Florence. London with its fairy-tale orange fogs, and Florence with its built up bridges and the gray leaves of the olive alleys on the hills remained forever alive in me, so they feel to me like the motherlands of my spirit.[73]

Vengerova's stay in Italy gave birth to three major articles, "Sandro Botticelli," "The Meaning of Dante for the Contemporary World" ("Znachenie Dante dlia sovremmenosti"), and "Francis of Assisi" ("Frantsisk Assiiskii"). They link the important social and spiritual changes in the Renaissance world with the world view and art expression of late nineteenth century Europe as reflected in Symbolism. "Sandro Botticelli" was first published in 1895, in *The Herald of Europe*.[74] "The Meaning of Dante for the Contemporary World" appeared in 1896 in *The World of God*,[75] whereas the first publication of "Francis of Assisi" took place, together with the second publication of the other two, in Vengerova's first volume of her three-volume work, *Literary Portraits*, in 1897.

"Sandro Botticelli"

"Sandro Botticelli" is a fascinating article. In order for a reader to understand not only the beauty of Botticelli's paintings, but also their "revolutionary" meaning, Vengerova places him within the history of his native city, Florence, discussing the evolution of its art and architecture in the framework of political struggles and self-affirmation. She traces the evolution of Florentine art and culture from Giotto, "the complete representative of the first period of the Renaissance in art,"[76] and his school, to the Academy of Plato (founded by Cosimo Medici), whose spirit influenced art, philosophy, and the attitude of individuals toward life, Church, and God. She explains the development of an individualist spirit among the Florentines and stresses that the art represented in Botticelli's paintings is the synthesis of the "evolved" Florentine spirit:

> The poets of the time of Lorenzo the Beautiful mainly represent . . . individuals of his period as angels, but these angels are pictured with very sceptical faces. Their representation determines . . . the spiritual and moral atmosphere of the fifteenth century: the presence of a duality and scepticism blended with the transports of spirituality. The previous naivety has disappeared from life and has been replaced by a broad and many-sided experience. Kind and cruel people of the previous century have been replaced by complicated personalities, hiding in themselves the ability for the highest spiritual aspirations and for deep downfalls; when they leave life, they do not leave it with an inexperienced and ignorant soul, but with the soul filled with experience and clear understanding of life and what it can bring. Among these people and this life, art was born; and that art became the synthesis of the ideas by which it was created. . . . Each artist of that period absorbed in his art the influence of the historical conditions and the moods it created in his soul, and we can trace it using the example of Botticelli.[77]

Vengerova attributes two major achievements to Botticelli's art. First, it reflects the importance of individual moods. The only motive that governs it is Botticelli's world perception, his soul, his individuality. Secondly, he creates a new understanding of beauty, which is the reflection of both his own ideas and those of the period. According to Vengerova, Botticelli's beauty does not manifest either medieval naivete nor the Greek fascination with purely exterior beauty. His beauty emphasizes the inner world of an individual and stresses its complexity. As Vengerova suggests, "Botticelli created a new ideal of a purely spiritual beauty, which reflects the life of the soul, and is a symbol of profound thoughts and mysterious moods."[78]

Vengerova divides Botticelli's life into three major periods. Each represents a stage in his inner evolution and results in different creative expressions. The first period is when Botticelli, in the 1450s, studied under Fra-Philippo Lippi and Veroccio, who was also the teacher of Leonardo da Vinci. Botticelli met Fra-Philippo Lippi in Veroccio's atelier and they quickly became close friends. During this period his works did not yet take an independent direction.

The second period began in the 70s when Botticelli freed himself from the influence of his teachers and was able "to bring to art his own inner world."[79] This was a long period in Botticelli's life as well as the most brilliant. During this time, he created works under the influence of the literature of the period and developed a psychological approach to the characters of his paintings. Vengerova beautifully illustrates her point by describing the new type of Judith created by Botticelli:

> The Biblical heroine, Judith, is painted by Botticelli not as celebrating victory over the enemy, but as an individual thinking about the meaning of her deed after its accomplishment. Botticelli is interested exclusively in the psychological side of the subject, in the state of the soul which unites such a political murder with the contemplation of the higher truth, when the heroic deed is understood as fruitless in confrontation with eternity. . . . The deed of Judith, accomplished for the liberation of her people, came out of a meek . . . soul; she accomplished her civic duty in a simple and peaceful way, without any involvement of personal feeling. She did not go to the camp of the enemy as an angry avenger, . . . but as a meek servant of God, who fulfills all His wishes. . . . When she went to fulfill God's wish, she did not do it out of pride; and now at the moment of the victory, she does not have any feeling of triumph. . . . The faithful servant of God encountered death and fell deep into thoughts of its mystery. . . . She turned her head back and it is not

the scene of murder that she sees. Now when the duty is accomplished, it is the mood of contemplation that is awaking in her and, forgetting the present, she still thinks about the eternal. All Botticelli's madonnas of that period carry the same stamp of duality, a non-acceptance of the earthly with an inability to merge with the heavenly. The feeling that is the most pronounced in them is the feeling of doubt and deception, and only in the depth of their dark mood shines something new, leading toward the heights, toward the inaccessible, but close to the ideal of the soul. . . . These contrasts make the paintings of the second period symbols of duality, of the searching and deeply disappointed soul.[80]

Vengerova explains that under the influence of Savanarola, one of the fighters against Humanism and the Medici, Botticelli entered into the third period of his creative work.[81] The few paintings of this last period are much darker than those of the second period, and they reflect both his despair in confronting the finality of the earthly existence and his faith for a better future.

This article was significant for Russian readers, especially for the Symbolists. The interest in Botticelli had been renewed earlier in the nineteenth century by Walter Pater in his book, *Renaissance*. He specifically asks what it is about Botticelli's paintings that give a modern viewer a unique aesthetic pleasure. In answering this question, he was the first in the nineteenth century to revive interest in Botticelli and to stress the closeness of Botticelli's works to modern times in its representation of spirituality.

When Vengerova introduced Russians to Botticelli, she stressed that in his "philosophy" of painting and in his "psychology," he was the closest painter to their times. He was a painter of moods and of the complexity of the human soul and, like the Pre-Raphaelites inspired by him, recreated a new canon of beauty, the beauty of the inner life. By introducing Botticelli, Vengerova introduced through his works the issues that she believed were important in the art and literature of her time, such as the philosophy of the inner life and its expression in art, Symbolist issues that she championed. By doing so, she underlined her belief that Symbolism was not a completely new movement, but rather one with roots in many earlier literary and artistic movements, movements which created great art and influenced the evolution of European civilization.

"The Meaning of Dante for the Contemporary World"

In this article, Vengerova, as with Botticelli, gives a thorough description of Dante's epoch, biography, and periods of literary creativity, while also offering analyses of his works. The essential aim is to explain the ways in which Dante was close to Vengerova's own time and especially to the movement of Symbolism. She asserts that what differentiates Dante from his predecessors is that he is a fighter for inner individual freedom – the essence of the Renaissance. Contrary to the ideas of Medieval times, when all individuality was under the yoke of the Church, Dante dared to articulate the importance of individual freedom and expression. Vengerova writes:

In politics, although he [Dante] remains an active person, he . . . becomes the first independent freedom lover. . . . Love for freedom leads Dante from its outward toward its inward understanding. . . . For that reason, on the one hand, he revolts against the imposition of both mundane and spiritual representatives of power, and, on the other hand, he prophesies the inner freedom of an individual, the return within oneself and the manifestation of all hidden strengths of the soul. Dante is the first bearer of an individualism that marks the culture of the new coming centuries, and that is what makes him particularly dear and close to us. From the moment when Dante began to speak in the name of freedom, of knowing himself as an individual, the slavery of the Middle Ages came to an end. . . . It opened the path toward a free art, lyrical poetry, and philosophy, which from now on dared to discuss the relationships of an individual with eternity, to talk about the discovery of the hidden mysteries of the world, . . . and the freedom of the human soul.

. . . An individuality, freed in the outer forms of existence and in its inner life, should discover its vocation. This is the idea that pervades Dante's great poem, "Divine Comedy," in which Dante indicates the path that the individual should take going from the temporal toward the eternal. In this way, philosophical meaning penetrates the announcement of freedom, of which Dante, in all his creativity, can be seen as the first prophet. [82]

Although Dante was known in Russia before Vengerova's article,[83] she gave a fresh perspective on Dante and his works. She introduced him, his works, and his ideas, from the perspective of the *fin de siècle*, as a precursor of the Pre-Raphaelites and of the Symbolist movement in Europe. By doing so, she stressed one more time the continuity between the Symbolist trend and the Florentine Renaissance.

"Francis of Assisi"

This article offers an additional perspective on the commonalities of the Renaissance and Symbolism. According to Vengerova, the role of individualism in both periods is associated with revolt against the establishment and strength to affirm one's own beliefs and apply them to life. She sees Francis of Assisi, the founder of the Franciscan order, as a forerunner of Symbolist spirituality, and stresses his new mysticism. He established his own relationships with God and for that reason creates his own religious order. His faith was independent of the yoke of the Church. She sees in his attitude a revolt against the rigidities of organized religion, against the establishment – a revolt that later was at the basis of Symbolism. She summarized this idea in one sentence: "What expressed itself by the triumph of the individual over the state, by the individualism . . . [in the case of Francis], started with the deed of renunciation and asceticism."[84]

Contemporary Italian Literature

Vengerova returned to Italy a few more times. During her second visit, in April of 1895, she wrote from Florence to her sister Isabelle:

> I have received your letter already in Florence, where I arrived a
> few days ago and where I plan to stay 2-3 weeks. Of all Italy this is
> the place where I feel the best – as if it were a motherland of my
> soul. Every corner, every painting says so much to my heart, and
> the tranquil beauty of the Florentine nature awakes in me all
> spiritual strengths. I am delighted that I came here the second
> time. It is no longer the novelty that attracts me, but the meaning
> of the surroundings that opens only during a more intimate
> acquaintance. [85]

She returned to Italy in 1897 and again in 1901, when she spent the bulk of her time in Rome. Her visits to Italy produced three additional articles. They are less striking than the articles about the Renaissance, but yet represent an interest and show that turn-of-the-century Italy was exposed to the same ideas that predominated in other European cultures at that time. In 1895, she published in *The Northern Herald* the short article, "A Letter from Italy: The Art Exhibit in Italy" ("Pis'mo iz Italii: khudozhestvennaia vystavka v Venetsii"), [86] then in 1904, "Italian Literature" for *New Encyclopedic Dictionary* (*Novyi entsiklopedicheskii slovar'*) [87] and in 1910, "D'Annunzio" [88] on the Italian Symbolist writer, Gabrielle D'Annunzio, whom she knew personally. That article appeared as a part of the third volume of her book, *Literary Portraits*.

"A Letter from Italy: The Art Exhibit in Italy" describes an exhibit of contemporary painting drawn from all over Europe. Vengerova emphasizes the presence of a new trend in art, of paintings that do not represent the paintings of "genre," but reflect the moods of the inner lives of the painters, of their particular perceptions of the world.

"Italian Literature" gives a detailed listing of contemporary Italian poets, prose writers, and dramatists. Vengerova makes a brief analysis of their works, but she especially praises the works of D'Annunzio because for her he embodies the contemporary spirit of individualism; he "praises extreme subjectivity and aesthetics, and expresses contempt toward the masses in the name of the superman."[89] The article, which is dedicated entirely to D'Annunzio, further develops the previous idea. In addition, she gives a very thorough description of D'Annunzio's life and works and explains in more detail the ways he represented the Modernist movement, the herald of extreme subjectivity, and the adoption of Nietzsche's ideas.

These articles on contemporary Italian culture are of interest in large part because Vengerova was the first in Russia to introduce contemporary Italian culture and to emphasize its specificity and relation to the general European movement of Symbolism. Her articles on the Italian Renaissance, on the other hand, are more striking and interesting because they not only show the Renaissance contribution to the evolution of Symbolist ideas, but also establish the continuity between the old and the new so that Symbolism appears as a contemporary form of the Renaissance.

GERMAN SPEAKING COUNTRIES

Vengerova had close relationships with German speaking countries. Both German and Russian were her native languages. Although she used German in her profession as a critic, she states in one of her letters that "For my main works I never need Germany . . . I do not like Germany."[90] Nonetheless, she translated a great deal of literature from German into Russian, often using the manuscripts of contemporary writers, many of whom she knew personally. She also wrote many articles about German culture and German avant-garde writers. Her sister Isabelle lived in Austria for many years and was a part of Austrian artistic society. As a result, Zinaida Afanasievna had an entry into her sister's circle, met many authors, and often obtained their manuscripts of plays and novels.

Vengerova frequently traveled to Austria to visit her sister and to Germany to visit her family friends, Luise Flax and her husband.[91] Luise was a translator of Russian literature into German. Vengerova made extensive use of contacts in German speaking countries, as she did in France and England, to obtain the material she needed to introduce Austrian and German literature to Russia. In one of her letters to her sister, Vengerova wrote:

> I beg you: bring the literary novelties! . . . I can get Hauptmann's book here. It is better if you get something more sensational; the best is something that has not been published yet. I need it for an article in *The Russian Word (Russkoe Slovo)*. The newspaper will pay for the right to use the material. The best is to find something that is not dramatic, but literary – but first class. Schnitzler is good . . . or maybe some memoirs. We need a sensation. Try! [92]

In another letter Vengerova told Isabelle she was translating a book by Lou Andreas Salomé on Nietzsche and asked her for articles by Salomé, Hauptmann and other Austrian and German writers.[93] She eventually wrote articles on "Hauptmann," "Wedekind," and "Schnitzler."[94] In 1904, she published an encyclopedia article on Nietzsche and translated a number of books written about him, including one by Salomé.[95] She was also interested in the Austrian writer, Jacob Wasserman, and translated many of his works from German into Russian.

Vengerova published a few articles dedicated to general discussions of German culture and German literary criticism, such as "On the West. The City of the Outside Culture. From Germany" ("Na zapade. Gorod vneshnei kul'tory. Iz Germanii."),[96]and "Individualism in the Modern Literature" ("Individualism v sovremennoi literature"),[97] which discuss *fin de siècle* relationships between the idea of individualism as it is reflected in literature and in the role of inner freedom. In Austria, Vengerova also collaborated with a German journal, *Magazin für die Litteratur des Auslands*, where she published articles about "young" Russian literature.

Individualism and Symbolism

Vengerova's interest in Leo Berg's book, *Superman in Modern Literature (Der Übermensch in der modernen Literature)*, which she discusses in her article, "Individualism in Modern Literature," is not accidental. Individualism was considered at the turn of the century to be the basis of the new literary and artistic movements and carried a flavor of mysticism among Russian Symbolist writers and poets. Berg's book is an exploration of individualism in literature and philosophy – an overview throughout centuries – with an emphasis on the role of Nietzsche in the development of the idea of extreme individualism, which influenced the literary and artistic movements of the *fin de siècle*.

Vengerova addresses the potential dangers of individualism and explains that the purpose of Berg's book is to show how to avoid those dangers and make individualism a constructive and positive experience for the society:

> The idea of a superman, isolated from Nietzsche's complete teaching, became a romantic protest against all moral prohibitions. At the moment when one neglects the demands of morality, begins to despise the masses, and starts to believe in oneself exclusively, one's hands are freed, and everything is permitted: it is possible to live without any limits; the ideal of the renunciation from the earthly becomes the easy way to reach purely earthly goals. The superman turns into an egoist and an epicurean. The goal of the critic is to struggle against that misunderstanding. Leo Berg does it partly in his historical sketch in which he discusses the appearance of the notion of the superman – the final stage of the most basic aspirations of contemporary culture. [98]

In her discussion of Berg's book, Vengerova explains the history of individualism and especially stresses its positive, mystical, and constructive sides, because it is through these aspects that individualism can lead to the positive growth of an individual, to his perfection, and, at the same time, to the enhancement of society.

In all her other articles on German and Austrian culture and literature, Vengerova builds on the ideas of individualism and illustrates its different manifestations. This idea is presented in the article, "On the West. From Germany: the City of the External Culture," published in 1899. In this article, Vengerova asserts that in order to be an artist – a meaningful generator of ideas or works of art – one should reach a level of inner independence from society, which is one of the forms of individualism. She uses the example of the city of Berlin, which she perceives as an ugly city without individuality, without a soul, because it is a city that came into being as a result of the sensibilities and the ideas of the state, of the masses, of the Franco-Prussian War, and not as a work of art by individuals. Building on that idea, she explains that because the German popular culture of that period was soulless, it created a strong negative reaction in artists, philosophers, and writers, who had souls and individuality. The greater the gap between the inner world of the intellectual and artistic elite, and the masses and their values, the stronger is the revolt and the more powerful and profound are the voices embodied in artistic works:

> The German artists and writers live without any spiritual contact with the public. . . . Whereas Berlin exults at its easy victories, in literature and in art there is an incessant protest to be heard against this triumph. . . . The government and society were ready to transform all nations into severely drilled army units. . . . Discipline rules over the schools, universities, manners, and morals of society, even over the interior lives of families. . . . Life passes in severely organized order like robots. . . . The triumph of this discipline in life is so considerable that it seems that there is no phenomenon which does not enter into the well-determined time frame. . . . It is just the reverse in literature where the human being is glorified. . . . Literature is imbued with the cult of the personality . . . and the tragic struggle against all final earthly desires, the aspiration toward

the attainment of freedom of the spirit, the renunciation of the will of others, opposition to the contentment and petty self-admiration of the Berlin crowd. [99]

In this article, Vengerova glorifies the role of an artist as prophet, rebel, individual, precursor of the superman, who, by not sharing the views of the masses, is able to withstand social pressure in order to create a more perfect world and therefore to enhance society and lead it toward moral perfection. She explains that the powerful role of an artist is only possible when the artist does not merge with the social environment. She contrasts German society with the French, in which, she believes, society's intellectual elite, and especially the artists, share the views and the spirit of the masses, and do not rebel against their mentality. As a result, those who ought to be prophets, that is the artists and philosophers, instead of concentrating on the essential content of the work of art, concentrate on its form, on appearance. Society decays and falls into mediocrity. In France, no apostles and no conscious aspirations are produced to lead the masses toward spiritual fulfillment and human perfection.

Futher,ore, Vengerova discusses the idea of Beauty, a central notion of Symbolism. She stresses the importance of spirituality in beauty. She believes that form is the artist's only tool to translate his artistic vision. Real beauty and real art always have a spiritual component because they express the inner world of an artist, the only immortal part of the human being, which in itself is a part of the divine. For this reason, she asserts that Berlin, built as a manifestation of the culture and ideas lacking in spiritual content, represents an absence of *real* beauty.

Vengerova's articles on individual German and Austrian writers, such as Hauptmann, Schnitzler, and Wedekind, are instructive. She liked these writers and often mentioned them in her personal correspondence. The person she seemed to like the most, as a writer and a person, was Arthur Schnitzler. She wrote:

I am completely in love with his [Schnitzler's] works. . . . In his works there are scenes surprisingly subtle. It seems to me that you [Isabelle Vengerova] met him [Schnitzler]. How is it that you did not fall in love with him? He is probably intelligent and sensitive – I am charmed by him.[100]

Later she added to her previous impressions, "He is a charming person in personal relationships. I even told him that."[101]

In her article about him, Vengerova stresses Schnitzler's attitude toward freedom and individualism, and his attitude toward art. She shows that, although these were typical issues for the turn of the century, Schnitzler discusses them from an unusual perspective. She demonstrates that he questions the importance of extreme individualism: of being faithful solely to one's own aspirations, and to one's own view of freedom. He is a subtle writer who does not give easy answers, but shows that life requires a balance and those who dismiss its social aspects and only follow their own immediate needs would eventually pay. It is important to preserve one's own individuality, but without destroying others. Life is a circle, and without balance there is always a retribution of one sort or another. Even so, Schnitzler believes that each individual has his own path to follow and must find his own balance.

Vengerova also demonstrates that Schnitzler questions a major idea of art, that art is more important than life. The turn-of-the-century artists believed that art had a mystical function, because through art an artist communicates with eternity and gives it an earthly shape, whereas physical life is perishable. She demonstrates that Schnitzler did not believe that art was above life. In his works, he represents the danger of a competition between art and life, and shows that art might become destructive and useless when it becomes more important than life or serves as the only purpose of human existence.

Vengerova's article on Schnitzler is of interest to the Russian audience because it prepared the public for the reading of his works in Russian, and showed a way of dealing with the latest issues of

Symbolism and *fin de siècle* culture. This article is also interesting since it demonstrates that Vengerova herself is beginning to question some of those same cultural assumptions.

In the articles on Wedekind, "Frank Wedekind" and "Wedekind's Satires," Vengerova, in addition to introducing the Russian public to Wedekind's works, explores another fashionable turn-of-the-century issue: revolt. In discussing Wedekind's works in "Frank Wedekind," she emphasizes that he uses a naturalistic device for Symbolist purposes. She believes that he depicts life in such an ugly manner in order to show the ugliness of a perishable physical existence in contrast to the eternal.

Vengerova is convinced that this idea also manifests itself in Wedekind's satires. In the article, "Wedekind's Satires," she endeavors to prove that by mocking society, people's social aspirations, and the vanity of human life – in short by mocking the temporal – Wedekind yearns for the eternal. Furthermore, she states that the bulk of Russian critics misunderstand Wedekind. They find his works insulting and do not see that his representation of life's ugliness is directly related to his revolt against the temporal.

In the articles on Hauptmann, Vengerova stresses Hauptmann's link with Ibsen who, according to her,

was the first to say that if the individual is searching for himself, then the family in its traditional structure would seem to him narrow; he [Ibsen] developed his theory of individualism by confronting individuality with its various forms of social slavery, . . . and had the courage to cry for the liberation of an individual within himself.[102]

She explains that Hauptmann's plays follow Ibsen's tradition and also express the struggle of an individual to be freed from society's chains, although Hauptmann's works are much darker than Ibsen. Ibsen believes that an individual might have enough strength to become independent of society, whereas Hauptmann shows the individual's aspiration toward this independence as well as his inability to reach it. For Hauptmann, this ability to see but not achieve independence is humanity's fatal flaw. Vengerova writes:

That struggle of an individual for distant ideals within a world of conditional goods, . . . he [Hauptmann] embodies in the tragedy of a human being, awakened for the awareness of his personal spiritual freedom, but awakened at a time when he is surrounded by the indestructible walls of the human house. [103]

To prove her point, she lists a range of works that represent that theme. Among them the work of Jakob Wassermann, one of her favorite authors:

I am reading Juden V.Z. I have not finished yet. I have not read for a long time a book that was conceived in such an interesting way. It has a great deal of Romanticism. . . . The book is real, very intelligent. The mixture of the visionary with the real is quite artistic, the psychological views of Jews and their roles are sometimes striking. I am withholding final judgement. But I will make Wasserman known. What pity that it is quite "uncensored," hardly possible for translation. [104]

In 1912, she wrote:

I absolutely need the novel by Wassermann. I am asked for it by the publishing house. They will pay for the manuscript. That is why I am asking you to send me his manuscript immediately after the reception of this letter, so I find it on my arrival, at the following address: Miss Vengerova c/o Prince Bariatynsky, 95, Bedford Court Mansions, London W.C." [105]

Although she translated many of Wassermann's works into Russian, she never wrote a critical piece about him.

In addition to Austria and Germany, Vengerova had semi-professional relationships in Switzerland. She visited that country on numerous occasions, mainly for pleasure, but still was able to write an article, "Arnold Böcklin," [106] about a Swiss Symbolist painter.

She introduces the reader to the Symbolist aspects of Böcklin's painting, especially the negative attitude toward rationality, which, in his paintings is reflected through descriptions of nature as an elemental force that governs the world, including the human being.

Vengerova never spent much time in the German speaking countries. Her heart was more attracted toward England, Italy, and even France, and in these countries she either lived or extensively traveled. Ironically, the circumstances of the Russian Revolution of 1917 and the massive emigration of the cultured classes from Russia in the early 1920s brought Vengerova to Berlin. There she settled for a number of years and became one of the founders and active members of the blossoming center for Russian culture, The House of the Arts.

CHAPTER IV

EXODUS

In 1917, the Russian Revolution turned Vengerova's world upside down, transforming life in Russia for decades. "The dictatorship of proletarians," the Bolsheviks' motto, brought hope to some and despair, poverty, and fear to many others. Intellectuals, writers, and poets such as Zinaida Hippius and Dmitry Merezhkovsky, Aleksandre Blok, Valery Briusov, Andrei Bely, and Zinaida Vengerova, who before the Revolution were against the monarchy and "saw revolution as a cataclysm that would provide an outlet for 'revolutionary destructive' and 'revolutionary creative' powers,"[1] soon began to feel differently about it. Once Hippius began to witness the elimination of individual freedom, the persecutions, and the almost complete economic collapse, she wrote that the kingdom of the Antichrist had been established and the power of darkness had fallen over Russia.[2] This was the realization of many. Millions of people, hoping to return once the Bolshevik regime was overthrown, fled to Western Europe between 1917 and 1924. Many of them never thought that it was to become a final departure. Vengerova was one of them.

Vengerova left Russia in 1921. She tried to obtain permission to leave in May of 1921, but only managed to reach her desired destination, Berlin, in September of 1921. To be able to leave Russia, one needed to have a Soviet passport, on which would be noted the destination and a visa for that country. When she applied for the passport, Germany, although the most accepting of the newly forming Soviet Russia, had not yet signed the Treaty of Rapallo, and German authorities were not very cooperative. The treaty was signed in April of 1922 and in that treaty Germany was the first among major European countries, to officially recognize the Soviet government. Later, that recognition made Berlin the first stopping point for many Russians, including many literary figures. Some of them were leaving Russia for good, but others came from the new Soviet Russia to visit Germany because at that point it was the only Western ally of the newly forming Soviet Russia where Soviets were allowed to travel.

In Moscow, Vengerova succeeded in obtaining a passport and an authorization to leave Russia because of the connections she had, although she had to wait in Moscow for two months, from 8 May to 8 July. On her passport, her final destination was noted as Germany and she was allowed to leave Russia by reason of illness that could not be treated in the Soviet Union. She was, in fact, seriously ill after the Revolution, but had she not known the "right" people she would never have been able to get an authorization obtain a passport.

Once she procured the passport, she was supposed to stay in Moscow for many more months waiting for the visa to Germany,[3] but she was lucky enough to get a visa to Latvia, at first for five days and then, once in Latvia, because of the intervention "of a multitude of acquaintances,"[4] her visa was renewed and she was able to stay in Riga until she received a visa to Germany.

Originally she hoped that in Latvia she would be able to receive a visa directly to France, because she did not have any interest in settling in Germany. She received a great deal of help with obtaining a French visa from the husband of her friend Sonia Balakhovskaia, Eugène Petit, who occupied an important position in the French government at that time and later helped many Russians – especially Russian intellectuals, writers, and artists – to emigrate to France. While in Riga, it appeared to be impossible for Vengerova to obtain a visa to France without stopping in Germany. Thus, she decided to go to Germany for two weeks, the necessary time, she believed, to obtain a visa – then to leave Germany for good and to settle in France or England. Despite her intentions, her emigration happened in a very different way.

In Riga, she received a visa to Germany and a number of letters from Balakhovskaia warning her that it would not be easy to establish herself professionally in Paris, whereas in Berlin there were many Russian literary ventures and Vengerova would have a better chance to find a professional place there. Moreover, she was badly treated in the French consulate in Riga.[5] Consequently, she decided to be flexible: to go to Germany, to see what the situation was there, and to stay there for a while; if the situation seemed favorable, then she would decide what she would like to do and where she would like to go.

Because of Germany's sympathetic attitude toward the young Soviet Russia and the Soviet government, Berlin became a special place for Russians and was a center of Russian culture abroad between 1921 and 1923. As noted, it was both a meeting place of Russians visiting from Soviet Russia and those leaving Soviet Russia for good. As a result, many publishing houses were founded in Berlin by the representatives of both sides, Reds, or Soviets and Whites, or non-Soviets. Those who represented the Soviets usually had a main office in Petrograd or Moscow. This was the case of the publishing house of Grezhbin,[6] and of Gorky's publishing venture, *World Literature (Vsemirnaia literatura)*.[7]

BERLIN

After her arrival in Berlin in 1921, Vengerova worked for both of those publishing houses because their profiles suited her interests and qualifications: translations of Western European literature into Russian and introductory articles about writers she translated. That was, after all, something that she had done all of her professional life and something she believed in: it was her mission to help Russian people in Soviet Russia, isolated from culture and "normal" life, to have some access to the cultural and literary life in the

West. It was her way of alleviating cultural hunger and the burden
put on the people by the Russian Revolution and its consequences.
That attitude and the fact that she worked for the Soviet publishing ventures was not well received by her friends in Paris. For instance, Zinaida Hippius, who escaped from Russia illegally in 1919
with one suitcase, leaving her previous life behind, was not "very
sympathetic" toward Vengerova's cooperation with the Soviets. She
wrote in a letter to Balakhovskaia: "Minsky wrote me at Wiesbaden
that he was leaving. There [in Berlin] Zinaida Afanasievna and
there [in Berlin] is a nest of traitors."[8]

Hippius' view of the situation affected Balakhovskaia, who wrote
an accusing letter to Zinaida Afanasievna. This was a dangerous
circumstance which could have affected Vengerova's emigration to
France, because Balakhovskaia's husband, Eugène Petit, as well as
many other writers, poets, and artists, was helping Vengerova to
obtain a visa. Her reply gives a vivid account of her life and work in
Berlin, as well as her views:

Sonia,
1. I do not publish a journal. 2. I do not get any money for the
publication of any journal. Right after my arrival to Berlin, I began
to work for a small journal, devoted exclusively to Western literature, whose purpose is to introduce the reader in Russia to the cultural life of the West. The journal is published by Nauchno-
tekhnicheski otdel [the department of Technical Sciences]. . . . I
was invited to participate in the editing of the journal; I write
articles – and feel happy – remembering too well how hungry I was
for culture while I was still in Russia: thinking that I will bring happiness to people in Russia who will read about the books and the
trends of Western ideas. The little journal (2 _ feuillets per month)
has not yet appeared. When the first issue comes out, in about
three weeks, I will send it to you, and you will read my article about
Steiner,[9] about the German theater, and you will see that I am
involved in my regular occupations.
    The work in this little journal is not my only occupation, partly
because it is not enough to live on. There is a large emigre Russian-

American publishing house here, which involved me in an important literary work: translations, editing books, collections of my
own articles. I promised them that if I have enough energy, I would
write for them to America (in English) and in the future there is the
idea of lectures in America, which my publishers would like to
organize for me. That, e.g. the work for my publishing house, is the
main source of my earnings. . . .

I am giving you an exact description of all that because I believe
that you have the absolute right to ask me questions if there is gos-
sip that reaches you. Probably if *passons le mot*, "I was sent by the
Bolsheviks to publish a journal," I would not have asked Evg. Iu.
[Eugène Petit] to help me move to France. But you can see that my
work, as always, is outside any kind of politics, and I do not have
"the Bolsheviks' money," except the honorarium for articles,
which, like the payment for work for *World Literature* (*Vsemirnaia
literatura*), because I work for it from here, comes from State Book
publishing (Gosudarstvennogo Knigoizdatel'stva). That is the way
for all of us who work here, thinking about people who stayed in
Russia and work there.[10]

Vengerova also worked for some publishing houses that were not
associated with the Soviet government. One of them was *The
Argonauts (Argonavty)*. At *Argonauts*, she and Nikolai Minsky headed
the literary section. In January of 1922, Vengerova wrote to Sonia:

In *The Argonauts* there are not any German banquets. There are,
though, German publishers, and one Russian sponsor, who has
English money.[11]

She also worked for the Russian newspaper, *Golos Rossii*, published
by "White" Russians and for the publishing house, *The Skify
(Skify)*, founded by the members of the Social Revolutionary
Party,[12] the left *esery*. Whenever and wherever she was able to do
her work, she did so independent of the political convictions of the
organization. On 22 September 1921, Vengerova wrote to Sonia:

On your advice, I began to look for earnings in Berlin – [and it is quite important] – for my future travels. Many publishers offer me work. Here, there are not many people who are well educated. As a result, there is a lots of freelance work . . . more than needed. In addition, there are requests from America to send essays. . . .
  Nik. Maks. [Minsky] also intends to come here. . . . And he will have lots of work. I am writing to him already about two offers, and that is before I had a chance to talk to the chief editor. From all that, it follows that in the meantime I should stay in Berlin. But I do not intend to settle here forever. That is why it is so important for me to obtain the visas to England and France.[13]

Already on 11 October 1921, Vengerova was very much involved in the Russian literary life of Berlin:

I am [in Berlin] already so much involved in literary work as if I never left Petersburg of the old days. We are publishing a new journal *The Herald of Western Literature (Vestnik zapadnoi literatury)*, for Russia, and I am busy trying to make it interesting. I am very fond of this work and, of course, I immediately immersed myself in the ocean of the literary and ideological life of the West, something that I missed so much in Russia. There is another publishing house, purely literary, that involved me in the center of its activities. I only need energy to manage everything.[14]

Because many publishing ventures started but often had economic problems, the life of those who worked for them was not secure, especially in 1923, when Russians began to leave Berlin because of the change in the German economy:

Everybody [all publishing houses] complains about not having any paper for printing, and nothing is published except the announcements about the forthcoming books. Alas, it seems to be the characteristic feature of Russian publishing houses in Berlin. There are many of them, but many have only a facade: they chat a lot, try to seduce, sometimes they even give an advance. But that does not really give any real results.[15]

While Vengerova was working for a variety of publishing houses in Berlin and was trying to write about Western European literature for Russians in the new Soviet Union, she was involved in an activity which might be considered as one of the most important of her literary contributions to the Russian life and culture in Berlin: her involvement with The House of The Arts (Dom Iskusstv), an important center for Russian literary and cultural life between 1921 and 1923.

Before The House of the Arts opened, Berlin already had a few literary centers, the most famous of which was The Union of Russian Journalists and Writers in Berlin (Soiuz russkikh zhurnalistov i literatorov v Berline), mainly concerned with matters such as copyright and other literary activities. In September 1921, it held a literary evening in memory of a Russian poet, Aleksandr Blok, who had died the previous month in the Soviet Union. There was also the society, Russil, Russian Art and Literature (Russkoe Iskusstvo i Literatura), which sponsored weekly meetings consisting of literary readings, concerts, and performances of theater, opera, and ballet.

The House of the Arts, however, was a much more important venture. Vengerova was among its founders in November 1921. Together with poets and writers including N. M. Minsky, Andrei Bely and A. M. Remizov, she served as an organizer and later a program administrator. The name of The House of the Arts was borrowed from a Petrograd version of The House of the Arts, founded in 1919. Its purpose was to have weekly literary gatherings and also to assist needy writers. In January 1922, the journal, *The New Russian Book (Novaia Russkaia Kniga),* described the function and the purpose of Berlin's House of the Arts:

> The House of the Arts is going to be an apolitical organization pursuing only cultural aims, the defense of legal and material interests of literary and artistic figures both abroad, as well as inside Russia, and keeping in contact with writers living in Russia. In addition,

The House of the Arts sets as one of its tasks the establishment of weekly evenings at which not only members and guests of the "house" could meet, but at which new works of writers could be read, musical compositions could be performed, etc.[16]

The success of The House of the Arts was confirmed by the Soviet writer Ilia Erenburg,[17] one of the members, who wrote: "In Berlin there existed a place which reminded one of Noah's ark, where the clean and the unclean could meet in peace; it was called the House of the Arts. . . ."[18] When Vengerova was reproached for her cooperation with the Soviet Union in working with the Soviet writers, she explained that The House of the Arts was a neutral place:

I do not entirely understand what you are writing about Erenburg. I do not have any common work with him; I know him mainly through our *House of the Arts*, where he reads his poetry and the poetry of others – mainly the poetry of the young Russian poets. . . . It is outside of any politics, as is the whole life of our House of the Arts. That is the particular character of Russian intellectual life in Berlin. Here we are closer to Russia, and love for culture, for the Russian cultural cause predominates over political passions. All politics is in the newspapers, whereas the meetings, large and lively, concentrate on the questions which are indirectly related to Russian creativity, and to questions of spirit. Those who come from Paris, except people outside of the newspaper, preoccupied by the interests of the party, find the local atmosphere particularly free.[19]

Minsky was elected president of The House of the Arts and Vengerova its treasurer. Its weekly meetings hosted many speakers and literary events from December of 1921 to October of 1923.[20] Vengerova organized one of the major events, held on March 20, 1922 when The House of the Arts was at the height of its popularity. In it, Thomas Mann gave a public lecture to benefit writers in Petrograd. He read a paper entitled "Goethe and Tolstoy," and at the end of the evening performance read from his *Das Eisenbahnunglück*. Vengerova delivered the evening's opening remarks, which she had written with Minsky, given that she was familiar with Mann's works.[21] It was, in Thomas Bayer's words, "the . . . milestone of The House of Arts."

Although The House of the Arts was an apolitical organization, it ended its existence for political reasons. By the fall of 1922, relations between the writers of the Soviet block and their sympathizers, and those who did not accept the Soviet regime, began to deteriorate. At the same time, many other Russian philosophers and writers were expelled from Russia and came to Berlin. Thus, a new society was formed, The Writers' Club (Dom pisatelei), which included mainly those who rejected the Soviet regime as well as the more recently arrived writers and philosophers. If The House of the Arts was inspired by The House in Petrograd, The Writers' Club received its inspiration from a similar organization in Moscow because the bulk of the expelled writers were from there. In the summer of 1923, the economic situation in Germany became extremely bad due to hyper-inflation and, in the fall of 1923, the organizers of The House of the Arts, as well as of The Writers' Club, left Germany. Some returned to Russia, some moved to Paris and others, like Vengerova, to London.

In November 1923, Vengerova obtained a visa to England through the assistance of an English writer whom she had befriended, Hugh Walpole.[22] She had obtained a visa to England where she worked for different publishing houses as a freelance translator and an editor of Russian literature. That November she wrote a revealing letter to Balakhovskaia in which she described her activities in London. She expressed her political views and her overall attitude toward the situation in Russia and the fate of Russian emigres. These views reflected her ignorance and her idealism in relation to the real situation in Soviet Russia in the late 1920s and 1930s, and her continual attempt to remain in touch with the Soviet Union:

You are asking me a question that is difficult to answer in a letter. . . . I shall tell you in just a few words, because I really wish very much that you understand me: "I am not giving my soul to the

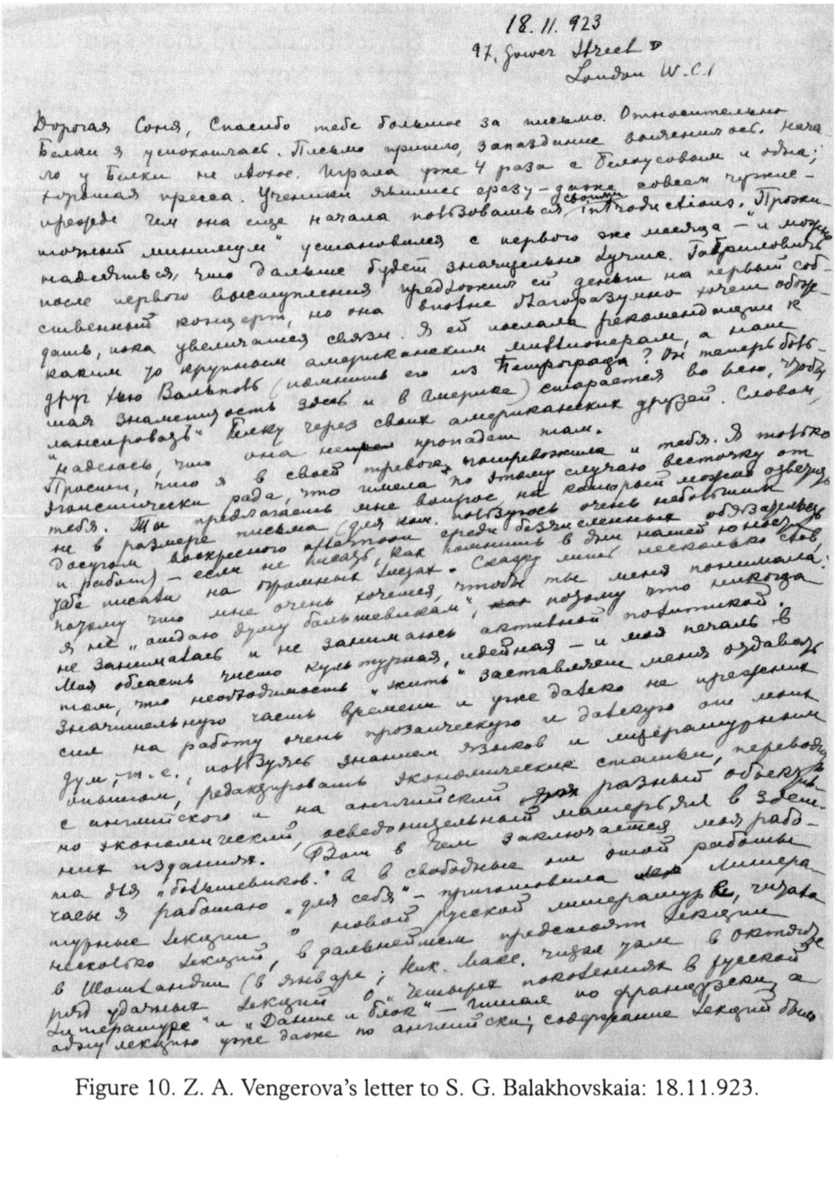

Figure 10. Z. A. Vengerova's letter to S. G. Balakhovskaia: 18.11.923.

Bolsheviks," because I never was involved in active politics and I am not involved in it now either. My area is purely cultural, the area of ideas – and I am sad that the necessity to live obliges me to give the bulk of my time and vanishing strength to very prosaic work, which is far from my thoughts. Using my knowledge of languages and my literary experience, I edit articles on economics and translate from English and into English a variety of . . . material related to economics in the local publishing houses. That is my work for "the Bolsheviks." And during the time I have free from that work, I work "for myself." I am preparing some new literary lectures about the new Russian literature that I will give in Scotland (in January). . . . Here [in London] I am invited after Christmas to give a lecture to the local Shakespeare society at the University. My theme is "Hamlet in the Making of Russia." When I finish that lecture, I will send it to you before it is published. In that, I will lecture vaguely about the historical paths of the Russian intelligentsia and that will be partly the answer to your questions about me.

In the meantime, I am repeating that I am not giving my soul to the Bolsheviks, or to politics in general. As far as my sympathies are concerned, they are certainly not on the side of a "putrid" emigration, but on the side of Russia, which, in terrible suffering, is giving birth to a new life. I absolutely do not support the present policies; I see and know all horrors and mistakes; I know it better than you do there in Paris, but I understand that the present needs of Russia are not the same as the ideas of the foreign intelligentsia regarding Russia and its future. It is not a question of "the freedom for an intelligentsia" to have political conversations (inside of Russia they do not think about it); the question is in the real help to Russia so it will be able to get up and stand on its feet. Whoever is guilty of the past (this is a special and long conversation), *now* first of all it is vital to avoid discord and new civil wars and to direct all strength to rebuilding the country. This is the true responsibility of each Russian who does not think of personal interests, but about Russia. In the meantime, the new generation, the new intelligentsia that is coming from the people, is growing up, an intelligentsia which is thirsty for knowledge. They are taking over all the university programs, all the artists' and literary studios, etc. That intelligentsia is completely different from us; it is active without having a

169

"broken heart" and it is to that intelligentsia that belongs the future of Russia.

You in Paris do not see new young Russians (I see and know many of them). You only hear the hissing of the people who have been thrown in the sea. That is why you are in such a fog regarding Russia. If, like us, you heard the professors who come from Russia. . . .

We are all, of course, the victims of these changes. Do you remember just at the beginning of the revolution when we often discussed it? I was telling you that I felt myself part of the dying Babylonian culture, but it does not stop me from being able to understand and to accept what I see, what comes to replace us in the eternal active movement of history. And I feel myself no lesser a victim than those in your entourage who sadden you. Think for a minute how many close people I lost, what kind of orphan I have become, and how dispersed is that small homeless group of people who remain. Think for a minute about my life, to what future I am condemned, and my approaching old age (in the previous times, I could peacefully earn my living by my literary profession) . . . and you would agree that I did not gain anything in these changes, but just the opposite. And if despite it, I feel a lively connection with the new (not with what is, but with what will be), it has deep roots in my consciousness.[23]

THE PARISIAN ARCHIVE OF PRINCE URUSOV

During her years abroad Vengerova published two works: "The Parisian Archive of Prince Urusov" ("Parizhskii arkhiv kniazia Urusova"), and memoirs of her meetings with the youngest daughter of Karl Marx, Eleonora Aveling. "The Parisian Archive of Prince Urusov" is devoted to Urusov's archive, located in the Musée Carnavalet in Paris. The archive contains a rich collection of material on Flaubert that Urusov hoped to use for a book, *Notes on Flaubert*, never written, because of his death in 1900. Prince Urusov was an unusual personality. He was a lawyer, famous for his articles about art and literature. Close to the Symbolists, he especially valued the Russian Symbolist poet Konstantin Balmont. Urusov became Balmont's close friend and protector. Urusov's scholarly passion was for Flaubert and, among literary scholars, he was known as one of the most knowledgeable Flaubert specialists. He collected everything related to Flaubert, including first editions of his books, as well as many published and unpublished articles about him. The archive also contained important correspondence with a variety of people who had known Flaubert.

Vengerova opens the article with a history of the literary relations between France and Russia and goes on to describe the archive, Urusov's role as a Flaubert scholar, and his relationships with those who were close to Flaubert, whom he knew personally or through correspondence. She explains that although Urusov was involved in literary activities in Russia,[24] these can only be fully appreciated if one is familiar with Urusov's archive of Flaubert and his work on him. In the final part of her work, Vengerova published a few of Urusov's articles on Flaubert that previously had been unpublished, and a few excerpts from some of his articles. She also contributed her own translations of unpublished letters, written to Urusov by different people associated with Flaubert, such as Mme. Commanville, Flaubert's niece.

Although it seems that Vengerova remained faithful to her earlier interests – that is, to the cultural relations between Russia and Western European countries, and to the period when the Symbolist movement blossomed in Russia – this work is different in spirit from the articles she wrote before her emigration, when she was an active part of the Symbolist movement. In earlier days, all of Vengerova's articles emphasized the spiritual aspect of literature and its revolutionary role in relation to a previously existing literature. This work, however thorough and erudite, does not introduce the reader to the spirit of the epoch in which Urusov lived, as did her other articles, but deals solely with the facts. Vengerova sent "The Parisian Archive of Prince Urusov" to the Soviet Union and it was published in *Literary Heritage* (*Literaturnoe nasledstvo)* in 1939.[25] To make her article publishable she had to avoid the depiction of the turn-of-the-century ideas which were perceived by the Soviets as politically dangerous.

VENGEROVA'S MEMOIR OF HER MEETING
WITH ELEONORA AVELING

Vengerova's second work, her memoir of her meetings with Eleonora Aveling, was written in 1933 during a stay in Paris and sent to the Institute of K. Marx and F. Engels in Russia. In 1963, a Soviet scholar named K. Seleznev published in the literary journal, *Questions of Literature (Voprosy literatury)* an article, "Eleonara Marx and Literature" ("Eleonora Marx i literatura").[26] This article is partly based on the information found in Vengerova's memoir, and quotes the parts of her work dealing with Aveling's literary career, as well as their common literary interests.

Vengerova's memoir, like her article on Urusov's archive, reveals her nostalgia for the cultural richness and liberal views of her youth, as well as her positive attitude toward Soviet Russia. Because of her emigration, she was protected from the horrors of the post-revolutionary period and unaware of the devastating later developments of the Soviet system and society. For that reason, she had plenty of opportunities to idealize Soviet Russia and the "new" Soviet people and society. Zinaida Hippius, who was extremely intolerant of the Bolsheviks and much more perceptive than Vengerova in that respect, wrote about Vengerova's attitude in a letter to Balakhovskaia:

> Do you know, dear Sonia, what was hard, among other things? To break off with old friends. We have so many of them, many who lost their minds and took the side of the Bolsheviks. For instance, Zina Vengerova. In essence she only deserves pity, but to see her is impossible, especially because she is unable to understand anything, but *is able* to harm.[27]

LAST YEARS

In the late 1920s Vengerova lived in Paris on Square Henri Carpeau in the 18th arrondissement and in 1937, after Minsky's death from cancer, moved to New York. There she lived with her beloved sister, the pianist Isabelle, who at that time had already become a well-known piano teacher at the Curtis Institute in Philadelphia. Vengerova died in New York on June 30, 1941. During the last years of her life, she suffered from Parkinson's disease. Isabelle wrote about it to Balakhovskaia on 5 April 1942: "Zina died on June 30, 1941 after a long illness and despite the efforts of the best specialists on Parkinson's disease – a cruel illness of the gradual atrophy of muscles and nerves."[28]

Vengerova's death was announced in obituaries in a number of Russian newspapers, including one published in New York, *New Russian Word (Novoe russkoe slovo)*. Although they provided limited information about Vengerova's life, these publications are signs of her continuing status as a public figure: she was remembered and recognized by cultured Russians, especially those who knew her work before the Revolution. Many had read her articles and books on Western European literature as well as her translations from English, French, German, and Italian.

CONCLUSION

Zinaida Vengerova was an unusual person for her time, and her contribution to both Russian and world culture is significant. Through her efforts as a cultural ambassador between Western European cultures (English, French, German, Italian, Austrian and even Scandinavian) and Russia, she introduced Russians to European literature and art, and, to a lesser degree, the English, French, and Austrian literatures to the Russian culture of the turn of the century. It was an important task because through the subtleties of literature and art, people gain understanding of each other, become closer, and are thus better able to cooperate.

At the turn of the twentieth century, there was a great deal of animosity and misunderstanding among European nations. For most Europeans, Russia, especially, represented a mystery. On the one hand, Europeans saw many wealthy Russian aristocrats come to Europe to spend their money at the casinos in the luxurious resort towns. On the other hand, the Russian peasants, recently risen from serfdom, were seen as ignorant and brutal. Russians were Christians, but their Christianity was different from that of Western Europe, appearing archaic and impenetrable. As a consequence, the Russian was often perceived as a mysterious and savage beast, polished only by a superficial patina. In Western Europe little was known about the actual complexity of the Russian soul, mentality, life, and culture. As knowledge of literature and art spread, Russia became, for the West, less mystifying and better understood -- an important basis for the evolution of future positive relations between West and East. Vengerova's efforts to introduce and interpret Russian literature to Europe helped to change the existing clichéd image of Russians.

On the other hand, although, many educated Russians were able to travel to the West and many spoke French -- and probably had a better knowledge of Western Europe than the average Western European had of Russia -- there were still many areas of misunderstanding. In particular, many Russians did not have wide access to the newer European literature and were not aware of intellectual thought and artistic trends that predominated in Europe in the second part of the nineteenth century. For Vengerova, discovering new literary and art works and writing about them was her profession and her passion. She followed the latest events in literature, often as a foreign correspondent, and read the latest literary works in their original languages, sometimes while still living in Western Europe, sometimes, wherever she was located, by receiving the books or manuscripts by mail, or through friends and relatives living in different European countries. As a result, long before these works reached Russia in either their original languages or translations, they became known to Russians through Vengerova's articles. For Vengerova, writing about Western European culture was a way to broaden the minds of Russians, influence their tastes, and help them to better understand the mentality of people living in the West.

Vengerova's role as cultural ambassador, however, had a particular slant because her goal was not only to write about the latest literary works and events taking place in Europe but to introduce them from a specific point of view. She was a Symbolist who lived her beliefs in Symbolist ideas and introduced literature and art primarily from that perspective. Her goal was to initiate cultured Russians, including Russian artists, poets and writers, to the Western European movements of Decadence and Symbolism. This initiation contributed to the formation of Russian Symbolism and, through her championing of Symbolism, helped to shape a new sensibility in art and literature, and even a new way of approaching life.

Vengerova believed that Symbolism was more than merely a literary and artistic trend; it was a philosophy of life. For her, the foundations of Symbolism went back to the roots of human culture and could be traced in all important artistic and literary works. Consequently, she eagerly limited her work to writing articles on those whom she perceived as representatives of the Symbolist world view. In all her criticism she stressed the main features of Symbolism and Decadence: the importance of the inner life, the soul of the creator, and its extension and manifestation in the creative work.

Vengerova emphasized the revolt that various individuals, starting with Francis of Assisi, made against the demands of society; she celebrated their courage to be attentive to and follow their own aspirations in order to build a more perfect world. Thus, some of Vengerova's articles, such as those on Francis of Assisi or William Morris, discuss how the dissatisfaction and the rejection of society led them to envision and strive for a new and better world. Some articles show the connection between the artists, poets, and writers who, by revolting against the reality surrounding them in academic art or literature, created a new art and literature, entirely the product of their imaginations. The article on French Symbolist poets demonstrates that Verlaine's and Rimbaud's ways of writing poetry do not depict, in a required academic way, the events of the surrounding world, but reflect the wealth of their own imaginations through the unconventional rhymes and words that echo the music of their souls. Some articles, such as those on Sandro Botticelli, Dante Gabriel Rossetti, or William Blake, emphasize the mystical connection between the inner world of the artists' imaginations and the invisible divine reality. Vengerova, as well as other representatives of the *fin de siècle*, perceived an artist and his world as vehicles for the manifestation of divine reality on earth, the work of art represented for them an embodiment of the divine Beauty.

Vengerova made a clear distinction between Symbolism and Decadence. Although both movements sprang from the same root, they have different outcomes. Decadence reflects an overall unhappiness with the surrounding world and a desire to withdraw from it through the imagination and fleeting moods or sensations. Decadence does not offer, however, any solution for this general dissatisfaction with the world, whereas Symbolism shares this dissatisfaction with the outer world, and offers a solution: it aspires to create a better earthly world through action, yet also values the intangible, the eternal divine world, whose manifestations in symbols and signs it seeks on earth and whose perfection it uses for the creation of a new Kingdom of God on earth. That is why, in writing about Guy de Maupassant's "Boule de Suif," Vengerova underscores Boule de Suif's self sacrifice for the sake of "humanity," embodied in her compatriots, as a symbol of the divine Beauty. Whereas the moral ugliness of her companions, who first use Boule de Suif, and then reject her, represents an earthly world, a false social morality, a Kingdom of Darkness on earth.

Beauty and imagination in Decadence mean goals in themselves. They awaken emotions, reactions, and lead to reveries and intensification of the life of the spirit. Beauty in Symbolism means revelation: it opens an invisible horizon and offers a gate to the discovery of the divine. Imagination in Symbolism is associated with the inner world of the creator, not for the sake of pure excitement but because it is perceived as an extension of the spiritual world -- the inner world being the *only* eternal part of a human being. Death in Decadence meant an escape from the general dissatisfaction with life. Death in Symbolism is Platonic in nature. It is an entrance into a new and more perfect life. Through death, the soul is united with the heavenly world from which it originated. For that reason, Vengerova believed that works of art and literature which sprung from an artist's inner world and focused on the significance of the inner life of his characters, usually dealt with universal issues, the issues, that will always be of importance and value for humanity. Whereas works that describe historical events or social reality, or otherwise concentrate solely on the outer form instead of the essence, would eventually perish because the external would change and eventually loose its meaning. Vengerova often demonstrates this by citing the phenomenon in literature that neglects the importance of content and concentrates only on form. One of the striking examples is her article "Literary Criticism in France"("Literaturnaia kritika vo Frantsii"), which, like her other articles, introduces her readers to Western European culture, and in this case, to French literary criticism. In this article, Vengerova, using different examples, demonstrates that any literary criticism which lacks the content and mainly strives to impress the reader merely by its form will not have any future and will be forgotten with the change of fashion.

Vengerova's work as a whole can be seen, to a large degree, not only as a promulgation of Western European literature and art in Russia, but as a first turn-of-the-century application of the Symbolist philosophy to literature, and as a first study of the Symbolist and Decadent movements at a time when they were only in the process of being shaped and established. Her way of perceiving Western European Symbolism and the different features of that movement contributed to shaping Russian Symbolism when it was in its early stages.

Vengerova was also important as a woman writer. Although there were many talented and important women writers among Modernists, Vengerova's style of life, her independence, her travels alone throughout Europe, and her type of writing were unusual for a woman of her time. Her life and writings were an important contribution to establishing new ways of perceiving women as independent individuals, as human beings deserving the same rights and opportunities as men. Her style of life was in many ways a reflection of her philosophy on women's issues. Her articles on women like Helena Blavatskaia and Georges Sand, or her translation of *Autobiography* by Annie Besant, show her interest in and identification with strong and independent women. The articles, "Feminism and Woman's Freedom" and "The Russian Woman," reflect her preoccupation with women's conditions and are an attempt to question the social roles, positions, and perceptions of women by themselves and by society. In these articles, however, Vengerova uses her typical "Symbolistic" approach, which concentrates on what she defines as the depth and content of the issue, instead of form. She moves "from inside out," believing that in order to change people's ways of thinking, it is important to understand an issue first, then provide an alternative perspective on that issue, because only through awareness and education change is possible. The outside changes are the most effective when they are applied to a society that is mentally ready for them.

The study of Vengerova's works and life offers insights into the Russian Symbolist spirit and allows us to trace the evolution of the literary relationships between Western Europe and Russia at the turn of the century. From this study, we also learn how Western European ideas, the ideas representing the Decadent and Symbolist trends, penetrated Russia and influenced the development of Russian literary schools and styles. To understand Vengerova and her milieu is to understand the shaping of Russian Symbolism and new Russian tastes in literature and art, which, because of the Russian Revolution, were lost.

Fortunately, Russian turn-of-the-century culture was planted in Western European culture and enriched by Russian turn-of-the-century often Symbolist artists who settled in the West. Only now, after the collapse of the Soviet Union, Russians living in their homeland are rediscovering their lost culture and endeavoring to bring back to life the period in which Vengerova lived and the culture to which she belonged. That rediscovery might, as in Vengerova's own time, influence the tastes, culture, and lifestyle of the Russian people, and lead to a new generation that will produce a vibrant art and literature, partially redeeming the lost years of the Soviet regime. At the beginning of the 21st century, perhaps because of her role as cultural ambassador, Vengerova will also be given a respectful place in the West.

NOTES

1 Briusov, Valery. "O iskusstve," *Collected Works (Sochineniia)*, Moskva, khuduzh-estvennaia literatura, 1987, page 41. All translations of Russian texts, if not noted otherwise, are by Rosina Neginsky.
2 Ibid., page 38.

INTRODUCTION

1 The end of the Symbolist period coincided with the Russian Revolution of 1917.
2 *Russian Writers 1800-1907: Biographical Dictionary (Russkie pisateli 1800-1907: biografichesky slovar')*, M., Sovetskaia entsiklopediia, 1989, page 412.
3 Vengerova, Zinaida. *Literary Portraits (Literaturnye kharakteristiki)*. Kn. I, St. Petersburg, 1897; kn. II, St. Petersburg, 1905; kn. III, St. Petersburg, 1910. *English Writers of the Nineteenth Century (Angliiskie pisateli XIX veka)*. Izd. "Prometei," Saint Petersburg, 1913.
4 Neginsky, Rosina. *Letters of Z.A. Vengerova to S.G. Balakhovskaia-Petit (Pis'ma Z.A. Vengerovoi S.G. Balakhovskoi-Petit), Revue des Études Slaves*, LXVII, 2-3, 1995.
5 One serviceable definition of Modernism is "a general term applied retrospectively to the wide range of experimental and avant-garde trends in the literature (and other arts) of the early 20th century. . . . Modernist literature is characterized chiefly by a rejection of 19th-century traditions and of their consensus between author and reader: conventions of realism . . . or traditional meter. Modernist writers tended to see themselves as avant-garde disengaged from bourgeois values, and disturbed their readers by adopting complex and difficult new forms and styles." See Chris Baldick, *The Concise Oxford Dictionary of Literary Terms*, New York: Oxford University Press, 1991.
6 Glinsky, Boris. "Illness or Publicity" ("Bolezn' ili reklama"), *Istorichesky Vestnik*, 1896, N 2, pages, 632-633.
7 Vengerov, S. A.(ed.) *Russian Literature of the XX century, 1890-1910 (Russkaia literatura XX veka, 1890-1910)*, Moskva., 1914, page 136.
8 Diaghilev ballets – with its innovations in dance, music, sets and costumes – influenced the evolution of the dance culture all over the world.
9 Dmitry Filosofov in his letter to Vengerova, written 31 March 1899, asks

Vengerova to write an article for *The World of Art*: "Maybe you will find it possible to prepare a small article for *The World of Art* that would discuss Péladou's objections to L. Tolstoy? . . . You know the size of our articles. For that you need only look through several issues and take into consideration the size of articles by Merezhkovsky, Soloviev, and other contributors to the section, 'Literary Events.'") IRLI, fond 39, inventory 700, page 1.

10 Moréas, Jean. "A Literary Manifest"("Un manifeste littéraire"), *Le Figaro*, 18 Septembre, 1886, literary supplement (le supplément littéraire).

11 Vengerova, Zinaida."Symbolism in its Modern Understanding" ("Simvolism v ego sovremennom ponimanii"), *Dnevniki pisatelei*, 1914, N2.

12 Vengerov, S.A. (Editor). *Russkaia literatura XX veka, 1890-1910*, Moskva, 1914, page 136.

13 Andrew Wilton mentions in his article, "Symbolism in Britain," that many late nineteenth century artists took up the theme of Keats' "Lamia" (1819). In this poem, the beautiful Lamia takes revenge for her murdered children by murdering the children of others, and also seduces young men in order to kill them in their sleep by sucking their blood. The origin of this character comes from the image of Lilith, a woman-demon from the Apocrypha, who becomes Lamia in the Latin translation of the Bible, *Vulgata*, and whose image Dante Gabriel Rossetti tried to recreate in some of his paintings. Keats' description of Lamia, with his emphasis on eyes and throat, stresses his vision of Woman as that of an exotic beast, the superimposition of pleasure and pain. Today Keats is perceived as a forerunner of Aestheticism.

14 Vengerova, Zinaida. "The Poets-Symbolists in France" ("Poety-simvolisty vo Frantsii"), *Vestnik Evropy*, 1892, book IX, page 115.

15 Briusov, Valery. *Iz moei zhizni*, Moskva, 1927, as quoted in Ch. Rosenthal's article "Zinaida Vengerova: Modernism and Women's Liberation," *Irish Slavonic Studies*, Fall 1987, page 98.

16 Vengerova, Zinaida. "New Utopia" ("Novaia utopiia." William Morris i ego posledniaia kniga), *Severny Vestnik*, book VII, pages 249-256.

17 Vengerova, Zinaida. "The New Trends in English Art" ("Novye techniia v Angliiskom iskusstve"), *Vestnik Evropy*, 1895, book V, pages 192-235.

18 Vengerova, Zinaida. "M. Maeterlinck: The Tragic Beginning in Maeterlinck's Plays" ("M. Maeterlinck. Tragicheskoe nachalo v piesakh Materlinka."), *Beginning (Nachalo)*, 1899, books I-II, pages 155-172.

19 Vengerova, Zinaida. "Introduction" ("Predislovie"), *Literary Portraits (Literaturnye kharakteristiki)*, St. Petersburg, 1897, pages I-II.

20 Bogdanovich, A. "Critical Notes" ("Kriticheskie zametki"), *The World of God (Mir Bozhii)*, 1897, N3.

21 Overall, the review, published in the journal, *The Herald of Europe*, is positive, though the author is skeptical of Vengerova's perception of modern literature and art as a "second Renaissance:"

> The book contains articles submitted by Vengerova to various journals. The collection aptly reflects Mme. Vengerova's salient interest. She pays particular attention to currents in European poetry – so-called Pre-Raphaelism, Symbolism, Decadence, and Aestheticism (Ibsen, Hauptmann). She explains her point of view and her choice of authors in the introduction. We would have difficulties in finding in this contem-

porary poetry a "second Renaissance." ("Literaturnye kharakteristiki. Zin. Vengerovoi. StP., 1897,"*Vestnik Evropy*, 1897, N 1-2, pages 867- 869).

22 A.K. "Zinaida Vengerova. Literaturnye kharakteristiki, St.Petersburg, 1897," *Istorichesky Vestnik*, 1898, N 9, page 1107.

23 Bogdanovich, A. "Kriticheskie zametki," *Mir Bozhii*, 1897, N3, page 5.

24 The second volume includes the following articles: "Maeterlinck as an artist and a thinker" ("Maeterlinck kak khudozhnik i myslitel"), "E. Zola," "A. France," "G. Kahn," "G. Rodenbach," "E. Verhaeren," "H. de Régnier," "J. Ruskin," "W. Morris," "W. Pater," "G. Senkevitch," "F. Wedekind."

25 For instance, in an article published in the journal *Obrazovanie (Education)*, E. Koltavarskaia supported Vengerova in her attempt to bring the latest movement in world literature to the attention of the Russian public. She generally agrees with Vengerova's view of the Decadents and Symbolists and appreciates Vengerova's efforts to share those views with the Russian audience. She also shares Vengerova's criticism of the conservatism of Russian literary criticism in the face of these new literary movements:

> Mme. Vengerova's book presents a thoughtful evaluation of the characteristics of many outstanding modern writers. These are famous literary names like M. Maeterlinck and Gustave Kahn on the one hand, and Emile Zola and H. Senkevich on the other. From the first pages of the book, one is, however, aware that the author's main focus is on the representatives of new literary movements. They determine the character and flavor of the book. . . . Mme. Vengerova is passionately sympathetic with these new movements, and in her essays she analyses them and endeavors to protect them from the common accusation that . . . these new writers *lack ideas and principles*. This attempt is very understandable, because among the multiplicity of prejudices which fill our critical literature, the most prevalent is that which invalidates any theory labeled "Decadent." Many are too willing to ascribe such terms as "decadence" and "decadenshchina" to anything which tries to break away from the old framework and to manifest new forms and expressions. Any author to whom such epithets are attributed, would, regardless of talent, be treated with mockery and derision. . . . Mme. Vengerova sees in this new literary movement a clearly traced path from Aestheticism, the cult of beauty, through philosophy to religion, with its purpose to explore the most important human problems through an understanding of human psychology. ("Zin. Vengerova. Literaturnye kharakteristiki. Kniga vtoraia., StP, 1905," *Obrazovanie*, N 11-12, v. 14, 1905, pages 147-148).

26 Unfortunately because of the war and the Revolution, *English Writers (Angliiskie pisateli)* is the only volume that has ever been published.

27 For instance, Andrei Levinson, in his article "Z.A. Vengerova. Sobranie sochinenii," published in *Modern World (Sovremenny Mir)*, 1913, N 2, page 145, emphasizes that Vengerova is irreplaceable in her role as ambassador and propagator of Western literature in Russia, and in fostering understanding and acceptance of the complexity of Symbolism:

> The main merit of Z.A.Vengerova lies in her acceptance of the difficult task as an intermediary between Western European and Russian literature. She has executed this task with knowledge, initiative, and outstanding tenacity. Her articles about the newest literary schools are valuable for the interchange of ideas. . . . She was one of

the first (if not the first) to talk about Verlaine, the French Symbolists, the English Utopists, and Aesthetes, with sympathy and knowledge.

28 Wilton, Andrew. "Symbolism in Britain," in *The Age of Rossetti, Burne-Jones and Watts. Symbolism in Britain 1860-1910*," Tate Gallery Publishing, 1997.

29 Ibid., pages 11-33.

30 Ibid., page 21.

31 Symons, Arthur. *The Symbolist Movement in Literature*, London, 1899.

32 Wilton, Andrew. "Symbolism in Britain," in *The Age of Rossetti, Burne-Jones and Watts. Symbolism in Britain 1860-1910*," Tate Gallery Publishing, 1997, page 25; quoted from C.K. Hyder (ed.), *Swiburne as Critic*, 1972.

33 Yeats, W.B. *Ideas of Good and Evil*, London & Stratford-Upon-Avon, 1903.

34 Vengerov, S.A. (ed.). *Russian Literature of the XX century, 1890-1910 (Russkaia literatura XX veka, 1890-1910)*, Moskva, 1914, page 136.

35 The fifth canto tells the story of two lovers, Paolo and Francesca, discovered by Paolo's brother and Francesca's unloved husband, Sigismondo Malatesta da Rimini, and killed by him.

36 Vengerova, Zinaida."Russian Woman" ("La femme russe"), *Revue des revues*, 1897, September.

37 Vengerova, Zinaida. "Feminism and Woman's Freedom" ("Feminism i zhenskaia svoboda"), *Obrazovanie*, books V-VI, pages 73-90.

38 Huysmans described Odilon Redon's and Gustave Moreau's works in his novel, *Against Nature (A Rebours)*.

39 Briusov, Valery. "O iskusstve," *Sochineniia*, Moskva, khudozhestvennaia literatura, 1987, page 38.

CHAPTER I

1 All translations from Russian and French, as previously mentioned, if not noted otherwise, are by Rosina Neginsky.

2 There are uncertainties related to Vengerova's place of birth. In the letter from Riga to her friend Sofia Grigorievna Balakhovskaia, written on the 17th of August [1921], Vengerova writes: "By the way, they [The French Ministry of Foreign Affairs] are able . . . to make a new passport for me to enter France on the basis of many *papiers d'identité*, diploma, etc, including the old French diploma – *équivalence de baccalauréat* [equivalent of the French baccalauréat], delivered in Paris. Maybe it is for the best – in this *équivalence* it is marked that I was born in Helsingfors." (See *Pis'ma Z.A. Vengerovoi k S.G. Balakhovskoi (Letters of Zinaida A. Vengerova to Sofia G. Balakhovskaia-Petit)*, *Revue des Études Slaves*, Paris, LXVII, 1995, letter N 57). Nevertheless, in her "Autobiographical Note" (S.A. Vengerov, *Russkaia literatura XX veka, 1890-1910*, M., 1914, page 135) she says that she was born in Sveborg.

3 The essay was submitted to the publishing house by Zinaida Vengerova. Before the submission of the essay, Paulina Iulievna wrote to Zinaida: "I repeat one more time my request to think well before you give my article to be printed. I will not be at all upset; it is dear to me as my personal memory. Since it has been written, it will become part of my memoirs; in any case, it will find its interest and its apprecia-

NOTES

tion. And if you, Zinochka, are very busy, you should not spend your precious time for that. I only ask that you return to me the article by registered letter, if the editorial staff be fastidious about it."Institut Russkoi Literatury, rukopisnyi otdel (IRLI), fond 39, inventory 519, page 55, no date.
4 Ibid., page 55.
5 Ibid., page 45.
6 Neginsky, Rosina. Introductory article to *Pis'ma Z.A. Vengerovoi k S.G. Balakhovskoi-Petit, Revue des Etudes Slaves,* Institute d'Etudes Slaves, Paris, LXVII/1, 1995, p. 189.
7 The letter was written on 3 July, 1908. The original of the letter is located at IRLI, fond 39, inventory 1049.
8 Slonimsky, Nicolas. *Perfect Pitch,* Oxford University Press, Oxford, New York, 1988.
9 Neginsky, Rosina. Introductory article to *Pis'ma Z.A. Vengerovoi k S.G. Balakhovskoi-Petit (Letters of Zinaida A. Vengerova to Sofia G. Balakhovskaia-Petit), Revue des Études Slaves,* Institute d'Études Slaves, Paris, LXVII/1, 1995, page 189.
10 In the excerpt from the letter to Sonia Balakhovskaia-Petit, translated below, Vengerova gives us an overview of the situation related to her father's death, and the role her father played in the city:

Dearest Sonichka, I have been here [Minsk] for three days, an entire eternity. You know what happened – I came a day after the funeral of my father. When the telegram was sent, he was already deceased from the heart attack. Do you remember Saturday, during dinner time, when I suddenly told you that I wished to be at home – it was the hour of his death – Saturday, 7 pm. The day before he still was full of joy and healthy, we had guests, danced – then he did not feel well that night and the next day, and now it is the end. You and I, my dear, once talked about the horror of the word "end" – I know what it means. I do not have either feelings of grief or tears. I became a stone. My God, Sonia, it is such a strange word "the end." Periodically I enter my father's study. There are candles under his portrait, there on the table are wreaths from his grave, black ribbons of the official wreaths, and those inscriptions, Sonia, "to the memory of A.L. Vengerov" etc. – Where to take strength, Sonia, to think in advance for the sake of life?
It is the sympathy of the city that supports mother – a funeral that had 15 thousand people; everybody's concern; everybody's recognition of the service that father did for society. She believes in the reward; she thinks that he will be rewarded. It appears that it was mainly the last meeting of the council, where he was terribly worried by somebody and from where he came away completely shattered, that had an effect on him. It was a theme of speeches at his grave. Obituaries, articles in the local newspapers, have a good effect on my mother – I only see that next to my father's name is always added "deceased." Letter of 2 of April, 1892, from Minsk.

11 Ibid.

We all children came here. Mother, thank God, tries to be strong, my sisters are in good health. Semen and Mark are busy taking care of business - only at nights Semen's nerves let go. Maria does not look good; her *fiancé* does not leave her alone, even for a minute. But she looks . . . pale; . . . you would not have recognized her. And all that happened within a week.

12 Nicolas Slonimsky in his *Perfect Pitch,* Oxford University Press, Oxford, New York, 1988. page 31, depicts his uncle "Semyon" (Semen) in the following terms:

185

NOTES

The most famous among my mother's relatives was her brother, my uncle Semyon Afanasievich Vengerov, professor of Russian literature and editor of the collected works of Pushkin, Shakespeare, Schiller, and other classics published in profusely illustrated editions. His most significant contribution, however, was *a critical biographic dictionary of Russian writers*, which was never published but remained in the state of 'cartothèque,' consisting of tens of thousands of 'fiches,' or filing cards, containing information on Russian writers, including personal communications from such giants as Tolstoy and Turgenev. Students to this day make a pilgrimage to the Vengerov 'cartothèque' for their research work.

The honor in which Uncle Semyon's name is held among Russian intellectuals is indicated by its passing mention in Vladimir Nabokov's novel, *Ada*, in which his name is spelled in full, but the dates of his life are deliberately altered, making him a nonagenarian at death. As often in his writings, Nabokov manipulates his army of intellectual Poltergeister bent on pointless mischief in order to confuse and mislead the innocent reader with malice aforethought. But who except me and a handful of specialists in Russian literary criticism would penetrate the murky intent of this futile mystification?

13 Vengerov was known for his *Russian Literature in its Modern Representatives. Critico-Biographical Essays. I.S. Turgenev, 1877 (Russkaia literatura v eiu sovremennykh predstaviteliakh. Kritiko-biograficheskie etudy. I.S. Turgenev), The History of the Contemporary Russian Literature from Belinsky's death to our days, SPb, 1912 (Istoriia noveishei russkoi literatury. Ot smerti Belinskogo do nashikh dnei), In What is the Charm of the Russian Literature of the XIX Century? SPb, 1911 (V chem ocharovanie russkoi literatury XIX veka?).*

14 Vengerov also wrote a biographical essay about N.A. Nekrasov (1878), I.I. Lazhechnikov (1833), A.F. Pisemsky (1884), N.V. Gogol, and A.P. Chekhov. From 1891 to 1897 Vengerov was one of the managing editors of the literary section for the *Encyclopedic Dictionary of Brokgaus and Efron*, in which he published more than one hundered of his own articles, and the editor of *Biblioteka velikikh pisatelei (Library of the Great Writers)* in the publishing house of Brokgaus and Efron. From 1886 to 1904 he was publishing *Critical-biographical Dictionary of Russian Writers and Scientists* (SPb; the publication of the dictionary has not been finished), and from 1900 to 1917 he was publishing *The Historical Dictionary of Russian Writers* (vv. 1- 4, SPb.- St. Petersburg, stopping "Nekrasov.")

15 Minsky, Nicolai. "S.A. Vengerov," *Poslednie novosti*, 3 oct. 1920.

16 The excerpts of this letter are written down in Zinaida Vengerova's note book; no date, located at IRLI, fond 39, inventory 447; translated from Rosina Neginsky, *Pis'ma Z.A. Vengerovoi k S.G. Balakhovskoi-Petit, Revue des Etudes Slaves*, Paris, LXVIII/2-3, footnote 13 for the letter 22, page 476.

17 In his book *Perfect Pitch*, Oxford University Press, Oxford, New York, 1988, page 8, Nicolas Slonimsky describes his father in the following terms:

My mother always pictured my father as an unworldly intellectual who read Tacitus in the original Latin before going to bed, so that his mind was far away from the daily concerns of domestic life. . . . She liked to compare my father with Simeon Stylites, the medieval monk who spent most of his life sitting atop a column, surveying the bustling life below with philosophical equanimity.

I remember my father as an idealist. His own human fault was his tardiness in delivering to the printer his monthly magazine articles, written in a fine calligraphic hand. He often worked all night long to meet the deadline.

18 Ibid, page 186.

19 Famous composer, who was also a medical doctor. In her letter, Fanni Slonimsky remembers him "very vividly. . . . he was young and handsome. . . . At that time Borodin was better known as a chemist than as a composer; that was before he met Wagner who converted him definitely to music." Ibid, page 187.

20 Ibid, page 187.

21 For more about Isabelle Vengerova's emigration and establishment in the USA, see Rosina Neginsky, *Pis'ma Z.A. Vengerovoi k S.G. Balakhovskoi-Petit, Revue des Études Slaves*, Paris, LXVII/4, 1995, letter N 59, page 734, letter N 60, page 737, letter N 63, page 743, 745 (note N 45), letter N 64, page 747. See also Slonimsky, Nicolas, *Perfect Pitch*.

22 Neginsky, Rosina. *Pis'ma Z.A. Vengerovoi k S.G. Balakhovskoi-Petit, Revue des Études Slaves*, Paris, LXVII/2-3, 1995, letter N 29, page 489.

23 Schumann Clara [Josephine], maiden name Wieck, 1819-1896 - pianist, teacher and composer.

24 Neginsky, Rosina. *Pis'ma Z.A. Vengerovoi k S.G. Balakhovskoi-Petit, Revue des Études Slaves*, Paris, LXVII/2-3, 1995, letter N 30, page 491.

25 Ibid., letter N 33, page 499.

26 Stasov, Vladimir Vasil'evitch (1824-1904) - Russian music and art critic, art historian, honorary member of the St. Petersburg Academy of Sciences (1900).

27 Neginsky, Rosina. *Pis'ma Z.A. Vengerovoi k S.G. Balakhovskoi-Petit, Revue des Études Slaves*, Paris, LXVII/2-3, 1995, letter N 35, page 503.

28 Tartakov, Ioakim Viktorovich (1860-1923) - singer (baritone), teacher. Starting in 1909, he was a main director at the Mariinski theater in St. Petersburg.

29 Neginsky, Rosina. *Pis'ma Z.A. Vengerovoi k S.G. Balakhovskoi-Petit, Revue des Études Slaves*, Paris, LXVII/2-3, letter N 38, page 510.

30 Leshetitshki, Theodor (1830-1915) - Polish pianist and piano teacher. Starting in1862, he taught piano at the St. Petersburg conservatory.

31 Neginsky, Rosina. *Pis'ma Z.A. Vengerovoi k S.G. Balakhovskoi-Petit, Revue des Études Slaves*, Paris, LXVII/2-3, 1995, letter N 40, page 515. Isabelle knew Zinaida's literary friends and on numerous occasions Vengerova mentions the attitude of her literary friends to her talented sister. In the letter of October 15, 1900, Vengerova writes: "Balmont is sending you his hello. Now he thinks that he likes music and goes to listen to Belka (he does not court her though)." Or "She [Isabelle Afanasievna] has a new, almost-friendship with Zin[aida] Nik[olaevna] [Hippius], who is seduced by her purity after she was confronted with a lot of ugliness." Or in a letter of March 20, 1905 describing the *soirée* spent at Poliksena Solovieva, Vengerova mentions her sister to be with them and writes about her the following: "Today's soirée was strange – Belka's performance in the dim light, nice words lying in half-voice; my words, almost sincere – do you feel this mood?

32 Slonimsky, Nicolas. *Perfect Pitch*, Oxford University Press, 1988, page 190.

33 Minsky came from the village Gluboki, in Vilenkin's county. To be able to go to school he moved to Minsk and lived at Vengerovs' who were his distant relatives. He graduated from the Minsk Lycée in 1875 and was granted the golden medal. In

the autumn of 1875 he entered the law school at St. Petersburg University and successfully graduated in 1879.

34 Neginsky, Rosina. *Pis'ma Z.A. Vengerovoi k S.G. Balakhovskoi-Petit*, *Revue des Études Slaves*, Paris, LXVII/1, 1995, "Introduction," footnote 102, page 205.

35 Minsky, Nikolai Maksimovich.

36 Zinaida Vengerova.

37 IRLI, fond 39, inventory 779, page 64. This entry was probably made in 1901.

38 Vilkina's sister.

39 Elizavetino is a village not too far from St. Petersburg where Vengerova was spending her summer together with her friends, the Symbolist poets and writers, Hippius and Merezhkovsky.

40 IRLI, fond 39, inventory 779, page 64. This entry is probably made in 1901, page 70.

41 Ibid, page 187.

42 Ibid, page 100, 19 January, 1901.

43 Semen Afanasievich Vengerov, Zinaida's brother. See the beginning of Chapter One for more information about him. He disapproved of Zinaida's style of life and considered her moving in with the Minskys an imposition.

44 IRLI, fond 39, inventory 837, pages 111-113.

45 Here is the letter that Vengerova wrote to Vilkina in 1904. I quote here excerpts, translated from the original Russian:

> Dear Bela,
>
> Why do you not come to the lesson? You seem to be angry at me after you found out the joke I told you at the Slonimskys. But here there is a misunderstanding, and since there are many misunderstandings of this kind, I am happy to have an opportunity to finish with it, and explain to you how I perceive your "life happiness." It is a vain thought to think that I am standing in your way. . . . I sincerely wish that Nik. Maks. marry you. I thought it would happen naturally, without my obvious intervention. But now I see that assistance is necessary, and I come to you as an ally. You should not think that I do not treat you well and that I am jealous of N. M. I give you my word of honor that I do not have any reason for that. Your love seems to me so beautiful, that all my sympathies are on your side. . . . If you are afraid of N. M.'s friendship with me, I give you the complete warranty: I will not see him, not to make you grieve. Is this not the sufficient condition for you to be happy?
>
> Answer me, Bela, do you wish in these conditions to marry N. M.? I make you a formal offer in his place – believe me I have a right to it and let me act. Then in the near future I will be able to felicitate you – if you wish only at the distance, not to awake the fear.
>
> You can show this letter to N. M. In this letter there is nothing new for him – these are the confidences of our numerous conversations. But I think it is better not to show. I am saying seriously that I will arrange everything according to your wishes, if you let me act, instead of transforming all that into idle conversation.
>
> Think thoroughly and answer me.
>
> > Zina

This letter is located in IRLI, fond 39, inventory 837.

46 Essay.

47 Neginsky, Rosina. *Pis'ma Z.A. Vengerovoi k S.G. Balakhovskoi*, *Revue des Études Slaves*, Paris, LXVIII/2-3, footnote 4 for the letter 21, page 474. For the full document, consult IRLI, fond 39, inventory 179, pages 37-38.

NOTES

48 IRLI, fond 39, inventory 179, page 31.
49 See Chapter Two.
50 It is known that Vengerova did a number of translations from Spanish. Nevertheless, it was not possible to find any biographical data related to her study of this language. In her obituary though, published in the newspaper, *Novoe russkoe slovo* (*New Russian Word*) on 2 July 1941, there is a mention of her knowledge of Spanish. The author of the obituary writes about Vengerova: "Her specialty was Modern English literature. . . . Z.A. translated also from French, German, Italian, and Spanish languages."
51 Neginsky, Rosina. *Pis'ma Z.A. Vengerovoi k S.G. Balakhovskoi-Petit, Revue des Études Slaves*, Paris, LXVIII/1, footnote 10, "Introduction," page 191.
52 Vengerova, Zinaida. "Avtobiographicheskaia spravka" ("Autobiographical Essay") in *Russkaia literatura XX veka, 1890-1910*, ed. by S.A. Vengerov, M., 1914, page 135.
53 Ibid., page 136.
54 Letter to Sophia Grigorievna Balakhovskaia, Meudon, le 4.7.90, 4, Rue du Départ, BDIC.
55 Existed between 1905 and 1928, Gaideburov's theater was the first traveling Russian company. Gaideburov, Pavel Pavlovich (15/27 Feb., 1877 - 4 March 1960) was a Russian-Soviet actor and theater director.
56 Neginsky, Rosina. *Pis'ma Z.A. Vengerovoi k S.G. Balakhovskoi-Peit*, "Introduction," *Revue des Études Slaves*, Paris, LXVII/1, 1995, page 192.
57 Ibid.
58 Ibid.

CHAPTER II

1 Neginsky Rosina. *Pis'ma Z. A. Vengerovoi k S. G. Balakhovskoi-Petit, Revue des Études Slaves*, Paris, LXVII/2-3, 1995, page 460, footnote 1.
2 Boborykin, Petr Dmitrievich (1836-1921) – Russian prose writer.
3 IRLI, Zinaida Vengerova's letter to her sister Isabelle, Saint Petersburg, 5.01.95, Voznesensky 13, fond 39, inventory 1049.
4 For more information, see Clyman, Toby W. & Diana Green (ed.). *Women Writers in Russian Literature*, Greenwood Press: Westport, Connecticut, London, 1994.
5 Richard Sheridan (1751-1816) – Irish playwright.
6 Vengerova, Zinaida. "Sheridan," *Mir Bozhii*, 1893, book VIII, pages 33-46.
7 Evreinova, Anna Mikhailovna (1844-1919) – the first Russian woman who received a doctoral degree in law (University of Leipzig). Between 1885 and 1890, she published *The Northern Herald*.
8 Neginsky, Rosina. *Pis'ma Z. A. Vengerovoi k S. G. Balakhovskoi-Petit, Revue des Études slaves*, Paris, LXVII/2-3, 1995, letter 14, St. Petersburg, 21.9.1895, page 457.
9 Vengerova, Zinaida. *Literaturnye kharakteristiki (Literary Portraits)*, St. Petersburg, 1897, v. 1, pages 277-378.
10 Neginsky, Rosina. *Pis'ma Z. A. Vengerovoi k S. G. Balakhovskoi-Petit, Revue des Études slaves*, Paris, LXVII/2-3, 1995, letter 14, St. Petersburg, 21.9.1895, page 462, footnote 4.
11 Ibid., page 462, footnote 4.
12 See S. A. Vengerov (ed.). *Russian Literature of the XXth Century, 1890-1910*

NOTES

(*Russkaia literatura dvadtsatogo veka*), Tovarishchestvo "Mir," Moscow, reprint Wilhelm Fink Verlag, München, 1972, page 249.

13 Vengerova, Zinaida. "John Keats i ego poeziia," *Vestnik Evropy*, 1889, book X, page 539; book XI, page 62.

14 For more information, see Sonia I. Ketchian, *Keats and Russian Poets*, Birmingham Slavonic Monographs, N 33, Birmingham, U.K.: The University of Birmingham Press, 2001.

15 Vengerova, Zinaida. "Poety-symvolisty vo Frantsii. (Verlaine, Mallarmé, Rimbeau, Laforgue, Moreas), *Vestnik Evropy*, 1892, book IX, page 115.

16 See Introduction to this book.

17 Vengerova, Zinaida. "Novaia Utopiia (William Morris i ego posledniia kniga)," *Severny Vestnik*, 1893, book VII, pages 249-256.

18 See S. A. Vengerov (ed.). *Russkaia literatura dvadtsatogo veka*, Tovarishchestvo "Mir," Moscow, reprint Wilhelm Fink Verlag, München, 1972, page 249.

19 One of the newspapers.

20 BDIC, letter of 6/02/1893, St. Petersburg.

21 Vengerova was personally acquainted with Lou Andreas Salomé and was instrumental in introducing her to the members of *The Northern Herald*.

22 In a letter to her sister Isabella, Vengerova wrote about Lou Andreas Salomé:
Did you notice that I translate in *The Northern Herald* Salomé's book about Nietzsche? I like the mind of this woman very much. (IRLI, Inventory 39, list 1049a, page 102).

23 Gurevich, Liubov. "Istoriia *Severnogo Vestnika*" in *Russkaia literatura dvadtsatogo veka, 1890-1910*, ed. S. A. Vengerov, Tovarishchestvo "Mir," Moscow, reprint Wilhelm Fink Verlag, München, 1972, pages 254-255.

24 Glinsky, Boris. "Bolezn' ili reklama," *Istorichesky Vestnik* (*The Herald of History*), 1896, N 2, page 630.

25 Neginsky, Rosina. *Pis'ma Z. A. Vengerovoi k S. G. Balakhovskoi-Petit, Revue des Études slaves*, Paris, LXVII/1, 1995, page 196, footnote 43.

26 S.A.Vengerov (ed.), *Russkaia literatura dvadtsatogo veka, 1890-1910*, Tovarishchestvo "Mir," Moscow, reprint Wilhelm Fink Verlag, München, 1972, pages 240.

27 BDIC, letter of 29/12/1894, St. Petersburg.

28 Hippius, Zinaida. "Grizelda," *Severny Vestnik*, N 2, February, 1895, St. Petersburg.

29 B.D.I.C., letter of 25/01/1895, St. Petersburg.

30 Ibid., letter of 27 December, no year (probably the end of 1895).

31 Neginsky, Rosina. *Pis'ma Z.A. Vengerovoi k S.G. Balakhovskoi-Petit, Revue des Études slaves*, Paris, LXVII/2-3, 1995, footnote 4, page 462. Vengerova wrote about Volynsky in 1892: "The soul of the journal [*The Northern Herald*], who plays now a very important role as the executer of literary destinies, is a repulsive, insolent *zhid*."

32 Ibid., footnote 4, page 463. See also A.L. Evstigneev and N.K. Pushkarev, *Pis'ma Z. N. Hippius k A. L. Volynskomu, Minuvshee: istorichesky almanakh*, 1993, N 12, pages 328-329.

33 Ibid., pages 461-462.

34 Elizaveta Petrovna (1709-1761) – Russian Empress, the daughter of Peter the Great.

NOTES

35 Neginsky, Rosina. *Pis'ma Z.A. Vengerovoi k S.G. Balakhovskoi-Petit, Revue des Études slaves,* Paris, LXVII/2-3, 1995, letter 20, pages 470-471.

36 S. A. Vengerov (ed.), *Russkaia literatura dvadtsatogo veka, 1890-1910,* Tovarishchestvo "Mir," Moscow, reprint Wilhelm Fink Verlag, München, 1972, page 178.

37 Vladimir Soloviev's philosophy of the soul was heavily influenced by the philosophy of Plato.

38 As I mentioned earlier, for Russian Symbolists, beauty was inseparable from ethical values. For this reason, Vengerova, in her article on Guy de Maupassant, gives special attention to his short story, "Boule de Suif."

39 Ternavtsev, Valentin Aleksandrovich (1866-1940) – one of the main speakers of *Religious and Philosophical Gatherings,* worked on the interpretation of *The Book of Revelations.*

40 Vengerova in her letter calls *Philosophical and Religious Gatherings, Philosophical and Religious Society.*

41 Neginsky, Rosina. *Pis'ma Z.A. Vengerovoi k S.G. Balakhovskoi-Petit, Revue des Études slaves,* Paris, LXVII/2-3, 1995, letter 33, page 498.

42 B.D.I.C., letter of 22/01/1903, St. Petersburg.

43 Ibid., letter of 20/02/1903, St. Petersburg.

44 Volkonsky, Sergei Michailovich, prince (1860-1937) – theater activist and critic, the author of the book, *Moi vospominaniia (My Memoirs),* München, 1923, two volumes; director of the imperial theaters between 1899-1901; was close to the circle of *The World of Art.*

45 Neginsky, Rosina. *Pis'ma Z.A. Vengerovoi k S.G. Balakhovskoi-Petit, Revue des Études slaves,* Paris, LXVII/2-3, 1995, letter 34, pages 500.

46 Ibid., page 509.

47 Vengerova, Zinaida. "Pevetz vremeni. Henri de Régnier," *Novy Put',* N 4, April, 1904, St. Petersburg.

48 Vengerova, Zinaida. "Mistiki bezbozhiia. Emile Verhaeren," *Novy Put' ,* N 2, February, 1904, St. Petersburg.

49 Lermontov, Michail. *Major Poetical Works,* translated from the Russian by Anatoly Liberman, University of Minnesota Press, Minneapolis, 1983, page 55.

50 Neginsky, Rosina. *Pis'ma Z.A. Vengerovoi k S.G. Balakhovskoi-Petit, Revue des Études slaves,* Paris, LXVII/2-3, 1995, letter 37, pages 507.

51 Philosophical doctrine developed by Nikolai Minsky. Minsky asserts that God is dead, but he died while he was giving birth to the universe. Therefore, the universe possesses God's features, but is deprived of God. Humanity is able to sense God's features in the universe, but it is also endowed with the understanding of its own feebleness as opposed to God's power. Thus, the tragedy of humanity is the ability to sense and appreciate, and the inability to attain the ideal. Hence, Minsky believes that the role of mankind is to understand the world through contemplation, because in any case, action is useless. Vengerova was not a champion of meonism, but, unlike Hippius, she preferred contemplation to action.

52 Neginsky, Rosina. *Pis'ma Z.A. Vengerovoi k S.G. Balakhovskoi-Petit, Revue des Études slaves,* Paris, LXVII/2-3, 1995, letter 32, page 496.

53 Ibid., letter 33, page 498.

54 Tiutchev, Fedor Ivanovich (1803-1873) – Russian poet.

55 Baratynsky, Evgenii A. (1800-1844) – Russian poet.
56 Vengerova, Zinaida. "Hippius," *Mercure de France,* 1898, N 6, vol. 26, page 930.
57 Ibid., page 931.
58 Vengerova, Zinaida. "Zinaida Hippius," "The Saturday Review," 17 January, 1903, page 86.
59 Although Hippius, like Vengerova, believed in the necessity of the Revolution, Hippius understood immediately the destructive and dangerous precept of "Dictatorship of the proletariat," which later destroyed Russia. Thus, she with Merezhkovsky and their friend, Dmitry Filosofov, to save their lives and the sanity of their spirits, escaped Russia clandestinely to Poland in 1919, leaving everything behind and carrying just one suitcase. Later Hippius and Merezhkovsky, leaving Filosofov in Poland, moved to Paris, where they settled.

Vengerova, who also left Russia after the Revolution, emigrated through official channels to Berlin, as Germany was the only country that kept diplomatic relations with Russia after the Revolution, and where Russian cultural life bloomed in the early 1920's. In Berlin, Vengerova was one of the founders of the famous *House of the Arts,* whose purpose was to establish a collaboration between the Russian writers and poets, who stayed in Russia, accepting the new regime, and those who emigrated. That endeavor ended in 1923, and Vengerova moved to England and then to France. Despite emigration, Vengerova had sympathy for the Soviet Revolution, and for those who stayed in Russia, although she recognized and understood its destructive character. (See Chapter Four, Exodus).

Hippius disapproved of Vengerova's activity in Germany. She viewed this as support for the Soviets and their regime, that she, Hippius, loathed. Thus, in one of her letters to Sonia Balakhovskaia-Petit, Hippius wrote: "Minsky wrote to me. . . saying that he is leaving [Russia]. There [in Berlin] is Zinaida Afanasievna and the nest of traitors, alas."(See Rosina Neginsky, *Zinaida Hippius: Letters to S.G. Balakhovskaia-Petit (Zinaida Hippius:Pis'ma k S.G. Balakhovskoi-Petit), Russian Literature,* XXXVII, 1995, letter of 27 October, 1921, Paris, page 80.

Reacting to the allusion to Hippius' words that were partly conveyed to Vengerova by Sonia in a letter accusing her of collaboration with the Soviets, Vengerova wrote:

> What happened was supposed to have happened. . . . Merezhkovskaia will be intriguing against me, as soon as I arrive. She failed the great intrigues of "the world dimension," thus she is forced to be satisfied by little, e.g., by her favorite occupation: to spoil the relationships between people. . . . I am asking of you one thing, Sonia, if you are my friend: I will explain to you everything; whatever you wish, I will explain to you; my actions are entirely open and clear. They are concentrated on work. . . . But in front of anybody else I do not plan and do not wish "to justify" myself and I am asking you, since you are my friend, not to do it either. . . . Merezhkovskaia is welcome to think and to say whatever she wishes. She does not have a right to be a judge. Do not give yourself the satisfaction of justifying me in front of her. (See Rosina Neginsky, *Pis'ma Z.A. Vengerovoi k S. G. Balakhovskoi-Petit, Revue des Etudes slaves,* Paris, LXVII/4, 1995, letter 61, pages 739-740).

In emigration, Vengerova and Hippius never saw each other, although at one point they both lived in Paris.
60 Neginsky, Rosina. *Pis'ma Z.A. Vengerovoi k S.G. Balakhovskoi-Petit, Revue des Études slaves,* Paris, LXVII/2-3, 1995, letter 23, page 477.

NOTES

61 Diaghilev, Sergei Pavlovich (1872-1929) – art and theater Russian impressario. Diaghilev, after the journal ceased its existence in 1904, became known all over the world as an active promoter, impresario, and ambassador of avant-garde Russian culture of the turn of the century in the West, especially of Russian music and ballet, which had such a dramatic impact on the development of the European artistic culture of the early 20ᵗʰ century, including the world of fashion.

62 Shvartsman, Lev Isakovich (pen name Shestov, 1866-1938) – Russian philosopher. He was a relative of S.G. Balakhovskaia through the marriage of his sister, Sofia Isakovna Shvartsman (1862-1941) with Balakhovskaia's brother Daniil Grigorievich Balakhovsky (1862-1931). Vengerova was one of the first who appreciated Shestov's creative mind and his exceptional intellect. She was one of the first to write a book review on his first book *Shakespeare and His Critic Brandes (Shekspir i ego kritik Brandes)*, which was published in the journal *Obrazovanie (Education)* in January 1900. In the letter of 29 November, 1899 Vengerova wrote: "Here there is L. Shvartsman. We have many discussions. I like his exceptionally intellectual life. Everything he writes is deeply thought, interesting, and arguable." See Rosina Neginsky, *Pis'ma Z.A. Vengerovoi S.G. Balakhovskoi-Petit, Revue des Études slaves*, Paris, LXVII/2-3, 1995, page 460, footnote 1.

63 Muther, Richardt (1860-1909) – German professor and Art Historian. His book was published in German in 1893-1894 under the title *Geschichte der Malerei im XIX. Jahrhundert*, München.

64 Benois, Alexandr Nikolaevich (1870-1960) – Russian painter; member of Diaghilev's group.

65 Benois, Alexandre. *My Memoirs (Moi vospominaniia)*, vv. I-III, M., 1990, pages 517-518.

66 Artistic Art Criticism.

67 Neginsky, Rosina. *Pis'ma Z.A. Vengerovoi k S.G. Balakhovskoi-Petit, Revue des Études slaves*, Paris, LXVII/1, 1995, Introductory article, page 200.

68 Ibid., page 200.

69 *Mercure de France* was the journal that promulgated the "new" literature and new approach to arts. Vengerova had edited the section "Lettres russes"of *Mercure de France* between 1897 and 1899. Already in1892, Vengerova hoped to write in French for a French literary journal. In a letter to a friend, she writes: "Thank you for your information about the *Vie littéraire*. I would ask for nothing better than the collaboration with the Russian section. You know what attracts me – I would like very much to write in French." See Rosina Neginsky, *Pis'ma Z.A. Vengerovoi k S.G. Balakhovskoi-Petit, Revue des Études slaves*, Paris, LXVII/1, 1995, footnote N 68 to the introductory article, page 200.

70 Rozanov, Vasily Vasilievich (1856-1919) – writer, critic, philosopher, journalist.

71 Sologub, Fedor (real name Teternikov, Fedor Kuzmich, 1863-1927) – Symbolist poet, prose writer, playwright, translator.

72 *The World of Art* asked Vengerova to write an article about Pushkin for them for Pushkin's jubilee. The article that she wrote did not appear, however, in the journal. It was published much later, in 1907, in the first volume of *Biblioteka velikikh pisatelei* under the editorship of S.A. Vengerov.

73 B.D.I.C., letter of 11/10/1899, Raz'ezhaia, StP.

74 Later, at the third meeting of the Religious and Philosophical Gatherings, in March

1901, Merezhkovsky gave the same lecture. It was entitled "Lev Tolstoy and the Russian Church" ("Lev Tolstoy i russkaia tserkov") and was published in the journal *The New Path*, in February 1903, in the section dedicated to Religious and Philosophical Gatherings, pages 57-74.

75 Tenesheva (maiden name Piatkovskaia), Maria Klavdievna (1867-1929) – princess, social activist, collector, philanthropist, painter, author of *Impressions of My Life* (*Vpechatlienia moei zhizni*, published in 1991).

76 Mamontov, Savva Ivanovich (1841-1918) – business man, philanthropist; lost his fortune in 1899.

77 Weinberg, Petr Isaevich (1831-1908) – poet, translator, historian of literature.

78 Vengerova, Zinaida. *Literaturnye kharakteristiki*, St. Petersburg, 1910, pages 300-305.

79 Ixkul von Hildenbrand, Varvara Ivanovna (maiden name Lutkovskaia, 1846-1929) – a lady of high society, who supported the arts. She had a famous literary salon at her house between 1880 and 1900. Her first husband was a Russian diplomat, N.D. Glinka-Mavrin. After she divorced him, she married another diplomat, Baron Ixkul von Hildenbrand, who died in 1894. She tried writing in the 1880's, but soon understood that it was not her area. Thus, she became active in the social arena, and she opened her own publishing house, "Pravda" ("Truth"), in which she published, partly under the influence of Leo Tolstoy, the texts of important writers adapted for the general public. In this publishing house, between 1891-96, she published sixty four books, which included works by Tolstoy, Chekhov, Korolenko, and many others. They all were printed in I. D. Sytin's publishing house. The poet Khodasevich in his memoirs wrote about Ixkul and her salon:

> Baronessa Varvara Ivanovna Ixkul belonged to the type of those exceptional women who would charm the old and the young, the rich and the poor, aristocrats and peasants. Among her admirers it was possible to find the representatives of foreign monarchs and Russian revolutionaries. In her salon, known at one point to all of St. Petersburg, she united the people of very different parties and social status. There are rumors that at one time she was receiving at her salon the very strict minister of interior affairs, and at the same time she was hiding in her apartment a person wanted by the police. With the Empress Aleksandra Fedorovna she kept good relationships until the last days of the monarchy. Both the admirers and the enemies of Rasputin loved her. (Khodasevich V., *Vospominania o Gorkom*, Biblioteka "Ogon'ka,"1989, N 44, pages 20-21.)

80 Neginsky, Rosina. *Pis'mz Z.A. Vengerovoi k S.G. Balakhovskoi-Petit*, *Revue des Études slaves*, Paris, LXVII/3, 1995.

81 Berdiaev, Nikolai. *Samopoznanie*, YMCA, Paris, 1983, pages 177-178.

82 Ibid., pages 176-177.

83 Neginsky, Rosina. *Pis'ma Z.A. Vengerovoi k S.G. Balakhovskoi-Petit*, *Revue des Études slaves*, Paris, LXVII/4, 1995, letter 44, page 702.

84 B.D.I.C., letter of 9/09/1896, Nevsky/corner of Liteiny, StP.

85 Neginsky, Rosina. *Pis'ma Z.A. Vengerovoi k S.G. Balakhovskoi-Petit*, *Revue des Études slaves*, Paris, LXVII/2-3, 1995, letter N 23, page 477.

86 Vengerova, Zinaida. "Lettres Russes," *Mercure de France*, Oct – December, vol. 32, 1899, page 279.

87 Vengerova, Zinaida. Ibid., vol. 28, page 551.

88 Ibid., page 481.
89 Ibid., page 481.
90 Vengerova, Zinaida. "Lettres Russes," *Mercure de France*, vol. 26, page 925.
92 Neginsky, Rosina. *Pis'ma Z.A. Vengerovoi k S.G. Balakhovskoi-Petit*, *Revue des Études slaves*, Paris, LXVII/4, 1995, letter 4, page 217.
93 Nikolai Minsky's play that was published in *The World of Art*.
93 Schnitzler, Arthur (1862-1931) – Austrian writer, playwright. Vengerova knew him personally. See her article "A. Schnitzler" in her book *Literaturnye kharakteristiki (Literary Portraits)*, vol. 3, St. Petersburg, 1910.
94 Chumina, Olga Nikolaevna (1862-1909) – Russian poet, prose writer, dramatist, translator and theater critic.
95 IRLI, fond 30, inventory 1049 a, pages 19-20; letter of 28 September, probably 1899, Raz'ezhaia 39, St. Petersburg.
96 Vengerova, Zinaida. "Ob otvlechnnom v teatre," *Zavety*, 1914, book II.
97 Ibid., page 6.
98 Vengerova, Zinaida. "Stanislavsky," *Entsiklopediia Brokgauza i Efrona*, St. Petersburg, 1897.
99 Stanislavsky, Konstantin Sergeevich (real name Alekseev, 1863-1938) – leading Russian actor, stage director, theater teacher, founder and director of the Moscow Art Theater, MHAT (1898).
100 Vengerova, Zinaida. "Stanislavsky," *Entsiklopediia Brokgauza i Efrona*, St. Petersburg, 1897, page 697.
101 Kachalov, Vasily Ivanovich (real name Sverubovich, 1875-1948) – one of the great Russian actors.
102 Moskvin, Ivan Mikhailovich (1874-1946) – Russian actor.
103 Knipper, Olga Leopardovna (1868-1959) – Russian actress; Chekhov's wife.
104 D'Annunzio, Gabrielle (1863-1938) – Italian writer and playwright. See Vengerova's article about him in the third volume of her book *Literary Portraits*, book III, StP, 1910.
105 Shaw, George Bernard (1856-1950) – British writer and playwright. He was originally from Ireland. See Vengerova's article "B. Shaw" in *The Herald of Europe*, 1914.
106 Neginsky, Rosina. *Pis'ma Z.A. Vengerovoi k S.G. Balakhovskoi-Petit*, *Revue des Études slaves*, Paris, LXVII/1, 1995, Introductory article, pages 202-203.
107 Vengerova, Zinaida. "Moskovskie Theatry," "Novaia Zhizn'," N XII, 1912.
108 Ibid., page 262.
109 Ibid., page 265.
110 Ibid., page 266-267.
111 Neginsky, Rosina. *Pis'ma Z.A. Vengerovoi k S.G. Balakhovskoi-Petit*, *Revue des Études slaves*, Paris, LXVII/1, 1995, Introductory article, footnote 92, page 203.
112 Shchepkina-Kupernik, Tatiana Lvovna (1874-1952) – Russian writer, poet, playwright, translator; the grand daughter of actor M.S. Shchepkin.
113 Neginsky, Rosina. *Pis'ma Z.A. Vengerovoi k S.G. Balakhovskoi-Petit*, *Revue des Études slaves*, Paris, LXVII/1, 1995, LXVII/2-3, letters NN 15-17, pages 459-465.
114 These strikes took place in October 1905. It started with the strike of railway workers who demanded the convocation of the Constituent Assembly. This strike

caused the signing of the Manifest, which gave a right to the people to have a parliament and to determine laws.
115 *Chernaia sotnia* (Hundred Black) is the nickname of the merchants who sold the cheapest produce at the market. Among these people, the extreme right party of "Soiuz Mikhaila Arkhangela" ("The Union of Archangel Michael") or otherwise called "Soiuz Russkogo naroda" ("The Union of Russian People") recruited those who expected to conduct the pogroms and the disorders in the streets.
116 The name of the Bolsheviks until 1918.
117 Neginsky, Rosina. *Pis'ma Z.A. Vengerovoi k S.G. Balakhovskoi-Petit, Revue des Études slaves*, Paris, LXVII/4, 1995, letter 41, page 693.
118 S.A. Vengerov (ed.), *Russkaia literatura XX veka: 1890-1910*, Moskva 1914-16, reprint 1972, Wilhelm Fink Verlag München, pages 357-363.
119 Ibid., pages 360-362.
120 Hippius, Zinaida. *Rossia-Gruziia: spletenie sudeb; Dmitry Merezhkovsky (Russia-Georgia: the Interlacement of Fates)*, v. 2, Tbilisi, Merani, 1991, page 252.
121 For more details, see Chapter I.
122 Neginsky, Rosina. *Pis'ma Z.A. Vengerovoi k S.G. Balakhovskoi-Petit, Revue des Études slaves*, Paris, LXVII/4, 1995, letter 43, page 700.

CHAPTER III

1 Sonia Balakhovskaia-Petit. See Chapter I for more information about her.
2 Vengerova's letter of 27.6.1911, 28, Rue Poussin, Paris, 16 to her sister Isabelle Afanasievna Vengerova. IRLI, fond 30, inventory 1049.
3 Minsky was forced to leave Russia because of his involvement in the publication of the newspaper, *New Life* (*Novaia zhizn'*), run by Social Democrats such as Lenin and Gorky. For more details, see Chapter II.
4 Sturgis, St. Matthews. *Passionate Attitudes*, Macmillan, London, 1995, page 15.
5 See the novel by Huysmans, J.K. *Against Nature (À Rebours)*.
6 Nordau, Max. *Degeneration*, University of Nebraska Press; Reprint edition, November 1993.
7 Vengerov, Semen (ed.). *Russkaia literatura XX veka, 1890-1910*, M., 1914, reprint Wilhelm Fink Verlag, Munchen, 1972, page 136.
8 Ibid.
9 Vengerova, Zinaida. "P. Verlaine, "*Severny Vestnik*, 1896, book II, pages 271-287.
10 Vengerova, Zinaida. "Gustave Kahn," *Literaturnye kharakteristiki*, volume 2, St. Petersburg, Prometei, 1905.
11 Vengerova, Zinaida. "J.K. Huysmans," *Literaturnye kharakteristiki*, St. Peterburg., 1897, pages 261-263.
12 Vengerova, Zinaida. "Gustave Kahn,"*Literaturnye kharakteristiki*, St. Petersburg., Prometei, 1905, pages 155-151.
13 Maeterlinck, Maurice. *Sochineniia* in three volumes, in L. Vilkina's translation. "Introductions" are by N. Minsky, Z. Vengerova, V. Rozanov; StP., izdanie M.V. Pirozhkova, 1906.
14 Vengerova's article about Emile Verhaeren appeared in 1904 in the Russian Symbolist journal, *The New Path (Novy Put')* and was later published in the sec-

ond volume of Vengerova's *Literary Portraits*, appearing in 1905 in St. Petersburg. In 1913, Valerii Briusov wrote an article about Verhaeren, "Dante sovremennosti," and claimed in the footnote that he was the first to introduce Verhaeren to the Russian public. The reality, however, was different; Briusov was the first to translate Verhaeren's poems in Russian, but Vengerova was the first to write about Verhaeren and to explain to the Russian public who Verhaeren really was.

15   Although the article on Rodenbach is constructed in the same way as all of Vengerova's other articles on Belgian poets and writers, its special feature is in observing the cultural exchange that began to establish itself between France and Belgium. It is only today, at the end of the 20th century and beginning of the 21st, that we begin to be aware of the cultural closeness that existed between two countries and the influence that Belgium had on French Symbolism. Vengerova, though, was already aware of that at the end of the 19th and beginning of the 20th centuries, and extensively mentioned it in her articles about Belgian poets.

16   For more details, see Chapter II.

17   Wengueroff, Zinaida. "La femme russe," *Revue mondiale*, Sept. 1897, p. 489-499.

18   Vengerova, Zinaida. "Feminism i zhenskaia svoboda," *Obrazovanie*, 1898, v. 7 (N 4), pages 73-90. For the English translation of the article see the Encyclopedia, *Russian Women Writers*, v. 2, pages 892-907.

19   Vengerova, Zinaida. "Blavatskaia," *Biographical Dictionary of Brokgaus and Efron (Biographicheski slovar' Brokgauza i Efrona)*, v. 3, 1892, pages 301-315.

20   *Severny Vestnik*, 1895, book I, pages 137-152; book II, pages 219-248; book III, pages 224-263; book IV, pages 209-239; book X, pages 186-199; book XI, pages 137-152.

21   Steiner, Rudolf (1861-1925) - Austrian by birth, was the head of the German Theosophical Society from 1902 until 1912. In 1912, he formed his own Anthroposophical Society.

22   Letter from St. Petersburg, 12/25.1.1908, Thursday. IRLI, fond 30, inventory 1049.

23   Letter from 77, rue Varenne, Paris, 3.6.1908, Sunday. IRLI, fond 30, inventory 1049.

24   Letter from Edinbourg Hôtel-Paris, 20, rue de Trévise, Paris, 2/15 October 1908. IRLI, fond 30, inventory 1049.

25   Ibid., Letter from London, 7, Bayley Street, Bedford Square, W.C., 17.7. 1910.

26   Ibid., Letter from Paris, 28 rue Poussin, Paris 16, 3.8.1911.

27   Neginsky, Rosina. *Pis'ma Z.A. Vengerovoi k S.G.Balakhovskoi-Petit, Revue des Études Slaves*, LXVII/1, 1995, letter 10, page 229.

28   Vengerova, Zinaida. "William Blake," *Literaturnye kharakteristiki*, St .Petersburg., Prometei, 1897, page 155.

29   Vengerova, Zinaida. *Angliiskie pisateli XIX veka*, St. Petersburg, 1913, page 9.

30   Vengerova, S.A. (ed.). *Russkaia Literatura XX veka*, Wilhelm Fink Verlag Munchen, 1914, pages 136-137.

31   Although Vengerova was one of the first to write an article about Wilde, she was not the first. When she published her first article, Wilde was already known in Russia. Before her, in 1893, Prince Sergei Volkonsky published an article "Art and Morality" ("Iskusstvo i nravstvennost") on English Aestheticism and Oscar Wilde, and then in 1895, Akin Volynsky published another article on Wilde, which for a while was considered a first article that initiated Russian readers to

NOTES

English Aestheticism and Oscar Wilde. However, as Betsy F. Moeller-Sally points out in her article, "Oscar Wilde and the Culture of Russian Modernism," the first translation of Wilde in Russia appeared only in 1897. The bulk of the translations came out only after 1903, and Wilde's *Complete Collected Works* in Russian were published in 1912. Vengerova's article, however, was very important. In addition to being a literary critic, Vengerova was a translator, thus her first article on Wilde, published the same year as a first translation of Oscar Wilde in Russian, could be seen as an introduction to this translation. Whereas her second article, published in 1913, right after the appearance of Wilde's *Complete Collected Works* in 1912 under the editorship of Kornei Chukhovsky is a conclusion to Wilde's fame in pre-revolutionary Russia.

32 Moeller-Sally, Betsy F. "Oscar Wilde and the Culture of Russian Modernism," *Slavic and East European journal*, Vol. 34, No. 4 (1900): p. 461.

33 Vengerova, Zinaida. "Oscar Wilde," *Angliiskie pisateli deviatnadtsatogo veka*, vol.1, St. Petersburg, 1913, page 181.

34 Wilde states that "To the critic the work of art is simply a suggestion for a new work of his own, that need not necessarily bear any obvious resemblance to the thing it criticizes. The one characteristic of a beautiful form is that one can put into it whatever one wishes, and see in it whatever one chooses to see; and the Beauty that gives to creation its universal and aesthetic element, makes the critic into creator in his turn, and whispers of a thousand different things which were not present in the mind of him who carved the statue or painted the panel or graved the gem." Although by Wilde's time, in 19th-century England that idea was widely used, Wilde was the first to formulate it.

35 Vengerova, Zinaida. "Oscar Wilde," *Angliiskie pisateli deviatnadtsatogo veka*, vol.1, St. Petersburg, 1913, pages 183-184.

36 See Chapter II, "Saint Petersburg."

37 See F. Moeller-Sally, Betsy. "Oscar Wilde and the Culture of Russian Modernism," *Slavic and East European Journal*, Vol. 34, No. 4, 1900, pages 466-467.

38 Neginsky, Rosina. *Pis'ma Z.A. Vengerovoi k S.G.Balakhovskoi-Petit*, *Revue des Études Slaves*, LXVII/1, 1995, page 219.

39 Vengerova, Zinaida. "Avtobiographicheskaia spravka," *Russkaia literatura XX veka, 1890-1910*, ed. by S.A. Vengerov, Moskva, 1914, page 136-137.

40 In 1898, Vengerova included a part of that article in her essay "Modern English Painting" ("Sovremennaia angliiskaia zhivopis'"), published in *Education* (*Obrazovanie*), book II.

41 As I mentioned earlier, today it is universally accepted that the Pre-Raphaelites can be called The English Symbolists. It was a term used in 1997 at the exhibit of the Pre-Raphaelite paintings, *English Symbolism: The Age of Rossetti and Burne-Jones*, at the Tate Gallery in London and at previous exhibits of the second part of the 20th century. But it was not the term that was used to designate the Pre-Raphaelites in the early 1890s. Vengerova, however, uses this terms in her discussion of the Pre-Raphaelites and already in the1890s classified them as such.

42 Vengerova, Zinaida."Preraphaelitskoe bratstvo," *Literaturnye kharakteristiki*, Prometei, St. Petersburg, 1897.

43 Ibid.

NOTES

44 The article "Modern English Painting" describes the exhibition of English paint-
    ing in Saint Petersburg, in the Society for the Encouragement of Arts. Since the
    exhibition contained a number of the Pre-Raphaelite paintings, Vengerova con-
    centrated on the paintings and history of the Pre-Raphaelite movement and its
    contribution to the evolution of art and ideas:
    The historical meaning of the Pre-Raphaelites is dual; first, creative and then educa-
    tional. The creative meaning of the Pre-Raphaelites is in the fact that its members
    were truly great painters - the most remarkable painters of our century. . . . The Pre-
    Raphaelites aspired to bring to art an ethical content.

45 In addition, this book also includes the article "Oscar Wilde and English
    Aesthetes," a number of revolutionary articles about the new trends in French lit-
    erature, "The Symbolist Poets in France," "Paul Verlaine," "J.K. Huysmans;" an
    article, "Henrik Ibsen," that gives a new unconventional view of the works of the
    Norwegian playwright; an article on German playwright "Henrik Hauptmann,"
    and three remarkable articles on Italian Renaissance culture and its influence on
    the art and literature of the *fin de siècle.*

46 Vengerova, Zinaida. *Angliiskie pisateli XIX veka,* volume 1, Prometei, St.
    Petersburg, 1913.

47 Vengerova, Zinaida. "John Ruskin," *The Herald of Europe (Vestnik Evropy),* 1900,
    book VI, pages 674-692.

48 Interestingly, the early article, "John Keats and his Poetry," Vengerova's first arti-
    cle, which set the tone for her future works, was not included in either *Literary
    Portraits* or in *English Writers of the Nineteenth Century.* The reason for that is
    unknown, although it is possible to suppose that she considered her first article to
    be still a student work, since she wrote it when she still was a student, too imma-
    ture to be included in a collection of a professional writer and literary critic.

49 Taken from Roy E. Gridley, *The Browning and France,* 1982, p.170 and here cited
    from *The Age of Rossetti, Burne-Jones and Watts. Symbolism in Britain, 1890-1910,*
    Tate Gallery Publishing, page 288.

50 Ibid.

51 Ibid, page 22.

52 That ecstasy also reminds one of Salomé's ecstasy over the head of Jokanaan in
    Wilde's play "Salomé."

53 Here are the parts of Browning's poem, "Porphyria's Lover," whose spirit later
    reappears in Symbolist poetry:
    That moment she was mine, mine, fair,
    Perfectly pure and good: I found
    A thing to do and all her hair
    In one long yellow string I wound
    Three times her little throat around,
    And strangled her.
    No pain felt she;
    I am quite sure she felt no pain.
    As a shut bud that holds a bee,
    I warily oped her lids: again
    Laughed the blue eyes without a stain.
    And I untightened next the tress

> About her neck; her cheek once more
> Blushed bright beneath my burning kiss.

Here is Rossetti's Sonnet "Lilith:"

> The rose and poppy are her flowers; for where
> Is he not found, O Lilith, whom shed scent
> And soft-shed kisses and soft sleep shall snare?
> Lo! As that youth's eyes burned at thine, so went
> Thy spell through him, and left his straight neck bent,
> And round his heart one strangling golden hair.

54 Vengerova, Zinaida. "Robert Browning," *Literaturnye kharakteristiki*, Prometei, St. Petersburg, 1897, page 106.

55 One of the reasons Blake was so little appreciated is because his poetry is integral with his art, and in the early 19th century, there was no way to economically reproduce the art with commercial printing, so that awareness of his books tended to be limited to the few that could afford hand-colored copies of the books.

56 Rossetti's enthusiasm also inspired his brother, W. M. Rossetti to write in 1875 an introduction to a collection of Blake's poetical works. Between 1868 and 1893, Edwin Ellis and William Butler Yeats published a three-volume collection of Blake's work. In one of these volumes Ellis and Yeats explain the philosophical theories of Blake and their symbolism. In 1903, Yeats included in his book *Ideas of Good and Evil*, two articles that he wrote about Blake in 1897 and 1898, "William Blake and the Imagination," "William Blake and his Illustrations to the *Divine Comedy*." Finally in 1910, Yeats reprinted the *Poetical Works of William Blake* and wrote for it a long introductory article. As Andrew Wilton points out:

> Blake figures regularly in modern literature on Symbolism as a precursor of the movement. . . . The Symbolists responded to the vigorous spirituality expressed through his personal mythology, a spirituality placed in firm opposition to the material world, which Blake rejected as Death. Burne-Jones, Spencer Stanhope, Simeon Solomon, and William Blake Richmond frequently show Blake's influence. (Andrew Wilton, "Symbolism in Britain," *The Age of Rossetti, Burne-Jones and Watts. Symbolism in Britain, 1860-1910*, Tate Gallery Publishing, 1997, page 25.

57 Vengerova, Zinaida. "Robert Browning," *Literaturnye kharakteristiki*, St. Petersburg, Prometei, 1897, page 44.

58 Vengerova's article on Blake was the first and the most thorough introduction to Blake in Russia. In 1905, the Russian Symbolist poet, Balmont, also wrote an article on Blake, "Blake, a Founder of English Symbolism," but the article was quite insignificant. Contrary to Vengerova's article, which gives a thorough examination of Blake's works and explains their importance for the contemporary artists, poets and writers, Balmont's article does not give any specific information about Blake. His introduction to Blake is limited to Balmont's own impressions of Blake's works, which might be considered interesting only because that introduction came from the pen of a poet who later became famous and is considered today as one of the most important poets of Russian Symbolism. It is possible to assume, however, that Balmont's first acquaintance with Blake took place through Vengerova's article, since Balmont did not know any English.

59 Moscheles, Felix (1833-1917) - English painter. He mainly painted landscapes and portraits.
60 Monkhouse, Allan (1858-1936) - English playwright, literary and art critic.
61 Ford, Isabelle Ormiston (1860-1924) - English writer and translator.
62 Hambourg, Michail (1855, Iaroslavl', Russia - 1916, Toronto, Canada) - pianist, taught at Guilhall School of Music in London between 1890-1910. Together with his son Boris (1885, Voronezh, Russia - 1954, Toronto), violoncellist, he founded in Toronto the Hambourg Conservatory of Music. His older son, Mark (1879, Boguchar, Russia - 1960, Cambridge) was a pianist and musicologist. The middle son, Jan (1882, Voronezh - 1947, Tour, France) was a violonist.
63 See Seleznev, K. "Eleonora Marx i literatura", *Voprosy literatury*, N 9, 1963.
64 "Fond of Free Russian Press" was founded by Stepniak in 1891 in London for the propagation in Russia of the revolutionary literature.
65 Mendelson, Stanislaw (1858-1918) - Polish political activist and publicist. He participated in many European political movements.
66 Neginsky, Rosina. *Pis'ma Z.A. Vengerovoi i S.G.Balakhovskoi-Petit, Revue des Études Slaves*, LXVII/1, 1995, letter 2, pages 212-213.
67 Vengerova, Zinaida. "Tolstoy's Last Days," *Fortnightly Review*, v. 95, 1911, pages 289-299.
68 Letter from London, 17.7.1910, Bedford Square, W.C., to her sister Isabelle Afanasievna Vengerova. IRLI, fond 30, inventory 1049.
69 Neginsky, Rosina. *Pis'ma Z.A. Vengerovoi k S.G.Balakhovskoi-Petit, Revue des Études Slaves*, LXVII/4, 1995, letter 48, page 711.
70 Neginsky, Rosina. *Pis'ma Z.A. Vengerovoi k S.G.Balakhovskoi-Petit, Revue des Études Slaves*, LXVII/4, 1995, page 712.
71 Ibid., LXVII/1, 1995, p. 223, letter 7.
72 Ibid., page 225, letter 8.
73 S. A. Vengerov (ed.). *Russkaia literatura dvadtsatogo veka*, Tovarishchestvo "Mir," Moscow, reprint Wilhelm Fink Verlag, Munchen, 1972, page 137.
74 Vengerova, Zinaida. "Sandro Botticelli," *The Herald of Europe (Vestnik Evropy)*, 1895, book XII, page 767.
75 Vengerova, Zinaida. "The Meaning of Dante for the Contemporary World" ("Znachenie Dante dlia sovremennosti"), *The World of God (Mir Bozhii)*, 1896, book X, pages 177-189.
76 Vengerova, Zinaida. "Sandro Botticelli," in *Literaturnye kharakteristiki*, St. Petersburg, 1897, page 354.
77 Ibid., page 365.
78 Ibid., page 366.
79 Ibid., page 369.
80 Ibid., pages 377-379.
81 Savanarola, Girolamo (1452-1498) was a superior of the Dominican monastery, San Marco, in Florence. He acted against Medici, denounced the Pope's power, called the Church toward asceticism, and was very critical of Humanism in such a way that he even organized the burning of works of art. After the exile of Medici from Florence in 1494, Savanarola was instrumental in helping the establishment of the republic. In 1497 he was banished from the Church and burned.
82 Vengerova, Zinaida. "Znachenie Dante dlia sovremennosti," in *Literaturnye kharakteristiki*, St. Petersburg, 1897, pages 328-329.

83 For more information on Dante in Russia, see Polonsky, Rachel. "Dante and Russian Poetry," *The Cambridge review,* vol. 117, November 1996, pages 27-34.
84 Vengerova, Zinaida. "Francis Assiiski," in *Literaturnye kharakteristiki,* St. Petersburg, 1897, page 316.
85 A letter to Isabelle Afanasievna Vengerova, dated Firenze, Pension Giotti; Piazza Soderim, 17.4.95, IRLI, fond 39, inventory 1049.
86 Vengerova, Zinaida. "Pis'mo iz Italii: khudozhestvennaia vystavka v Venetsii," *Severny Viestnik,* 1895, book IX, pages 41-45.
87 Vengerova, Zinaida. "Ital'ainskaia literatura," *Novy entsiklopedicheski slovar,* 1904.
88 Vengerova, Zinaida. "D'Annuncio," *Literaturnye charakteristiki,* St. Petersburg, 1910.
89 Vengerova, Zinaida. "Ital'ainskaia literatura," *Novy entsiklopedicheski slovar,* 1904, page 53.
90 Neginsky, Rosina. *Pis'ma Z.A. Vengerovoi k S.G.Balakhovskoi-Petit, Revue des Études Slaves,* LXVII/4, 1995, page 742.
91 Flax Luise - translator from Russian into German language. She was a close friend of Vengerova's family. She specialized in the translation of many Russian writers into German. She collaborated with Merezhkovski, who met Flax through Vengerova. In one of his letters to Vengerova, he asked her to give him the address of Luise Flax in Berlin, because he hoped to contact Mme Flax regarding the translation in German of his article "L. Tolstoy and Dostoevsky. (See Rosina Neginsky, "Edited Correspondence of Dmitrii Merezhkovsky, Introduction and Commentaries," *Novoe literaturenoe obozrenie,* Moscow, May, N 12, pages 109-117, 1995, letter of 29 August/9 September, no year). Her husband was a German journalist, who specialized in the Balkans.
92 A letter to Isabelle Afanasievna Vengerova. IRLI, fond 39, inventory 1049 a, no date, just the day, Monday, page 54.
93 Ibid., 1896, page 102.
    Now I have a request for you: collect everything, written in the journals and newspapers, about "Florian Jeyer" by Hauptmann (except *Magazin für Literature*), and about Hauptmann in general and send it to me, if you can, immediately. Of course, it is better not to send the whole journals, but only the excerpts. . . . In addition, among Hauptmann's articles, I would have liked to have the sketch "Felix Hollander." I do not know where it was published. . . .
    Do you know where Lou Andrea Salomé published her critical articles (about theater)?
    Have you noticed in *The Northern Herald* that I am translating Lou Andrea Salome about Nietzsche - I like this woman for her mind.
94 The article "Hauptmann" first appeared in *The Herald of Europe* in 1896 (Zinaida Vengerova, "Hauptmann," *Vestnik Evropy,* 1896, book XI, pages 308-329) and then was published in the first volume of Vengerova's *Literary Portraits* (Zinaida Vengerova, "Hauptmann," *Literaturnye Kharakteristiki,* St. Petersburg, 1897, book one). In 1907, Vengerova published one more article on Hauptmann in *Niva,* and then this article together with an article "H. Hauptmann: Hauptmann's Fairy Tales" appeared in the third volume of Vengerova's *Literary Portraits* (Zinaida Vengerova, "H. Hauptmann. Hauptmann's Fairy Tales," *Literaturnye Kharakteristiki,* Saint Petersburg, 1910, book three). She published an article "F.

Wedenkind" in the second volume of her *Literary Portraits* (Zinaida Vengerova, "F. Wedekind," *Literaturnye Kharakteristiki*, St. Petersburg, 1910, book three), the articles "Wedekind's Satires" ("Satiry Wedekinda") and "Schnitzler" in her third volume of the same book (Zinaida Vengerova, "O. Schnitzler," *Literaturnye Kharakteristiki*, St. Petersburg, 1910, book three).

95 Rill, A. *Nietzsche as a Painter and a Thinker (Nietzsche, kak khudozhnik i myslitel')*, publication of the journal, *Education (Obrazovanie)*, St. Petersburg, 1898, in Vengerova's translation. Salomé, Lou Andrea. *F. Nietzsche in his Works (F. Nietzsche v svoikh proizvedeniiakh)*, The Northern Herald (Severny Vestnik), 1896, book III, pages 273-295; book IV, pages 253-272; book V, pages 225-239, in Vengerova's translation.

96 Vengerova, Zinaida. "Na Zapade. Gorod vneshnei kul'tury," *Obrazovanie*, 1899, book XI, pages 1-12.

97 Vengerova, Zinaida. "Individualizm v sovremennoi literature," *Obrazovanie*, 1898, book XII, pages 110-119.

98 Ibid., page 111.

99 Vengerova, Zinaida. "Na Zapade. Gorod vneshnei kul'tury," *Obrazovanie*, N 4, 1899, pages 2, 3.

100 Vengerova, Zinaida. "Individualizm v sovremennoi literature," *Obrazovanie*, 1898, book XII, page 116, St. Petersburg, 21 August [1898].

101 Ibid., 23/10 1910, 28, Rue Poussin, Paris 14e.

102 Vengerova, Zinaida. "Harhard Hauptmann," *Literaturnye kharakteristiki*, St. Petersburg, 1910, page 52.

103 Ibid., page 57.

104 Vengerova's letter: Staraia Siverskaia, 26 August [1898].

105 Ibid., 14/27 1912, StP.

106 Vengerova, Zinaida. "Arnold Böcklin," *Obrazovanie*, 1901, book 2, page 49.

CHAPTER IV

1 Pachmuss, Temira. *Zinaida Hippius An Intellectual Profile*, Southern Illinois University Press, Carbondale and Edwardsville Feffer & Simons, Inc., London and Amsterdam, page 193.

2 Ibid., pages 198-199.

3 Neginsky, Rosina. *Pis'ma Z.A. Vengerovoi k S.G. Balakhovskoi-Petit*, Revue des Etudes Slaves, Paris, LXVII/4, 1995, letter 57, pages 728: "I obtained a visa to Riga in Moscow and only for 5 days - and even that the Latvian consul gave as an exception for me, since without a visa to Germany, they do not let people enter Latvia."

4 Ibid., letter 57, page 728.

5 Ibid., letter 58, page 731: "Just in case, I went yesterday to the French consul; he asked brutally: 'D'où venez vous? Avec quel passeport?' And then he announced that he would pour a visa in 'un passport bolchviste, malgré toutes demandes du ministère.' I tried to explain to him that being Russian and arriving from Petrograd, I am unable to have any other passport but the one I have from Moscow, given to me for the reason of an illness. Then I added that in the meantime I was not asking for a visa, but only to send a telegram to the ministry, according to the telegram

NOTES

from E.Iul. that I have shown to him. But he did not want to have any discussions with me. . . . His secretary added, looking at me: 'Vous n'avez l'air malade.' (I answered him: 'Tant mieux - je voudrais ne pas en avoir aussi la chanson), probably seeing in my recovered well- rounded face the stigmas of Bolsheviks. But one person, who was witnessing that conversation, said to me: 'Obtenez un ordre des Affaires étrangères et le consulat n'aura qu'à se soumettre."

6 The situation of Grezhbin's publishing house and its decay is representative of the political changes that took place in Soviet Russia within a very short time. In 1919, right after the Revolution, Grezhbin, a co-owner of an important pre-revolutionary publishing house "Shipovnik," opened a publishing house in St. Petersburg and Berlin. That publishing venture existed until 1923, publishing the books commissioned by the official Soviet publisher, Gosizdat, until 1922. At first Grezhbin lived in St. Petersburg, but in 1921 he moved to Berlin, where he was an official representative of the Soviet organ, The International Book (Mezhdunarodnaia kniga) abroad. In 1923 he was ruined because the economic and political situation in Russia increasingly worsened, and Grezhbin's position was perceived with an increasing suspicion: he was accused by the Soviets to be an emigré and by the emigres to be a Soviet. Grezhbin finished his life in misery in Paris, in 1929.

7 The case of Vsemirnaia literatura was a little bit different. The idea of Vsermirnaia literatura, the publication of the collected works of European and American literature between the 18th and 20th centuries, belonged to writer Maxim Gorky. The realization of the project belonged to the above mentioned Grezhbin and Gorky. Originally, between 1917 and 1919, Vsemirnaia literatura was located in Grezhbin's apartment, but then it opened two branches, one the main branch, remained in Russia, and the second branch opened in Berlin because many intellectuals, people of literature, and writers were living in Berlin at that time and were able and willing to contribute to the publication in such a way that no one in the Soviet Union was able to do. This arrangement worked very well because the Russian emigres had knowledge and culture, were happy to do literary work, especially when it was pertaining to their subject matter and many of them needed money. Whereas Gosizdat – the Soviet Russian State publishing venture, had some money to spare for the realization of Gorky's project, but did not have qualified people to do it. The project, however, was interrupted in 1924 and never completed because of the lack of paper in the Soviet Union at that time.

8 Neginsky, Rosina. Pis'ma Z.A. Vengerovoi k S.G. Balakhovskoi-Petit, Revue des Études Slaves, Paris, LXVII/1, 1995, page 207 and footnote 107 on page 207. See also Chapter II, "Saint Petersburg."

9 Rudolf Steiner. See Chapter III.

10 Neginsky, Rosina. Pis'ma Z.A. Vengerovoi k S.G. Balakhovskoi-Petit, Revue des Études Slaves, Paris, LXVII/4, 1995, pages 739-740.

11 Ibid., page 742.

12 "Eser" is a name of a member of the Social Revolutionary party.

13 Neginsky, Rosina. Pis'ma Z.A. Vengerovoi k S.G. Balakhovskoi-Petit, Revue des Etudes Slaves, Paris, LXVII/4, 1995, letter 59, pages 733-735.

14 Ibid., letter 60, page 737.

15 Ibid., letter 63, page 744.

16 Beyer, Jr., Thomas R. "The House of the Arts and the Writers' Club Berlin 1921-

NOTES

1923," in Russische Autoren und Verlage in Berlin nach dem Ersten Weltkrieg, Berlin: Berlin Verlag A. Spitz, c 1987, page 13 and the footnote N 14.

17 Erenburg, Ilia Grigorievich (1891-1967) - journalist, writer, poet, translator.

18 Beyer, Jr., Thomas R. "The House of the Arts and the Writers' Club Berlin 1921-1923," Russische Autoren und Verlage in Berlin nach dem Ersten Weltkrieg, Berlin: Berlin Verlag A. Spitz, c 1987, page 14.

19 Neginsky, Rosina. *Pis'ma Z.A. Vengerovoi k S.G. Balakhovskoi-Petit, Revue des Etudes Slaves,* Paris, LXVII/4, 1995, letter 62, pages 741-742.

20 At first, in December of 1921, the regular meeting day was on Saturdays and then it was moved to Fridays.

21 In 1903, she had published a condensed version of her translation of *Buddenbrooks* in *The Herald of Europe (Vestnik Evropy)*. See *Vestnik Evropy,* 1903, book X, pages 682-727; book XI, pages 287-344; book XII, pages 741-790.

22 Hugh, Walpole (1884-1941) - English writer, literary critic.

23 Neginsky, Rosina. *Pis'ma Z.A. Vengerovoi k S.G. Balakhovskoi-Petit, Revue des Etudes Slaves,* Paris, LXVII/4, 1995, letter 63, pages 743-744.

24 For instance, in imitation of Flaubert's "sottisier," Urusov collected the linguistic "pearls" that he heard during his legal activities, and published the essays in the newspaper, "Poriadok."

25 Vengerova, Zinaida. "Parizhski arkhiv kniazia Urusova," *Literaturnoe nasledstvo,* v. 33-34, section "Russkaia literatura vo Frantsii" ("Russian Literature in France"), Moscow, 1939, pages 591-616.

26 Seleznev, K. "Eleonora Marx i literatura," *Voprosy literatury,* N 9, 1963, pages 199-204.

27 Neginsky, Rosina. *Zinaida Hippius: Letters to S.G. Balakhovskaia (Zinaida Hippius: Pis'ma k S.G. Balakhovskoi), Russian Literature,* XXXVII, 1995, letter of 15 April 1920 from Warsaw, page 78.

28 "Zina mourut le 30 juin 1941 après une longue maladie et malgré les efforts de meilleurs spécialistes du Parkinson disease – maladie cruelle d'atrophie graduelle des muscles et des nerfs."

SELECTED BIBLIOGRAPHY

ARCHIVES
Biliothèque de Documentation Internationale Contemporaine (BDIC), Nanterre, France.
Institute of Russian Literature, Pushkinski dom (IRLI), Saint Petersburg, Russia.

BOOKS AND ARTICLES
Ash, Russell. *Dante Gabrielle Rossetti*. Harry N. Abrams, 1995.
Babin S., Semibratova, I. *Sud'by poetov serebrianogo veka*. Moscow: Knizhnaia palata, 1993.
Balmont, Konstantin. *Sobranie sochinenii v dvukh tomakh (Collected Works in two volumes)*. Mozhaisk : Terra, 1994.
Baranova-Shestova, Natalia. *Zhizn' L'va Shestova (Lev Shestov's Life)*. Paris: La Presse libre, 2 vols, 1983.
Baudelaire, Charles. *Œuvres complètes (Complete Works)*. 2 vols. Paris: Gallimard, 1975.
Bely, Andrei. *Simvolism*. Moscow, 1910.
Vospominaniia o A. A. Bloke. Munich, 1969.
Na rubezhe dvukh stoletii. Moscow, 1989.
Nachalo veka. Moscow, 1990.
Mezhdu dvukh revoliutsii. Moscow, 1990.
Simvolism kak miroponimanie, ed. L.A. Sugai. Moscow, 1994.
Benois, Alexandre. *Moi vospominaniia (My Memoirs)*. Moscow, 1990.
Berdiaev, Nikolai. "Dekadenstsvo i misticheskii realizm." *Russkaia mysl'*, No 6, (1907), pages 114-23.
Ekzistentsial'naia dialektika bozhestvennogo i chelovecheskogo. Paris:

YMCA Press, 1952.

Mirosozertsanie Dostoevskago, Paris : YMCA-Press, 1968.

"O novom religioznom soznanii." *Voprosy zhizni*, 1905, 9.

Opyt eskhatologicheskoi metafiziki; tvorchestvo i ob'ektivatsiia. (The Meaning of the Creative Act). Paris: YMCA Press, 1947.

Samopoznanie; opyt filosofskoi avtobiografii. Paris: YMCA Press, 1983.

*Viekhi. Sbornik statei o russkoi intelligentsii (*Landmarks : a Collection of Essays on the Russian Intelligentsia*)*. Frankfurt: Posev, 1967.

Berg, Leo. *The Superman in Modern Literature*. London: Jarrold & Sons, 1916.

Besant, Annie. *H.P. Blavatsky and the Master of Wisdom*. London, 1907.

Beyer, Jr., Thomas R. "The House of the Arts and the Writers' Club Berlin 1921-1923," in Russische Autoren und Verlage in Berlin nach dem Ersten Weltkrieg, Berlin: Berlin Verlag A. Spitz, 1987.

Blake, William. *The Complete Poetry and Prose of William Blake*. Anchor, 1997.

Bobkoff, John Joachim. Russia's first decadent and expressionist: Konstantin Sluchevsky. Dissertation: Thesis (Ph.D. in Russian Language)—Vanderbilt University, 1975.

Borisova, L. M. *Na izlomakh traditsii: dramaturgiia russkogo simvolizma i simvolistskaia teoriia zhiznetvorchestva*, Simferopol: Tavricheskii natsio-nal'nyi universitet im. V.I. Vernadskogo, 2000.

Briusov, Valery. *Collected Works (Sochineniia)*, Moskva: Khuduzhestvennaia literatura, 1987.

Dalekie i blizkie, Moscow, 1912.

Dnevniki 1891-1910, ed. I. M. Briusova and N. S. Ashukina. Moscow, 1927.

Iz moei zhizni (From my Life), Moscow, 1927.

Browning, Robert. *The complete works of Robert Browning : with variant readings and annotations*. Athens : Ohio University Press, 1969.

Carbone M.C., Carassiti A. *Botticelli*. New York: Gramercy Books, 1994.

C. D. "French-Russian literary relations." *Handbook of Russian Literature* (ed. Victor Terras). New Haven, London: Yale University Press, 1985.

Chekhov, Anton. *Polnoe sobranie sochinenii i pisem*. Moskva: Gosudarstvennoe. izdatelstvo kudozhestvennoi literatury, 1944.

Clyman, Toby W. & Greene, Diana (ed.). *Women Writers in Russian Literature*. Westport, Connecticut, London: Greenwood Press, 1994.

Dante, Alighieri. *Bozhestvennaia komediia* (*Divine Comedy*). Sankt-Peterburg : Kristall, 1998.

La divina commedia. Milano: Ricciardi, 1957.

Vita Nuova. Moscow: Khudozhestvennaia literatura, 1985.

D'Annunzio, Gabrielle. Francesca da Rimini. New York: Frederick A. Stokes Company, 1902.

Nocturne & five tales of love & death. Marlboro, Vt.: Marlboro Press, 1988.

D'Annunzio (1863-1938). Catalogue de l'exposition. Paris: Édition de la Réunion des musées nationaux, 2001.

Donchin, Georgette. *The Influence of French Symbolism on Russian Poetry.* The Hague, 1958.

Ehrhardt, Ingrid (ed.), Simon Reynolds (ed.), Hans Henrik Brummer (ed.). Djurgarden, Stockholm, Sweden: Schirn Kunsthalle Frankfurt, Birmingham City Museum and Art Gallery, Waldemarsudde Museum: 2000.

Encyclopédie du Symbolisme. Peinture, Gravure et Sculpture. Literature. Musique. Somogy, 1988.

Ermilova, E.V. *Teoriia i obraznyi mir russkogo simvolizma.* Moscow: Nauka, 1989.

Fink, Hilary. *Bergson and Russian Modernism 1900-1930.* Chicago: Northwestern University Press, 1998.

Gaunt, William. *The Aesthetic Adventure.* London: Cardinal edition, 1975.

Garnett, Richard. *Constance Garnett: A Heroic Life.* London, 1991.

Grechishkin, S.S. and Lavrov, A. V. (eds.)."Pis'ma k L. N. Vilkinoi." *Ezhegodnik rukopisnogo otdela Pushkinskogo doma na 1973 god,* Leningrad, 1976.

Guerman. Mikhail. *Michail Vroubel. L'Annonciateur des Temps Nouveaux.* Saint-Petersbourg: Parkstone Aurora, 1996.

Gibson, Michael. *Symbolism.* Taschen America Lic, 1999.

Glinsky, Boris. "Illness or Publicity" ("Bolezn' ili reklama"). *Istorichesky Vestnik,* N 2 (1896).

Gofman, M. *Poety simvolizma,* St. Petersburg, 1908.

Greenhalgh, Paul. *Art Nouveau, 1890-1914.* Harry N. Abrams, 2000.

Hauptmann, Gerhart. *The dramatic works of Gerhart Hauptmann.* New York: B.W. Huebsch, 1912.

Hippius, Zinaida. *Chertova kukla. Proza, stikhotvoreniia, stat'i.* Moskva:

Sovremennik, 1991.
Dmitrii Merezhkovsky. v. 2. Tbilisi: Merani, 1991.
Stikhi i proza. Tula Priokskoe knizhnoe izdatel'stvo, 1992.
Zhivye litsa.Stikhi i dnevniki. v. 1. Tbilisi: Marani, 1991.
Zhivye litsa.Vospominania. v. 2. Tbilisi: Marani, 1991.
Huysmans, J.K. *Against Nature (À Rebours).* Paris: Gallimard, 1977.
A vau-l'eau. Paris : Union générale d'éditions, 1975.
En ménage. Paris : Union générale d'éditions, 1975.
En route. Paris: Gallimard,1996.
En rade. Paris: Gallimard,1984.
La Bas. Paris: Flammarion,1993.
La Cathedrale. Paris : Plon,1908.
Marthe : histoire d'une fille. Paris : Union générale d'éditions, 1975.
Ibsen, Henrik. Translated and introduced by Rolf Fjelde. *The complete major prose plays.* New York : Farrar, Straus & Giroux, 1978.
Ivanova, E.V. "Vengerova." *Russkie pisateli 1800-1917. Biographicheski slovar',* v. 1. Moscow: Sovetskaia Encyclopedia, 1989.
Khodasevich V. *Vospominania o Gorkom.* Moscow: Biblioteka "Ogon'ka," N 44 (1989).
Keats, John. *Poems.* New York: Everyman's Library, 1974.
Ketchian, Sonia I. *Keats and Russian Poets.* Birmingham Slavonic Monographs, N 33. Birmingham, U.K.: The University of Birmingham Press, 2001.
Kliuchevski, B.O. *Kratkoe posobie po russkoi istorii.* Moscow: "Rassvet," 1992.
"Kriticheskie zametki." *Mir Bozhii.* N 3 (1896).
Lacambre, Genevieve. *Gustave Moreau: between epic and dream.* Paris : Chicago: Réunion des musées nationaux; Art Institute of Chicago, 1999.
Lacambre, Genevieve. *Gustave Moreau.* Princeton University Press, 1999.
Le Monde de l'Art. Association artistique russe du début du XXᵉ siècle. Leningrad: Editions d'art Aurora, 1991.
Lermontov, Michail. *Major Poetical Works,* translated from the Russian by Anatoly Liberman. Minneapolis: University of Minnesota Press, 1983.
Le Symbolism dans les collections du Petit Palais. Paris: Musée du Petit Palais, 1989.
Le symbolisme russe. Bordeaux, Paris: Réunion des musées nationaux, 2000.

Levin, Yu.D. *Vospriiatie angliiskoi literatury v Rossii*. Leningrad, 1990.

Na rubezhe XIX i XX vekov: Iz istorii mezhdunarodnykh sviazei russkoi literatury, Leningrad, 1991.

Lucie-Smith, Edward. *Symbolist Art*. Thames & Hudson, 1985.

Maeterlinck, Maurice. *Sochineniia* in three volumes, in L. Vilkina's translation. "Introductions" are by N. Minsky, Z. Vengerova, V. Rozanov. St. Petersburg: izdanie M.V. Pirozhkova, 1906.

Mancoff, Debra N. *Jane Morris: The Pre-Raphaelite Model of Beauty*. Pomegranate, 2000.

Maupassant, Guy de. *Œuvres complètes*. Paris : L. Conard, 1908.

Minsky, Nikolai. "S.A. Vengerov." *Poslednie novosti*, 3 oct. (1920).

Moeller-Sally, Betsy F. "Oscar Wilde and the Culture of Russian Modernism." *Slavic and East European journal*, Vol. 34, No. 4 (1900).

Moréas, Jean. "A Literary Manifest" ("Un manifeste littéraire"). *Le Figaro*, 18 Septembre, (1886), literary supplement (le supplément littéraire).

Murray, Peter and Linda. *The Art of the Renaissance*. London, New York: Thames and Hudson, 1963.

Neginsky, Rosina. "Edited Correspondence of Dmitrii Merezhkovsky, Introduction and Commentaries." Moscow: *Novoe literaturenoe obozrenie*, N 12 (1995).

Neginsky, Rosina. *Pis'ma Z. A. Vengerovoi k S. G. Balakhovskoi-Petit (Letters of Z.A. Vengerova to S. G. Balakhovskaia-Petit)*. Paris: Revue des Études slaves, LXVII/1, LXVII/2-3, LXVII/4, 1995.

Neginsky, Rosina. *Zinaida Hippius: Pis'ma k S. G. Balakhovskoi-Petit. Russian Literature*, XXXVII, 59-92, (1995).

Nietzsche, Friedrich Wilhelm. *Basic writings of Nietzsche*. New York : Modern Library, 1992.

Nordau, Max. *Degeneration*. University of Nebraska Press; Reprint edition, 1993.

Odilon Redon. 1840-1916. Catalogue. Chicago: The Art Institute of Chicago, 1994.

Pachmuss, Temira. *Zinaida Hippius. An Intellectual Profile*. London and Amsterdam: Southern Illinois University Press, Carbondale and Edwardsville Feffer & Simons, Inc., 1971.

Pater, Walter. *The Renaissance*. Introduction by Arthur Symons. New York: The Modern Library Publishers, 1919.Prettejohn, Elizabeth. *The Art of the Pre-Raphaelites*. Princeton University Press, 2000.

Peterson, Ronald E. (ed). *The Russian Symbolists*. Ann Arbor: Ardis, 1986.

Polonsky, Rachel. "Dante and Russian Poetry." *The Cambridge review*, vol. 117, November 1996, pages 27-34.

English Literature and The Russian Aesthetic Renaissance. Cambridge University Press, 1998.

Régnier, Henri de. *Faces et profils. Souvenirs sur Villiers de l'Isle-Adam, Jules Laforgue, Stéphane Mallarmé*. Paris: J. Bernard, "La Centaine," 1931.

Poèmes anciens et romanesques, 1887-1889. Paris : Librairie de l'art indépendant, 1890.

Richardson, James. *Vanishing lives: style and self in Tennyson, D.G. Rossetti, Swinburne, and Yeats*. Charlottesville: University Press of Virginia, 1988.

Rill, A. *Nietzsche as a Painter and a Thinker (Nietzsche, kak khudozhnik i myslitel')*. Translated by Z. Vengerova. Saint Petersburg: Obrazovanie, 1898.

Rodenbach, Georges. *Bruges-la-morte*. Paris: E. Flammarion, 1904.

Rosenthal, Charlotte. "Zinaida Vengerova: Modernism and Women's Liberation." *Irish Slavonic Studies*, (Fall 1987).

Rossetti, Dante Gabriel. *The essential Rossetti*. New York : Ecco Press, 1990.

Salomé, Lou Andrea. *F. Nietzsche in his Works (F. Nietzsche v svoikh proizvedeniiakh)*, *The Northern Herald (Severny Vestnik)*, (1896), book III, pages 273-295; book IV, pages 253-272; book V, pages 225-239, in Vengerova's translation.

Saabianov, Dimitri. *Valentin Serov. Le premier maître de la peinture russe*. St. Petersbourg: Parkstone Aurora, 1996.

Shead, Richard. *Ballets Russes*. London: Apple Press Ltd, 1989.

Schnitzler, Arthur. *Plays and stories*. New York: Continum, 1982

Sherbinin, Julie De. *Chekhov and Russian Religious Culture: Poetics of the Marian Paradigm*. Chicago: Northwestern University Press, 1997.

Shopenhauer, Arthur. *Mir kak volia i predstablenie*. Moskva: "Moskovski klub," Moskva, 1992.

Seleznev, K. "Eleonora Marx i literatura." *Voprosy literatury*, N 9, 1963.

Slonimsky, Nicolas. *Perfect Pitch*. Oxford, New York: Oxford University Press, 1988.

Sologub, Fedor. *Melkii bes (Shabby Demon)*. Letchworth (Herts.); Bradda Books, 1966.

Tiazhelye sny: roman, rasskazy. Leningrad: Khudozhestvennaia literatura, 1990.

Tiazhelye sny. Severny Vestnik, 1895, books VII, VIII, IX, X, XI, XII.

Neizdannyi Fedor Sologub: stikhi, dokumenty, memuary. Lavrov, A.V., Pavlova, M. M. (eds). Moskva : Novoe literaturnoe obozrenie, 1997.

Soloviev, Vladimir. *Sobranie sochinenii (Collected Works).* Berlin: Zaria, 1924.

Literaturnaia kritika (Literary Criticism). Moscow: Sovremennik, 1990.

Strindberg, August. *Slovo bezumtsa v svoiu zashchitu. Odinoki. Piesy.* Moscow: Khudozhestvennaia literatura, 1997.

Sturgis, St. Matthew. *Passionate Attitudes: the English Decadence of the 1890s.* London: Macmillan, 1995.

Symons, Arthur. *The Symbolist Movement in Literature.* London, 1899.

The Age of Rossetti, Burne-Jones and Watts. Symbolism in Britain 1860-1910. London: Tate Gallery Publishing, 1997.

Tolstoy, Leo. *Selections.* Freeport, New York: Books for Libraries Press, 1970.

Veinberg, Petr. *Stranitsy iz istorii zapadnykh literatur.* St. Petersburg, 1907.

Vengerov, S.A. *Kritiko-biographicheskii slovar' russkikh pisatelei i uchenykh (ot nachala russkoi obrazovannosti do nashikh dnei),* 4 vols. St. Petersburg, 1889-1904.

Osnovnye cherty istorii noveishei russkoi literatury. St. Petersburg, 1909.

Russkaia literatura dvadtsatogo veka, 1890-1910. Moscow: Tovarishchestvo "Mir." Reprint München: Wilhelm Fink Verlag, 1972.

Vengerova, Zinaida. "Angliiskie futuristy." *Strieletz,* sbornik I, (1915).

Angliiskie pisateli XIX veka (English Writers of the Nineteenth Century). St. Petersburg: Izd. "Prometei," 1913.

"Arnold Böcklin." *Obrazovanie,* book 2 (1901).

"Bernard Shaw." *Vestnik Evropy,* (1914).

"Blavatskaia." *Biographical Dictionary of Brokgaus and Efron (Biographicheski slovar' Brokgauza i Efrona),* v. 3, 301-315 (1892).

"Feminism i zhenskaia svoboda." *Obrazovanie:* v.7, N 4, pages 73-90, (1898).

"Feminism and Woman's Freedom,"translated by Rosina Neginsky. *Russian Women Writers.* London, New York: Garland Publishing, v. 2, pages 892-907, (1999).

"Hippius," *Mercure de France,* N 6, vol. 26 (1898).

"Individualizm v sovremennoi literature." *Obrazovanie,* book XII, pages 110-119, (1898).

"Ital'ainskaia literatura." *Novy entsiklopedicheski slovar',* (1904).

"John Keats i ego poeziia." *Vestnik Evropy,* book X, page 539; book XI, page 62, (1889).

"John Ruskin." *Vestnik Evropy,* book VI, pages 674-692, (1900).

"Lettres Russes." *Mercure de France,* Oct - December, vol. 32, (1899).

Literary Portraits (Literaturnye kharakteristiki). Kn. I, St. Petersburg, 1897; kn. II, St. Petersburg, 1905; kn. III, St. Petersburg, 1910.

"Mistiki bezbozhiia. Emile Verhaeren." *Novy Put',* N 2, February, St. Petersburg, (1904).

"Moskovskie Theatry." "Novaia Zhizn'," N XII, (1912).

"Na Zapade. Gorod vneshnei kul'tury." *Obrazovanie,* book XI, 1-12, (1899).

"Novy idealism vo Frantsii. Roman Rolland." *Zavety,* book VIII (1913).

"Novaia teoriia o lichnosti Shekspira." *Vestnik Evropy,* book VI, 352-361, (1913).

"Novosti inostrannoi literatury." *Vestnik Evropy,* (1893-1909).

"Ob otvlechnnom v teatre." *Zavety,* book II, (1914).

"Parizhski arkhiv kniazia Urusova." *Literaturnoe nasledstvo.* v. 33-34 (1939).

"Russian literary criticism." Knight (ed.). *History of the Beautiful.*

"Russkaia literatura vo Frantsii" ("Russian Literature in France"). *The Herald of Europe,* Moscow, pages 591-616, (1899).

"Pevetz vremeni. Henri de Régnier." *Novy Put',* N4, April, St. Petersburg, (1904).

"Pis'mo iz Italii: khudozhestvennaia vystavka v Venetsii."*Severny Vestnik,* book IX, pages 41-45, (1895).

"Russian Woman" ("La femme russe"). *Revue des revues,* September, (1897).

"Russkii roman vo Frantsii." *Vestnik Evropy,* v. 34 (2), (1899).

"Shekspir i ego critic Brandes."*Obrazovanie,* January (1900).

"Sheridan." *Mir Bozhii,* book VIII, pages 33-46 (1893).

"Sovremennaia angliiskaia zhivopis'." *Obrazovanie,* book II (1898).

"Stanislavsky." *Entsiklopediia Brokgauza i Efrona.* St. Petersburg, 1897.

"Symvolism v ego sovremennom ponimanii." *Dnevniki pisatelei,* N 2 (1914).

"Teatre v sovremennoi Frantsii" ("Theater in the Contemporary France"). *Obrazovanie,* book III (1899).

"The Life and Death of Tolstoy." *Fortnightly Review,* (1910).

Verhaeren, Emile. *Les Campagnes Halluciinées. Les Villes Tentaculaires.* Archives du Future et Labor, 1997.

Verlaine, Paul. *Oeuvres poétiques complètes.* Paris: Gallimard. Bibliothèque de la Pléiade, 1962.

Veselovsky, Aleksei. *Zapadnoe vliianie v novoi russkoi literature.* Moscow, 1910.

Volkonsky, Sergei Michailovich. *Moi vospominaniia,* two volumes. München, 1923.

Volynsky, A. L. *Anton Chekhov. O simvolizme i simvolistakh.* Offprint of "Severny Vestnik," n°. 10, 11, and 12. St. Petersburg, (1898).

Zen'kovsky, B. B. *Istoria russkoi philosophii.* Paris: YMCA Press, 1948.

Yeats, W.B. *Ideas of Good and Evil.* London & Stratford-Upon-Avon, 1903.

Yeats, W.B. "Introduction" to *Poetical Works of William Blake.* New York : Carlton House, 1920.

Wanner, Adrian. *Baudelaire in Russia.* University Press of Florida, 1996.

Wedekind, Frank. *Four Major Plays.* Lyme, NH: Smith and Kraus, 2000.

Wilde, Oscar. *Complete Collected Works.* London, New York: Harper & Row, 1989.

Wilde, Oscar. *The Essays of Oscar Wilde.* New York: Cosmopolitan Book Corporation, 1916.

Wildman, Stephen. *Edward Burne-Jones, Victorian Artist-Dreamer.* Yale University Press, 1998.

Wood, Christopher. *The Pre-Raphaelites.* Seven Dials, 2001.

INDEX

"About the Abstract in the Theater," 99
"A Letter from Italy: The Art Exhibit in Italy," 148
"Alma," 98
"Angel," 80
"A Small Temptation," 100, 101
A Rebours, see *Against Nature*, 184
Academy of Plato, 143
Ada, 186
Against Nature, 112, 184, 196
Akhmatova, Anna, 90
An Autobiography, 118-119
Andreev, Leonid, 137
"Angels of Creation," 126
Angliiskie pisateli XIX veka, see *English Writers of the Nineteenth Century*, 29, 40, 131, 181, 197, 199
Anna-Niuta Ermolina, 96
Antichrist, 159
"Après-midi d'un faune," see "Faun's After-Noon," 36
Argonavty, see *The Argonauts*, 163
"Astarte Syriaca," 127-128
Austria, 60, 119, 151, 156
"Autobiographical Essay," 22, 24-25, 31, 57, 110, 126, 189
Aveling, Eleonore 8, 136-137, 170, 172
"Avtobiographicheskaia spravka," see "Autobiographical Essay," 189, 198

Balakhovskaia-Petit, Sofia Grigorievna, (Sonia), 15-16, 39, 58-59, 65, 71-72,

74, 91, 122, 160-162, 167-168, 172-173, 181, 184-185, 189, 192-193, 196, 205
Ballets Russes, 36
Baratynsky, Evgenii A., 84, 192
Bariatynsky (prince), 138, 156
BDIC., 190
Beardsley, Aubrey, 30, 35, 132
"Beata Beatrix," 33, 127
Beginning, 182
Bela (Bella), see Vilkina, Liudmila, 50, 120, 188
Belgian Symbolism, 8, 81, 115
Belka (Belochka), see also Vengerova, Isabelle Afanasievna, 45-47, 187
Bely, Andrei, 119, 159, 165
Benois, Alexandre, 87, 193
Berdiaev, Nikolai, 50, 92-93, 194
Berg, Leo, 151-152
Berlin, 8, 40, 42, 54, 87, 99, 108, 152-153, 157, 159-162, 164-167, 192, 202, 205
Bern, 50
Bernhard, Sarah, 48
Bernstein, Leonard, 23, 45, 47
Besant, Annie, 118, 179
Bestuzhev's Institute of Higher Learning for Women, 21, 39, 43, 48, 57, 65
Bestuzhevskie kursy, see Bestuzhev's Institute of Higher Learning for Women, 39, 43, 57
Bezrodnaia, Iulia, 48

Blake, William, 8, 24, 27, 30-31, 128, 133-135, 177, 197, 200-201
Böcklin, Arnold, 157, 203
Bolsheviks, 104, 159, 163, 169, 172, 196
Botticelli, Sandro, 8, 24, 27, 29, 31, 33, 71, 142-146, 177, 201
Brown, Madox, 32, 126
"Browning and his Poetry," 27, 128, 132-133
Browning, Robert, 8, 27, 128, 132-133, 136, 199-200
Burne-Jones, Edward, 24, 31-32, 35, 125-126, 184, 200

Conrad, Joseph, 135
Contemporary Italian Literature, 8, 148
Cosimo Medici, 143
"Critical Notes," 29, 182
"Critic as Artist," 124
Curtis Institute, 173

D'Annunzio, Gabrielle, 33, 148-149, 195
Das Eisenbahnunglück, 166
Daudet, Alphonse, 57
Davydova, Alexandra Arkadievna, 65
Decadence, 8, 22-23, 27, 79-80, 90, 94, 109-115, 123-125, 176-178, 182-183
Degeneration, 26, 109, 196
Diaghilev, Sergei, 23, 33, 36, 86-87, 134, 181, 193
Divine Comedy, 31, 33, 147, 200
Dobroliubov, Alexander, 69
Dom Iskusstv, see The House of the Arts,165
Dom pisatelei, see The Writers' Club, 167
Dostoevsky, Fedor, 49, 202
Duse, Eleonora (1858-1924), 99

Education, 66, 117, 183, 193, 198, 203
Ekonomicheskoe uchenie Karla Marksa, see Karl Marx's Teaching of Economy, 44
Elizavetino, 49, 52, 73, 188
Emigration, 8, 20, 40, 45, 48, 58, 105, 107, 119, 122, 137, 157, 161-162, 169, 171-172, 187, 192-193
Encyclopedic Dictionary of Brokgaus and Efron, 186
Engels, Frederick, (1820-1895) 136, 172
England, 7-8, 20, 22, 28, 31-32, 40, 54, 60, 84, 107, 118, 121-123, 128, 134-135, 137-138, 140, 142, 150, 157, 161, 164, 167, 192, 198
English Aesthetes, 125, 199
English Symbolism, 35, 128, 198, 200
English Utopists, 184
Entartgung, see Degenration, 26
Epstein, Judah, 41
Erenburg, Ilia, 166, 205
esery, 163
Evreinova, Anna Mikhailovna, 65, 189

Fanival, Dr., 136
"Faun's After-Noon," 36
Feminism, 7-8, 33-34, 117, 179, 184, 197
"Feminism and Woman's Freedom," 34, 117, 179, 184, 213
"Feminism i zhenskaia svoboda," see "Feminism and Woman' Freedom," 34, 184, 197
Fet, Afanasy, 67
Filosofov, Dmitry, 76, 87, 182, 192
First World War, 64, 102, 128
Flaubert, Gustave, 170-171, 205
Flax, Luise, 150, 202
Flaxman, John, 33
Flekser-Volynsky, Akim, 24, 65, 72
Florence, 32, 140-143, 148, 201-202
Fokine, Michel, 36
Ford, Isabell Ormiston, 135-136, 201
Fortnightly Review, 8, 137-139, 201
Foss, Lukas, 23, 45
Frampton, George, 35
France, 7-8, 13-14, 16, 20, 22, 26-27, 40, 55, 58, 60, 67, 84, 88, 95, 97-98, 107-109, 111-112, 114-116, 119-121, 137, 150, 153, 157, 160-164, 171, 179, 182-184, 192-193, 195, 197, 199, 201, 205
France, Anatole, 115

INDEX

Francis of Assisi, 8, 27, 142, 147, 177
Franco-Prussian War, 152
Free Russia, 137
French Symbolism, 8, 109-110, 112, 123, 197
French Symbolist art, 22
Fridays at Sluchevsky, 7, 89-90

Gaideburov, Pavel Pavlovich, 58, 189
Garnett, Constance, 135
Garnett, Edward, 135
Gautier, Théophile, 109
German expressionism, 24
Germany, 16, 20, 28, 60, 67, 119, 149-150, 152, 156, 160-161, 167, 192
Gilchrist, Alexander, 31, 134
Giotto (di Bondone), 143
Glinsky, Boris, 21, 69-70, 181, 190
"Goethe and Tolstoy," 166
Gogol, Nikolai Ivanovich, 186
Golos Rossii 163
Goncharov, Ivan Alexandrovich, (1812-1891) 135
Goncourt, Edmond de, 116
Gorky, Maxim, 103-104, 137, 161, 196
Grand Palais, 35
Grezhbin, 161, 204
Grusenberg, 105
Gumilev, Nikolai, 90
Gurevich, Liubov, 24, 39, 57, 63, 65-68, 70-71, 190

"Hamlet in the Making of Russia," 169
Hauptmann, Gerhard, 27-29, 67, 150, 153, 155-156, 199, 202-203
"Heartache," 97
Heavy Dreams, 96
"Heather Gabler," 65
Herzl, Theodor, 41
Hippius (Merezhkovskaia), Zinaida Nikolaevna, 7, 23-24, 40, 49, 55, 65, 70-72, 74-76, 79, 82-87, 90-91, 96-97, 105, 117, 132-133, 137, 159, 162, 172, 187-188, 190-193, 196, 205

Historical Dictionary of Russian Writers, 186
Holman, William, 32, 126
Huysmans, Georges Charles, dit Joris-Karl, 27, 29, 112-114, 184, 196

Iakovleva, Iulia, 48
Iavorskaia, Lidia Borisovna, 69, 102, 138; Lida, Lidia Iavorskaia, Lidia Borisovna, 102
Ibsen, Henrik, 24, 27-29, 65-66, 101, 155, 182, 199
Ideas of Good and Evil, 31, 184, 200
"Individualism in the Modern Literature," 150
"Individualism v sovremennoi literature, see Individualism in the Modern Literature," 150
Inferno, 33
Italian Literature, 8, 107, 148-149
Italy, 8, 22, 32, 39, 55, 58, 60, 72, 92, 140-142, 148, 157
Iunia, 49
Ivanov, Viacheslav, 7, 16, 24, 79, 90, 92-94
Ixkul von Hildnbrand , Varvara Ivanovna (Baronessa), 7, 91, 97, 194; see also Lutkovskaia, 194

Jean Floressas des Esseintes, 112
Jekwabb, 68
Joffrey Ballet, 36
"John Keats and his Poetry," 25, 67, 199
"John Keats i ego poeziia," see "John Keats and his Poetry," 25, 190
Judeo-Christian tradition, 32
Judith, 144

Kachalov, Vasily Ivanovich, 100, 195
Kahn, Gustave, 111, 114-115, 183, 196
Karl Marx's Teaching of Economy, 44
Keats, John, 25-26, 67, 182, 190, 199
Kiev, 44, 58
Knipper, Olga Leopardovna, 100, 195
Konotop, 42
Korsh Theater, 101

"Kriticheskie zametki," see "Critical Notes," 29, 182-183

Là Bas, 112
"La Femme russe," see "Russian Woman," 34, 117, 184, 197
La Jeunesse blanche, 116
La Mer élegante, 116
La Princesse Maleine, 115
La Vogue, 111
Laforgue, Paul, 26, 60, 67, 111, 190
Lake Geneva, 50
Lamia, 182
Latvia, 160
Lausanne, 50
Lavrov, Petr Lavrovich, 58
Lawrence, D. H., 135
Lazhechnikov, I. I., 186
Le Figaro, 115, 182
Le Règne du silence, 116
Le Temps, 68
Leighton, Frederic, 24, 33, 35
Lermontov, Michail, 80, 191
Les Débats, 68
Les Flamandes, 115
Les Flambeaux noirs, 115
Les Fleurs du mal, 109
Les Moines, 115
"Les Noces," see "The Wedding," 36
Les Soirs, 115
Leshetitshki, Theodor, 47, 187
Lettres russes, 40, 84, 88, 95, 97, 116, 193, 195
"Lev Tolstoy and the Russian Church," 194
"Lev Tolstoy i russkaia tserkov," see "Lev Tolstoy and the Russian Church," 194
Levinson, Andrei, 183
L'Hiver mondain, 116
Liadov, Anatol, 68-69
Library of the Great Writers, 186
Life of Blake, 31; Life of William Blake, 134
Lippi, Fra-Philippo, 144
Literary Circles 7, 64, 86, 89
Literary Heritage, 171

Literary Portraits, 27, 29-31, 40, 90, 126, 128, 142, 148, 181-182, 190, 195, 197, 199, 202-203
Literaturnoe Nasledstvo, see Literary Heritage 171, 205
Literaturnye kharakteristiki, see Literary Portraits 27, 40, 128, 181-183, 190, 194-197, 199-203
"Living and Dead," 84
Login ,96-97
Lokhvitskaia, Mirra, 90, 92
London 8, 32, 35, 39-40, 58, 60, 64, 102-103, 106, 108, 119, 122-123, 125-126, 129, 135-140, 142, 156, 167, 169, 184, 189, 196-198, 201
Lorenzo the Beautiful, 143
Lost Paradise: Symbolist Europe, 35
Luba (Gurevich, Lubov), 70
Lutkovskaia, see Ixkul von Hildnbrand, Varvara Ivanovna, 194

Mademoiselle de Maupin, 109
Maeterlinck, Maurice, 26-27, 67, 91, 115-116, 182-183, 197
Mallarmé, Stéphane, 24, 26, 67, 111, 116, 190
"Maly soblazn," see "A Small Tempta-tion," 100
Mamontov, Savva Ivanovich, 89, 194
Mania, Maria Vengerova, 42
Mann, Thomas, 166-167
Marx, Karl, 44, 58, 136, 170, 172, 201, 205
Maupassant, Guy de, 139, 178, 191, 211
Memoiren einer Grossmutter, see Memoirs of a Grandmother, 42
Memoirs of a Grandmother, 42
Mendelson, Stanislaw, 201
Mercure de France, 40, 84, 88, 95, 97, 116, 137, 192-193, 195
Meredith, George, 27-30, 128
Merezhkovskaia (Hippius Zinaida), 70-72, 83, 86, 192
Merezhkovsky, Dmitry, 23-24, 65, 70-71, 76, 78-79, 83, 87-91, 94-95, 159, 182, 188, 192, 194, 196, 202

Mikhailovsky theater, 120
Millais, John Everett, 32-33, 35, 126
Millerand, 58
Minsk, 39, 42, 48, 55, 57, 185, 187-189
Minsky, Nikolai, 8, 16, 23, 40, 43-44, 48-49, 51, 54-56, 65, 68-70, 87-88, 90, 95, 101, 103-108, 119-122, 137-138, 162-167, 172, 186-188, 191-192, 195-197
Minsky's Emigration, 8, 40, 107, 119, 122, 137
Mir Bozhii, see The World of God, 65, 182-183, 189, 201
Mir Iskusstva, see the World of Art, 23, 83
Mirbeau, Octave, 115
Mirrors, 84-85, 133
"Mistiki bezbozhiia. Emile Verhaeren," see "The Mystics of Godlessness: Emile Verhaeren," 79, 191
Mme. Commanville, 171
Modernism, 21-22, 34, 36, 137, 181-182, 198
Modernist ideas, 21
Modernist literature, 20, 24, 27, 181
Modernist writers, 21, 181
Modern World, 183
Monkhouse, Allan, 135, 201
Montreal, 35
Montreux, 50
Moore, Albert Joseph, 35
Moréas, Jean, 22, 24, 26, 67, 110-111, 125, 182
Moreau, Gustave, 35, 184
Morris, William, 8, 24, 26-28, 32, 67, 111, 115, 126, 128-130, 132, 177, 182-183, 190
Moscheles, Felix, 135, 201
Moscow Art Theater (MHAT), 100-101, 195
Moscow Theaters, 100
Moskovskie teatry, see Moscow Theaters, 100
Moskvin, Ivan Mikhailovich, 100, 195
Mune-Sully, 99
Musée Carnavalet, 108, 170

Muther, Richardt, 87-88, 99, 193
"Muzhiki," see "Peasants," 97

Nabokov, Vladimir, 186
Nekrasov, N. A., 186
Neo-Philological society, 23, 27, 94, 126
New Russian Word, 173, 189
"New Trends in English Art," 27, 126, 128, 182
New York, 36, 40, 45, 173, 181, 185-186
New York Times, 45
"New Utopia," 26, 67, 128-129, 182
Nietzsche, Friedrich, 69-70, 75-76, 84, 133, 137, 149-151, 190, 202-203
Nijinska, Bronislava, 36
Nijinski, Vaslav, 36
Nikolai Maksimovich, see Minsky Nikolai, 43, 56, 78, 95, 188
"Nora," 65-66
Nordau, Max, 26, 109, 111, 196
Novaia Russkaia Kniga, see The New Russian Book, 165
"Novaia Utopia,"see "New Utopia," 26
Novaia zhizn, see The New Life, 54, 103, 195-196
Novoe russkoe slovo, see New Russian Word, 173, 189
Novosti inostrannoi literatury, see The News of Foreign Literature, 39
Novosti, see The News, 68, 95
"Novye techeniia v angliiskom iskusstve," see "The New Trends in English Art," 27
Novy Put', see The New Path, 191

Obrazovanie, see Education, 66, 117, 183-184, 193, 197-198, 203
"Ob otvlechennom v teatre," see "About the Abstract in the Theater," 99
Oscar Wilde, 8, 24, 27, 123-124, 128, 198-199
"Oscar Wilde and English Aestheticism," 27, 124

"Palata 6," see "Ward 6," 97
"Paolo and Francesca da Rimini," 33

INDEX

Paris, 8, 13-14, 16, 35-36, 39-40, 54-55, 58, 60, 64, 68, 90, 103, 106-112, 115-116, 118-122, 137, 161-162, 166-167, 169-170, 172, 184-197, 203-205
"Parizhskii arkhiv kniazia Urusova," see "The Parisian Archive of Prince Urusov," 170
Pater, Walter, 128-129, 145, 183
"Peasants," 97, 175, 194
"Peer Gynt," 101
Perfect Pitch, 185-187
Petit, Eugène, 15-16, 35, 58-59, 61, 65, 121, 160, 162-163, 181, 184-185, 187-198, 201-202, 204-205
"Pevets vremeni. Henri de Régnier," see "The Singer of the Time," 79
Phaedrus, 51
"Phantoms of Life or Mirra," 58
"Pippa Passes," 132
Pisemsky, 186
Plato, 51, 57, 96, 143, 191
"Poet and the Crowd," 88
"Poets-Symbolists in France," 26, 182
"Poet i tolpa," see "Poet and the Crowd," 88
"Poety-symvolisty vo Frantsii," see "Poets-Symbolists in France," 26, 190
Polonsky, Iakov Petrovich, 89-90, 202
Portinari, Beatrice (Dante's Beatrice) 33, 127
Pre-Raphaelite Brotherhood 27
Pre-Raphaelite Movement 22, 124, 199
"Prizraki zhizni ili Mirra," see "Phantoms of Life or Mirra," 58
Psychoneurological Institute, 43
Pushkin's centennial, 88, 117
Pushkin, Alexander, 15, 88, 117, 186, 194

Quartier Latin, 109
Questions of Literature, 172

Redon, Odilon, 35, 184
Reds, 161
Régnier, Henri de 79-82, 111, 183, 191
Rejan, 99

Religious and Philosophical Gatherings, 23, 75-78, 82, 191
Remizov, A.M., (1877-1957) 165
Renaissance (Aesthetical, Italian, Second), 22, 28-29, 32, 86, 141-143, 145-149, 182-183, 199
Revolutionary Manifest, 105
Revue Contemporaine, 111
Revue de Deux Mondes, 68
Revue Indépendante, 111
Revue Wagnerienne, 111
Richmond, William Blake, 31, 200
Riga, 160-161, 184
Rimbeau, Arthur, 22, 67, 110, 190
Rite of Spring, 36
Rodenbach, Georges, 111, 115-116, 183, 197
Rollin, Morris, 111
Rossetti, Dante Gabriel, 8, 23, 26-27, 30-33, 35, 123, 125-128, 132-135, 142, 177, 182, 184, 198-200
Rozanov, Vasily, 78-79, 83, 87-88, 92, 125, 193, 197
Ruskin, John, 115, 129, 132, 183, 199
Russian Letters, 40, 84
Russian Literature of the XX Century, 43, 181, 184
Russian Novel and French Culture, 8, 119
"Russian Novel in France," 119
Russian Revolution, 64, 86, 103, 157, 159, 162, 181
Russian Symbolism, 43, 84, 95, 97-98, 111, 129, 132-133, 176, 179-180, 201
Russian Symbolist movement, 20-21, 70, 75; Russian Symbolists, 23, 75-76, 80, 82, 84, 91, 95-96, 98, 119, 125, 133, 141, 191
"Russian Woman," 34, 117, 180, 184, 189
Russil, Russian Art and Literature, 165
"Russky roman vo Frantsii," see "Russian Novel in France," 119
Russkoe Iskusstvo i Literatura, see Russian Art and Literature (Russil), 165

Saint Petersburg, 7, 15-16, 63, 65, 67, 69, 71, 73, 75, 77, 79, 81, 83, 85, 87, 89, 91, 93, 95, 97, 99, 101, 103, 105, 181, 183, 188-189, 195-204
"Sacre du Printemps," see also "The Rite of Spring," 36
Salomé, Lou Andreas, 69, 150, 190
Sand, Georges, 118, 179
Sandys, Frederick, 33, 35
Savanarola, Girolamo,141, 145, 201-202
Savoy, 30, 132
Scherman, Thomas, 23, 45
Schiller, Friedrich, 186
Schnitzler, Arthur, 99-101, 150, 153-155, 195, 203
school of "Olympians," 24
schools of Aesthetes, 24
Schumann, Clara, 46, 187
Stasov, Vladimir Vasil'evich, 46, 187
Seleznev, K., 172, 201, 205
Senkevitch, G., 183
Severny Vestnik, see The Northern Herald, 24, 39, 57, 182, 190, 196-197, 203
Shakespeare, William, 57, 94, 115, 169, 186, 193
Shaw, George Bernard, 100, 195
Shchepkina-Kupernik, Tatiana Lvovna, 69, 102, 196
Shelley, Percy Bysshe, 136
Sheridan, Richard, 189
Shestov, Lev, 58, 63, 87, 125, 193
Siddal, Elizabeth, (1829-1862) 127
Sigismondo Malatesta da Rimini, 184
Slonimsky, Nicolas, 41, 44-45, 47, 185-187
Slonimskys, 188
Slovo, see Word, 54, 108, 120, 150, 173, 189
Sluchevsky, Konstantin, 7, 89-90
Social Democrat party, 103; Social Democrats, 103-105, 196
Social Life in London, 8, 135
Soiuz russkikh zhurnalistov i literatorov v Berlin, see The Union of Russian Journalists and Writers in Berline, 165
Sologub, Fedor, 7, 68, 79, 90-92, 94-97, 117, 194

Solomon, Simeon, 31, 35, 200
Soloviev, Vladimir, 23, 45, 75, 87, 91, 125, 133, 182, 191
Solovieva, Poliksena, 23, 187
Sorbonne, 16, 39, 58, 60
Soviet Russia, 20, 160-161, 167, 172
Sovremenny Mir, see Modern World, 183
Spain, 55
Spinoza, Baruch, 57
Square Henri Carpeau, 172
St. Francis, 29
St. Petersburg, 21, 23, 27, 43-44, 48-49, 54-55, 57, 60, 64-66, 69-71, 73, 84, 87, 89, 91-95, 98, 101-102, 119, 126, 182, 188-191, 194-195, 197, 203
Stanhope, Spencer, 31, 200
Stanislavsky, Konstantin Sergeevich, 99-100, 195
Stasov, Vladimir Vasil'evich, 46, 187
State Book publishing, 163
Stepniak, Segei, 135, 201
Stock, Henry John, 35
Strinberg, August, 24
Superman in Modern Literature, 151
Sverubovich, see Kachalov, Vasily Ivanovich, 195
Swinburne, Algernon Charles, 30, 132, 134
Switzerland, 39, 50, 58, 156
Symbolism, 7-8, 21-22, 24-31, 35, 43, 65-66, 75, 80-82, 84-85, 90, 95, 97-98, 100, 109-112, 114-117, 124-125, 128-130, 132-135, 141-142, 146-147, 149, 151, 153, 155, 176-180, 182-184, 197-201
Symbolism and Feminism, 8, 117
"Symbolism in Britain," 30, 182, 184, 199-200
"Symbolism in its Modern Understanding," 24, 182
Symbolist Movement in Literature, 30, 132, 184
"Symvolizm v ego sovremennom ponimanii," see "Symbolism in its Modern Understanding," 24
Symons, Arthur, 30, 132, 184
Symposium, 51, 96

INDEX

Tartakov, Ioakim Viktorovich, 47, 187
Tate Gallery, 35, 184, 198-200
Tenesheva, Maria Klavdievna, 89, 194
Ternavtsev, Valentin Aleksandrovich, 77,
  191
Teternikov, Fedor Kuzmich, see Sologub,
  Fedor, 194
*The Age of Rossetti, Burne-Jones and
  Watts,* 35, 184, 200
The Argonauts, 163
The Banal Story, 135
"The Dawn of Days," 84
"The Day of the Daughter of Hades," 30
"The Doll House," 65
The Fruits of Philosophy, 118
the Hambourgs, 135
The Herald of Europe, 21-22, 25-26, 30,
  39, 44, 67-68, 110-111, 119, 126, 129,
  142, 182, 199, 201-202, 205
The Herald of History, 29, 70, 190
The Herald of Western Literature, 164
*The History of Painting of the Nineteenth
  Century,* 87
The House of the Arts, 40, 157, 165-167,
  205
"The Hymn of Workers," 104
"The Meaning of Dante for the Contem-
  porary World," 8, 142, 146, 201
"The Moon," 84
"The Motherland," 84
The News of Foreign Literature, 39, 44, 62
The New Life, 103, 105
The New Path, 24, 79, 81-82, 194, 197
The New Russian Book, 165
The News, 39, 44, 67, 98-99
"The New Trends in Symbolist Art,"
  127
"The New Trends in English Art," 27,
  126, 128, 182
"The New Utopia: William Morris and
  His Last Book," 128-129
The Northern Herald, 7, 24, 39, 57, 63,
  65-67, 69-70, 72, 112, 118, 148, 189-
  191, 202-203
The Pantheon of the Theaters, 99

"The Parisian Archive of Prince Urusov,"
  170-171
The Petty Demon, 96
"The Precursor of English Symbolism:
  William Blake," 128
The Pre-Raphaelites, 24, 26, 28, 32, 35,
  125-126, 129, 145, 147, 198-199
The Religion of the Future, 104
The Russian Word, 150
The Saturday Review, 84-85, 192
"The Singer of the Time: Henri de
  Régnier," 79
The Skify 162, 163
The Union of Russian Journalists and
  Writers in Berlin, 165
"The Wedding," 36
The World of God, 65, 142, 182, 201
The Writers' Club, 167, 205
Théâtre Libre, 65
Theosophical Society, 118, 197
Tiutchev, Fedor Ivanovich, 192
Tolstoy, Leo (Lev), 8, 137-138, 194, 201
"Toska," see "Heartache," 97
Treaty of Rapallo, 160
Turgenev, Ivan, 186

Urusov, 8, 170-172, 205

Vasilevsky, V. G., 57
Vengerov, Semen Afanasievich, 19, 43,
  70, 103, 188, 196
Vengerov, Volodia (Vladimir), 43-44, 96
Vengerova, Elizaveta Afanasievna (Lisa),
  47, 48
Vengerova, Isabelle Afanasievna (Belka,
  Belochka), 45-47, 187, 196, 201-202
Vengerova, Zinaida Afanasievna, 181-
  182, 184, 189-192, 194-203, 205
Veroccio, 144
Vestnik Evropy 21, 39, 44, 182-183, 190,
  199, 201-202, 205
Vestnik zapadnoi literatury, see *The Herald
  of Western Literature,* 164
Vicaire, 111
Victorian England, 118
Vienna, 39, 50, 55, 57

224

Vilenkin, see Minky, Nikolai, 23, 43, 47, 187
Vilkina, Liudmila, 46-48, 54, 120
Vinci, da Leonardo, 144
Vita Nuova, 33
Vitega, 94
Vitte, 94
Volkonsky, Sergei Michailovich, 99, 191, 198
Voprosy literatury, see *Questions of Literature*, 172, 201, 205
Vsemirnaia literatura, see *World Literature,* 161, 163
Vulgata, 182

Wagner, Richard, 187
Walpole, Hugh 167, 205
"Ward 6," 97
Wassermann, Jakob, 155, 203
Watts, Georges Frederic (1817-1904), 33, 35, 184, 199-200
Wedekind, Frank, 150, 153, 155, 183, 203
Weinberg, Petr Isaevich, 7, 90-91, 194
Western European literature, 20, 22, 25, 67-68, 90, 120, 129, 161, 165, 173, 179
Western European Writers of the 19th Century, 128

Whites, 161
Wilde's Aestheticism, 125
Wilde, Oscar, 8, 24, 27, 29, 123-125, 128, 198-199
"William Blake and the Imagination," 31
Wilton, Andrew, 30, 132, 182, 184, 200
"Witch," 84
Word ,54, 108
World Literature, 161, 163, 183
World of Art, 7, 23, 83, 86-89, 99, 117, 134-135, 182, 191, 194-195
World of God, 65, 128, 142, 182, 201

Yeats, W. B., 31, 134, 184, 200
Young Belgium, 115

"Zerkala," see "Mirrors," 72, 84
Zinaida Afanasievna, 13, 18, 37-38, 41, 45, 48, 56, 99, 107-108, 117, 120, 141, 150, 162, 192, see also Vengerova, Zinaida
Zinaida Nikolaevna, 7, 70-71, 73-74, 79, 83, see also Hippius-Merezhkovskaia
Zionist movement, 41-42
"Znachenie Dante dlia sovremmenosti," see "The Meaning of Dante for the Contemporary World," 142
Znanie, 88
Zola, Emile, 183

HEIDELBERGER PUBLIKATIONEN ZUR SLAVISTIK
B. LITERATURWISSENSCHAFTLICHE REIHE

Herausgegeben von Horst-Jürgen Gerigk, Urs Heftrich und Wilfried Potthoff

Band 1   Ewald Trojansky: Pessimismus und Nihilismus der romantischen Weltanschauung, dargestellt am Beispiel Puškins und Lermontovs. 1990.

Band 2   Alexandra Ioannidou: Humaniorum studiorum cultores. Die Gräkophilie in der russischen Literatur der Jahrhundertwende am Beispiel von Leben und Werk Innokentij Annenskijs und Vjačeslav Ivanovs. 1996.

Band 3   Dorthe G. A. Engelhardt: L. N. Tolstoy and D. H. Lawrence. Cross-Currents and Influence. 1996.

Band 4   Dagmar Burkhart / Vladimir Biti (Hrsg.): Diskurs der Schwelle. Aspekte der kroatischen Gegenwartsliteratur. 1996.

Band 5   Alexander Graf: Das Selbstmordmotiv in der russischen Prosa des 20. Jahrhunderts. 1996.

Band 6   Heike Gundacker-Lewis: Studien zum russischen Opernlibretto des 19. Jahrhunderts nach Vorlagen von Puškin. 1997.

Band 7   Alexander Götz: Bilder aus der Tiefe der Zeit. Erinnerung und Selbststilisierung als ästhetische Funktionen im Werk Bohumil Hrabals. 1998.

Band 8   Roberto Mantovani: Musa Ćazim Ćatić. Ein islamischer Autor der Literatur des Fin de siècle in Bosnien. 1998.

Band 9   Christoph Garstka: Arthur Moeller van den Bruck und die erste deutsche Gesamtausgabe der Werke Dostojewskijs im Piper-Verlag 1906-1919. Eine Bestandsaufnahme sämtlicher Vorbemerkungen und Einführungen von Arthur Moeller van den Bruck und Dmitrij S. Mereschkowskij unter Nutzung unveröffentlichter Briefe der Übersetzerin E. K. Rahsin. Mit ausführlicher Bibliographie. Geleitwort von Horst-Jürgen Gerigk. 1998.

Band 10   Neil Stewart: "Vstan' i vspominaj". Auferstehung als Collage in Venedikt Erofeevs *Moskva-Petuški*. 1999.

Band 11   Larissa Chiriaeva: Studien zu einer strukturellen Typologie des russischen und bulgarischen Zaubermärchens. 1999.

Band 12   Игорь Вишневецкий: Трагический субьект в действии: Андрей Белый. 2000.

Band 13   Dragan Buzov: Die Romane des Milan Begoviç. Zur Kontinuität der Décadence-Literatur des Fin de siècle in der kroatischen Literatur des XX. Jahrhunderts. 2000.

Band 14   Dittmar Dahlmann / Wilfried Potthoff (Hrsg.): Mythen, Symbole und Rituale. Die Geschichtsmächtigkeit der *Zeichen* in Südosteuropa im 19. und 20. Jahrhundert. 2000.

Band 15   Galina Thieme: Ivan Turgenev und die deutsche Literatur. Sein Verhältnis zu Goethe und seine Gemeinsamkeiten mit Berthold Auerbach, Theodor Fontane und Theodor Storm. 2000.

Band 16   Roman Katsman: The Time of Cruel Miracles. Mythopoesis in Dostoevsky and Agnon. 2002.

Band 17   Birgit Harreß: Die Dialektik der Form. Das mimetische Prinzip Witold Gombrowiczs. 2001.

Band 18   Темира Пахмусс: Зинаида Гиппиус: Hypatia двадцатого века.. 2002.

Band 20   Claus Jürgen Heinrich Tengemann: Das Unheil der Melancholie. Ein Beitrag zum Phä-
nomen des melancholischen Antihelden in der russischen Literatur des neunzehnten
Jahrhunderts unter besonderer Berücksichtigung von Saltykov-Ščedrins *Die Herren
Golovlev*, Aksakovs *Familienchronik* und *Die Kinderjahre Bagrovs des Enkels*, Tol-
stojs *Familienglück* und Bunins *Suchodol*. 2002.

Band 21   Gudrun Braunsperger: Sergej Nečaev und Dostoevskijs *Dämonen*. Die Geburt eines
Romans aus dem Geist des Terrorismus. 2002.

Band 22   Pavao Posilović: Cvijet od kriposti. Als Facsimile herausgegeben und eingeleitet von
Wilfried Potthoff. 2002.

Band 23   Темира Пахмусс: Страницы из прошлого. Нз переписки Зинаиды
Гиппиус. Составлние, редакция, комментарии и вступительные статьи
автора. 2003.

Band 24   Jens Herlth: Die Präsenz des Abwesenden. Zur Poetik von Iosif Brodskijs *Rimskie
elegii*. 2003.

Band 25   Wolfgang Weitensteiner: Das andere Leben. Zeit und Erinnerung im Werk Jurij
Trifonovs. 2004.

Band 26   Temira Pachmuss: Thought and Vision: Zinaida Hippius's Letters to Greta Gerell. Compiled, edited, with annotations and introductions by the author. 2004.

Band 27   Rosina Neginsky: Zinaida Vengerova: In Search of Beauty. A Literary Ambassador between East and West. 2004.

Band 28   Gabi Tiemann: Das Werk Emanuil Popdimitrovs im Rahmen des Fin de siècle. 2004.

www.peterlang.de

Peter Lang · Europäischer Verlag der Wissenschaften

Temira Pachmuss

Thought and Vision: Zinaida Hippius's Letters to Greta Gerell

Compiled, edited, with annotations and introductions by the author

Frankfurt am Main, Berlin, Bern, Bruxelles, New York, Oxford, Wien, 2004.
164 pp., 2 fig.
Heidelberger Publikationen zur Slavistik. B. Literaturwissenschaftliche Reihe.
Edited by Horst-Jürgen Gerigk, Urs Heftrich and Wilfried Potthoff. Vol. 26
ISBN 3-631-52755-1 / US-ISBN 0-8204-7323-5 · pb. € 34.–*

This volume of the letters of the Russian poet and religious thinker Zinaida Hippius (1869–1945) guides the reader through the upheavals in her life in exile (1919–1945). Her complex genre of epistolary art has its own inimitable technique and its own internal code of aesthetics. These letters in French reveal the inherent dialectics of Hippius's ideas and aspirations and identify features of continuity and change in her earlier thoughts and vision and her later attitudes. Hippius's letters also reveal her literary endeavor to glorify the idea of beauty, grace, and refinement in art.

Contents: Zinaida Hippius' contacts and meetings in Paris · Disagreements among the Russian exiles in Paris · Russian literature, art, religion, and language

Frankfurt am Main · Berlin · Bern · Bruxelles · New York · Oxford · Wien
Distribution: Verlag Peter Lang AG
Moosstr. 1, CH-2542 Pieterlen
Telefax 00 41 (0) 32 / 376 17 27

*The €-price includes German tax rate
Prices are subject to change without notice
Homepage http://www.peterlang.de